CAMBRIDGE STUDIES IN LINGUISTICS

General Editors · W. SIDNEY ALLEN · EUGENIE J. A. HENDERSON
FRED W. HOUSEHOLDER·JOHN LYONS·R. B. LE PAGE·F. R. PALMER
J. L. M. TRIM

The social differentiation of English in Norwich

In this series

Other volumes in preparation

THE SOCIAL
DIFFERENTIATION OF
ENGLISH IN NORWICH

PETER TRUDGILL

Lecturer in Linguistic Science
University of Reading

CAMBRIDGE

at the University Press · 1974

Published by the Syndics of the Cambridge University Press
Bentley House, 200 Euston Road, London NW1 2DB
American Branch: 32 East 57th Street, New York, N.Y.10022

© Cambridge University Press 1974

Library of Congress Catalogue Card Number: 73-77178

ISBN: 0 521 20264 7

Printed in Great Britain
at the University Printing House, Cambridge
(Brooke Crutchley, University Printer)

Contents

List of Maps and Abbreviations

MAPS

ABBREVIATIONS

Sociological

MMC   middle middle class

LMC   lower middle class

UWC   upper working class

MWC   middle working class

LWC   lower working class

Linguistic

IPA   International Phonetic Association

ME   Middle English

OE   Old English

Abbreviations

RP	Received Pronunciation
SED	*Survey of English dialects* by H. Orton and E. Dieth, Leeds, 1962–
CS	casual style
FS	formal style
RPS	reading passage style
WLS	word list style

Acknowledgements

This work is based on research carried out for my Edinburgh University Ph.D. thesis, which bears the same name as this abridged and revised text and was written under the supervision of Bill Jones and Jim Mather. I am greatly indebted to my supervisors for their help, advice and encouragement, and I am most grateful to both of them. I am also particularly grateful to Bob Le Page, who examined the thesis, and made a large number of very useful criticisms, comments and suggestions for improvement, many of which have been incorporated in the present text.

In addition, there are a number of other people to whom my thanks are due. In the first stages of this work I received considerable support from John Lyons, and I also had a small but vital piece of encouragement from Keith Brown. I would like, too, to thank King's College, Cambridge, and Edinburgh University for their financial support.

I must express my especial thanks to William Labov, who started it all, and from whom I have learned a great deal; Michael Garman, who read the entire manuscript of the thesis, and made some extremely valuable comments and suggestions; and John Laver, who provided invaluable assistance at one stage. I have also profited from discussions with Arne Kjell Foldvik, Erik Fudge, Bob Hodgart, and Gerry Knowles, and I have received other useful comments and advice from Frank Palmer, Ron Asher, and David Crystal. The following people have also been very helpful in providing research materials: S. Ellis, A. R. Emerson, S. F. Sanderson, P. M. Tilling, and especially R. I. McDavid and W. N. Francis. The latter's comments on the Norfolk dialect were also very helpful.

During the course of the survey itself I had occasion to be grateful to a number of people. I am particularly indebted to Adrian Hannah, who carried out ten of the interviews and made my task that much easier. I am also very grateful to Geoffrey Carter and Francis Kapherr, who helped with the sample of schoolchildren; my mother and father, who provided the board, lodging and transport which enabled me to complete the survey so quickly, and all the Norwich people who co-operated with me as informants – as well as the unforgettable gentleman who wouldn't help me because he didn't believe in universities.

Finally, I want to thank Carol Geddes and Jill Tozer for their typing, and Sandra Trudgill for so usefully acquiring a Norwich accent during the past few years, as well as for her encouragement and her help with the maps and graphs.

P.T.

Introduction

0.1 Sociolinguistics

Sociolinguistics can be characterised as the branch of linguistics which employs or is concerned with the methods, findings or subject matter of the social sciences. As, therefore, the social sciences are conventionally divided into the two main branches of social anthropology and sociology, so sociolinguistics can be regarded as consisting of anthropological linguistics and sociological linguistics. The work that is presented here can be considered under the heading of sociological linguistics, in this sense: what follows is a study in sociological urban dialectology. In so far as sociology is concerned with the study of complex urban societies and communities, we shall be dealing with the subject matter of sociology. Further, in the application of sampling techniques to linguistic problems and in the handling of problems connected with the concept of social class we shall be making use of the methods and findings of sociology. We shall also be making some reference to the methods, findings and subject matter of another of the social sciences: human geography. Although linguists have long been interested in what they have termed 'linguistic geography', they have most often ignored the advances that have been made in the field of theoretical geography itself. The concepts of central place and urban field, and the theories of location and diffusion (see Berry & Pred, 1961; Haggett, 1965; Hägerstrand, 1952) are all relevant for linguistic studies. In so far as an attempt will be made here to rectify this omission, the following can also be considered to be a work in geographical linguistics.

0.2 Sociological dialectology

It should be pointed out that sociological dialectology is not, and has not been, necessarily *urban*. For example, Kurath & McDavid (1961), in their investigations into the dialects of the United States, made some attempt to obtain informants from different social class backgrounds. As, however, their methods of securing informants cannot be considered sufficiently rigorous to satisfy the higher demands made by sociological theory in this field, their work is perhaps better described as social, rather than sociological, dialectology.

It is also true to say that urban dialectology is by no means necessarily sociological. Many linguists have attempted to describe the speech forms of urban areas without recourse to any of the methodology of sociology. The inadequacies in the work of these linguists, both linguistic and sociological, stem from the fact that they have, generally speaking, chosen to ignore the fact that most if not all speech communities are more or less socially and linguistically heterogeneous. This heterogeneity is, moreover, much more marked in urban areas than it is in other linguistic communities. For this reason the inadequacies of non-sociological urban dialectology are all the more serious.

The application of sociological techniques to linguistic material represents, historically speaking, an advance, in that it permits not only the recognition of the fact of linguistic diversity but also the development of a methodology for handling this diversity. Many nineteenth-century linguists, for instance, were totally uninterested in the heterogeneous nature of linguistic communities, and especially so since non-standard dialects were often considered to be debased forms of the standard (see Lyons, 1968, pp. 34–5). In their historical reconstructions of 'proto'-languages by the comparative method, moreover, no recognition was given to the fact that these languages must themselves have been internally differentiated.

Since that time, the heterogeneity of speech communities has generally been acknowledged. Many linguists, however, have contrived to avoid facing up to the fact of this heterogeneity. This practice was particularly characteristic of American linguistics in the 1950s. Hockett, for example, has stated that, in working with the comparative method to reconstruct 'a single language free from dialect variation', we are making 'a potentially false working assumption' (1968, p. 486). Hockett nevertheless makes this assumption. One knows, in other words, that languages are subject to internal differentiation, but, for practical reasons, one pretends that they are not. In the synchronic treatment of modern languages, moreover, methods were devised to permit the inconvenient fact of linguisitc diversity to be ignored. Great stress was laid, for example, on the fact that analyses were only relevant for a single idiolect (see Harris, 1951, pp. 9–11). (In the last decade, on the other hand, it has been shown that, in some cases at least, the idiolect is the least stable object for linguistic study, and that it can only be viewed as coherent against the background of the linguistic community as a whole (see Labov, 1966a).) Much of linguistic diversity was also dismissed as 'free variation'. (Later studies have shown that most of this variation is not at all 'free', but is on the contrary structured and socially determined in sociologically and linguistically interesting ways.) Chomsky's competence/performance distinction also avoids the variation problem.

Since the last war, however, and particularly in the United States, there has been a steady increase in the number of works which have both recognised and attempted to cope with the fact of the non-homogeneity of language. From the point of view of urban dialectology, undoubtedly the most important of these works is Labov's study of the speech of the Lower East Side of New York City (1966a). Labov, whose work will be mentioned frequently in the course of the following chapters, has applied sociological methodology to a linguistically heterogeneous community with results that have several important implications for linguistic theory. The following work can perhaps, therefore, be seen as part of the trend towards studies dealing with heterogeneous speech communities and attempting to deal with and draw conclusions from linguistic diversity.

0.3   The value of sociological urban dialectology

What is the value of sociological urban dialectology, and what are its aims? One of the most obvious results of this type of work is the accumulation of a whole new body of linguistic data. Labov has said that the interpretation of the term *sociolinguistics* to signify a new interdisciplinary field dealing with the description of the relations of language and society is 'an unfortunate notion, foreshadowing a long series of purely descriptive studies with little bearing on the central theoretical problems of linguistics or of sociology' (1966a, p. v). Labov's condemnation of 'purely descriptive studies' would appear to be somewhat over-severe. 'Purely descriptive studies' of rural dialects have long been regarded as legitimate and worthwhile linguistic pursuits. While they may have contributed nothing directly to the solving of problems of linguistic theory, they have added to the linguist's knowledge about language, and have provided data which has subsequently been turned to solving various linguistic problems (see, for example, the reference in Kiparsky, 1968, to Enderlin, 1911). In exactly the same way, sociological *urban* dialectological methods can make possible descriptions of urban speech that are in themselves of value and interest. They increase the body of linguistic data available to linguists, and for this reason should not be required to have any direct bearing on theoretical problems.

At the same time it must be recognised that one of the main aims of research of this type is to shed light on various aspects of linguistic theory. Studies which are able to do this are obviously of more value than those that are not. Sociological urban dialectology provides the linguist with a body of data that is not only large but also accurate. Some of the conclusions we shall arrive at on the basis of this kind of data in the present work – such as, perhaps, the conclusion that women use more 'correct' linguistic forms than men – may appear to be rather obvious. We can claim, however, that we have presented material in an exact and rigorous way, which proves, perhaps for the first time, that (in this case) sex differentiation of this type occurs in British English, and which demonstrates the exact nature and degree of the differentiation. This, we believe, is a useful advance.

The large amounts of data that are obtained in this way can be applied to many theoretical problems, and in this present work we shall attempt to make some comments on phonological theory, and to make some contribution to the theory of the diasystem. The fact that the data is drawn from a large, dynamic and complex community, which is characterised by many different types of social interaction and by various types of social change, also means that it is particularly useful in the study of linguistic change.

Sociological urban dialectology can also have the function – particularly in Britain, where little attention has so far been paid to this kind of work – of providing a description of the linguistic characteristics of the vast majority of the country's population. It would seem that the considerable amount of rural dialectological work that has been carried out in Britain has left the linguist singularly ignorant about the way in which most of the people in Britain speak. The aims of rural dialectology have, of course, been of a different nature. Many dialectologists have, legitimately, been concerned to record older dialect forms before they are lost for good. The result has been, however, a neglect of current speech forms which could have provided an excellent 'laboratory' for the testing of linguistic hypotheses. Rural dialectologists, too, can be accused of having neglected the heterogeneity that is present even in rural speech communities.

Material from sociological urban dialect studies can also be useful for practical purposes. Because we can now know, often for the first time, the exact nature of the linguistic characteristics of large sections of the population, it is possible to point more accurately to the sort of difficulties that can arise in the teaching of standard English to children who have some other variety of English as their native tongue (see Labov, 1966*b*; Fasold & Shuy, 1970; Baratz & Shuy, 1969) (if indeed we wish to do this at all – see Newmeyer & Edmunds, 1971). It is also possible that conclusions will emerge that will be of some value in the teaching of English as a foreign language. Urban dialectology demonstrates, for example, that RP is very much a minority accent, even in England. This suggests that the teacher of English should perhaps not concentrate so exclusively as is now usual on the teaching of this particular accent.

Sociological urban dialectology can also be of some value to sociology. It can shed light, for instance, on problems concerning the discreteness and continuity of social classes, on certain aspects of role and status, and on the class structure of the community generally. It can also provide material that can be used in the study of reference groups, normative pressures, and prestige patterns. (We shall have something to say in the following chapters, for example, on the nature of the class structure in modern Britain.) This kind of work can also be of use in pointing to some of the barriers that exist in the way of social and educational advancement for many members of our society. It has been shown, for example, that linguistic differences not only arise from social inequality but also help to reinforce it (see Lawton, 1968).

Mainly, however, we shall be concerned in this work with problems of interest to linguists and linguistics. The following work, which makes use of both sociological and dialectological techniques, is the first attempt that has been made to describe the speech of the urban area in question. It is also one of the first essays in British sociological urban dialectology. In the following chapters we shall first of all describe how the urban dialect survey was carried out. We shall then attempt to illustrate, in some detail, the exact nature of the heterogeneity of the linguistic community in question, and try to establish a theoretical framework for the description of all types of speech that occur in the urban area.

1 Norwich

1.1 Norwich and its setting

This work in urban dialectology and sociological linguistics takes the form of a study of the English spoken in the city of Norwich, England. More exactly, it is a study of the speech forms of the urban area associated with Norwich, since the newer suburbs, which form part of an organic whole with the older city, remain outside the administrative boundary of the county borough. The population of the built-up area of Norwich in 1967 was approximately 160,000, with about 118,000 actually within the city boundary.[1] This means that, at the moment, the nearest town to Norwich which has a population exceeding that of Norwich is Greater London, which is about 120 miles away by road. In fact, Norwich, although by no means one of the largest towns in England, is, as the above information may suggest, of considerable cultural and commercial importance for the surrounding area of Norfolk and indeed for East Anglia as a whole. Like many urban centres, it has acted as a goal for in-migration from the surrounding rural areas for much of its history. This is still true of today, although much of the movement into the city is now of the commuting type.

These factors have important linguistic consequences. The speech of Norwich is clearly founded on east Norfolk rural speech, but has become increasingly differentiated from more rural speech forms over the years. One can speculate that this differentiation has taken place, at least partly, as a result of the spreading of linguistic innovations, not gradually across country, but along the more important lines of communication from one member of the urban hierarchy (see Johnson, 1967, pp. 92–4; Dickinson, 1967, pp. 47–59) to another. On the other hand, Norwich also exerts considerable linguistic influence on its rural hinterland,[2] and cultural innovations of all kinds tend to spread from

---

[1] The data that follow have been taken from *East Anglia: A Study* (EAEPC, 1968).
[2] For an exposition of the concept of hinterland, see Johnson (1967, pp. 89–92), and Nystuen & Dacey (1961). For the similar term 'Umland' see Kant (1951), and for 'Urban Field' see Smailes (1957, ch. 7) and Dickinson (1967, p. 31). For linguistic influence of cities on hinterlands, cf. Halliday *et al.* (1964, p. 85).

Norwich outwards. It is, for example, a well-known fact amongst Norfolk people that 'Norwich people drop their *h*'s'. This is a linguistic fact which is striking even to the layman, as the rural accents of East Anglia, possibly alone in the south of England,[1] consistently preserve *h* in their phonological systems in all styles of speech. One can therefore assume, albeit tentatively, that '*h*-dropping' is a linguistic feature that has spread to Norwich from the Home Counties, leaving the surrounding rural areas unaffected, at least for some generations. (It is worth noting in passing that the linguistic changes due to diffusion that we are referring to here are of the type called by Labov 'linguistic changes from below' (Labov, 1966*a*, pp. 238, 379; 1965), that is to say, from below the level of conscious awareness. Linguistic changes 'from above' are likely to be of a normative type tending to modification in the direction of RP, due to the influence of RP-speaking prestige groups and the educational institutions.)

1.2 East Anglia

As a geographical, or indeed cultural or linguistic term, 'East Anglia' can only be very imprecise. The counties of Norfolk and Suffolk are certainly East Anglian, and in many usages the term refers only to these two counties. There has always been doubt, however, as to whether or not the Fenland should be considered part of East Anglia, and consequently some definitions have included all or part of the counties of Cambridgeshire, Huntingdonshire, Lincolnshire and Northamptonshire. Essex, which is culturally and geographically closely linked with Suffolk and Norfolk, has also been included, as have even Bedfordshire and Hertfordshire.

In setting up East Anglia as an economic planning region, the Department of Economic Affairs has recently redefined the area for its own purposes. It incorporates under this heading Norfolk, Suffolk, Cambridgeshire, Huntingdonshire and the Soke of Peterborough. Much of the statistical information in this chapter concerning 1966 or later years is taken from the first publication of the East Anglia Economic Planning Council (1968), and must therefore be taken to refer to East Anglia in this sense.

---

[1] 'The only remaining manifestation of the /h/ phoneme, initial prevocalic [h], began to be lost as early as the fifteenth century in many dialects. Its loss in the dialects south of the Humber (Vachek should have excepted East Anglia, where it is still very much alive) has resulted in the total disappearance of the phoneme in these dialects' (Francis, 1966).

Linguistically speaking, East Anglia, as a relatively homogeneous dialect area, has been shrinking gradually under the impact of the spread of Home Counties speech forms. It would seem, for instance, that it does not now make very good sense, except perhaps at the level of the very old, very rural speaker, to include Norfolk, and, say, Hertfordshire in the same region, as has been done previously. For this reason, 'East Anglian', as a linguistic term, must be employed in a rather restricted sense. To avoid confusion, the following conventions will be adopted in the linguistic sections of this work:

(a) 'Norfolk' linguistic forms will refer to the speech of central and eastern Norfolk and north-eastern Suffolk. This area is more or less co-extensive with the Norwich 'city region' proposed by the EAEPC (1968, ch. 6), but stretches further west to the edge of the Fenland, and probably includes King's Lynn.

(b) 'East Anglian' linguistic forms will refer to the speech of Norfolk, east Suffolk, and those parts of west Suffolk, eastern Cambridgeshire and north-eastern Essex which remain distinctively East Anglian, or relatively unaffected by the speech forms of the Home Counties.

These definitions are necessarily imprecise in the absence of any thorough dialect survey of the present-day speech habits of all sections of the communities in these areas.

1.2.1   Communications. Since the beginning of the industrial revolution, the history of East Anglia has been one of declining economic importance, and geographical isolation, followed in more recent years by population pressure and increasing cultural and economic influence from the south-east. Both the geographical isolation and the influence of the south-east are partly caused by and partly reflected in the communications networks that serve East Anglia. East Anglia, which lies between 40 and 120 miles distant from Greater London, is set apart from the main national centres of commerce and industry, and from the chief north–south road and rail routes leading from London. Throughout East Anglia transport communications are poor, and most of the main road and rail routes lead to London. Norwich itself, the most northerly of the four main East Anglian centres, suffers most from this isolation:

Norwich has become virtually the capital of East Anglia, the attractive, odd and curiously remote corner of Britain, cut off on three sides by the sea and on the fourth by British Rail. Although this is an ancient and not very funny joke, there is more than a grain of truth in its reference to the difficulties of communication with the rest of the country, and this has had a profound effect on the way in which Norwich developed over the years and will do so in the future. (Wood, 1968)

There are also, undoubtedly, linguistic effects, although it is difficult to know, without further study, exactly how railway timetables and road networks relate to cultural and linguistic diffusion, and what implications they have for the linguistic influence of the Home Counties in East Anglia. It has been shown, however, that isogloss bundles correlate closely with traffic network patterns in parts of the U.S.A.[1] In any case, in view of the generally poor communications system, it would not be surprising to discover that East Anglia is something of a relic area, linguistically speaking.

The East Anglian urban hierarchy is dominated by the four major centres of Norwich, Ipswich, Cambridge and Peterborough, and the three minor centres of King's Lynn, Great Yarmouth and Lowestoft, and Bury St Edmunds. In one classification of the urban hierarchy of England and Wales (Smailes, 1944), Norwich is described as a 'major city', Ipswich and Cambridge as 'cities', and Peterborough, together with King's Lynn, Great Yarmouth, Lowestoft and Bury St Edmunds, as a 'major town or minor city'. Each of these towns acts as a centre for shopping, social services, entertainment, and employment. According to the urban hierarchy theory of diffusion, which both human and linguistic geographers have recognised as valid (see Hägerstrand, 1951; 1952; 1965; 1967; Bunge, 1966, pp. 112–74; Bach, 1950, p. 136; Schwarz, 1950, p. 74; and DeCamp, 1958, p. 372), it can be hypothesised that linguistic innovations are likely to spread to Norwich from Ipswich and Cambridge, rather than or as well as direct from London. This is particularly so in view of the fact that the main lines of communication from London to Norwich, as outlined above, lie through these two towns. We can omit Peterborough as it lies outside lingustic East Anglia and is not on a direct route from London to Norwich.

(There is no *a priori* reason, incidentally, why linguistic innovations should not also spread to Norwich from, say, the Midlands via Peterborough. However, the increasing linguistic dominance of London is a fact which the casual listener can notice in the south of England from

---

[1] 'Most of the important dialect boundaries in the eastern United States fall along lines which are natural troughs in the network of communications.' Labov (1966*a*, p. 499, and see p. 502 n.).

TABLE 1.1. *Immigration to Norfolk, 1960*

London	680	Cambridgeshire	390
Middlesex	670	Hertfordshire	330
Essex	660	Sussex	270
Ely	570	Buckinghamshire	200
Surrey	480	Hampshire	190
Kent	440	Bedfordshire	180

TABLE 1.2. *Immigration to Norwich, 1960*

Middlesex	210	Lancashire	120
East Suffolk	190	Essex	100
London	140	Hertfordshire	100
East Sussex	130	Kent	100

Oxford to Dover, and even further afield. There is no reason to suppose that East Anglia will escape this influence, particularly in view of the system of communications and the evidence of influence already observed. There is in any case no sign of any linguistic influence from other directions.)

1.2.2   Immigration. The migration tables of the 1961 Census and the 1966 Sample Census (General Register Office, 1964; 1967) give further evidence of the cultural influence of the Home Counties on East Anglia and of the way this influence is effected. Immigrants (defined as persons who twelve months previous were living elsewhere) into the Eastern Region in the year to 1960 totalled approximately 152,130 or 4.1% of the population of the region. Something over one half of these had come from London and the South-Eastern Region (77,340). The next largest influx was from the North Midland Region (8,500). A further breakdown of figures shows that in the same period Norfolk received a total of 17,700 immigrants. Of these, 2,960 were in fact migrants from the county borough of Norwich. Of those coming actually from outside Norfolk, nearly half were contributed by the authorities listed in table 1.1. Figures for Norwich for the same period show a similar trend, with large numbers of immigrants from the south-eastern counties. The total number of immigrants into Norwich was 4,160, of whom 1,870 were from Norfolk. Of the rest, nearly half came from the areas shown in Table 1.2. This trend continues in the 1966 Sample Census figures, which indicate a further influx from the south-east. Of the total 1966 population of Norwich (116,350), 94,860 were born in East Anglia. Of the others, 9,340 were born in the South-Eastern Region, and only between 900 and 1,500 in each of the other six English regions.

1.2.3 Population. The population of East Anglia is both the smallest and least dense of the eight English planning regions. (This is, of course, one reason for the expansion of densely populated London in this direction.) The percentage increase in 1951–66 was the largest in the country, however, and this trend is likely to accelerate in the next fifteen-year period. The 1967 population of East Anglia was 1,611,910, of whom 576,430 (over one third of the total) were living in the north-east (Norwich) subdivision or city region. Half of this number were living in Norwich (118,610), Great Yarmouth (51,910), and Lowestoft (49,160). The Norfolk rural districts which contain the Norwich suburbs also had large populations: Blofield and Flegg (41,130), Forehoe and Henstead (31,200), and St Faiths and Aylsham (54,150). The region had a somewhat higher than average proportion of old people, particularly in the north-eastern subdivision. The 1961 Census shows that the age distribution of Norfolk is markedly older than that of England and Wales as a whole. The population aged under five (7.4%) was lower than that of England and Wales (7.8%). The proportion aged over sixty-five in Norfolk (13.8%) was considerably more than that of England and Wales (11.9%) and had risen since 1951 (12.6%). The population of Norfolk increased at a rate of 0.23% a year between 1951 and 1961, compared with 0.44% a year between 1931 and 1951. This places Norfolk forty-second in a list of sixty-two administrative counties in terms of annual increase 1951–61. The population of the largest East Anglian urban settlements (more or less continuously built-up areas) in 1966 was:

| Norwich | 160,000 | Cambridge | 105,000 |
| Ipswich | 129,000 | Peterborough | 81,000 |

An important factor in the future population is likely to be the organised London over-spill schemes which have already affected, for example, Peterborough, Ipswich and Thetford. There has as yet been no over-spill to Norwich. Depending on the size of any influx, linguistic influence may be effected in this way in the future.

1.2.4   Social and economic structure. East Anglia has a much higher percentage of people employed in agriculture than the country as a whole. It also has a higher proportion involved in the manufacture of food and drink; in construction; in professional and scientific services; and in public administration and defence. In all other fields, notably heavy industry, the proportion is less than that for the country as a whole. Unemployment has recently been quite close to the national level, but the Norwich and Peterborough regions have had higher rates than the Ipswich and Cambridge regions. It is also noteworthy that a below-average proportion of children stay on at school beyond the statutory leaving age.

In terms of earned income per income-tax case, East Anglia falls 8 % below the United Kingdom average, and has the lowest average for all regions of England and Wales. Investment income, however, is relatively high. Within East Anglia, both total net income and earned income are on average significantly lower in Norfolk than elsewhere. For total net income per tax case, the relevant 1964–5 figures were:

United Kingdom	£1,003 p.a.
East Anglia	£950 p.a.
Norfolk	£913 p.a.

The 1965–6 figures for earned income show an even bigger discrepancy:

East Anglia	£974 p.a.
Norfolk	£908 p.a.

(The next lowest East Anglian area was Cambridgeshire, with £969 p.a.)

1.3   Norwich

Norwich itself is generally thought to have grown up out of a number of Anglo-Saxon settlements made around the lower-most ford of the River Wensum, near its confluence with the River Yare. By 1066 it was one of the largest towns in England, with an Anglo-Danish population of about 5,500 (Green & Young, 1964), and indeed at this time east Norfolk was the most populous part of the country. By 1086, because o the effects of the Norman Conquest, the population had fallen to around

5,000, a large number of whom were Norman, French, Breton or Flemish. Subsequently, large numbers of Jews also arrived, but during the next 200 years many migrants were attracted from the surrounding countryside by the wealth of the city, and their influx reduced the alien proportion in the population. The cathedral was founded in 1094, and Norwich then became the administrative as well as ecclesiastical capital of the region. It was also the commercial capital of a fertile area producing wool and barley. At that time, trade routes eastward across the North Sea were as easy as those leading inland, because of the great distance from London and the swampy impassable nature of the Fens. There was a substantial immigration of Flemish weavers into the district in the fourteenth century and Norwich subsequently became the centre of a large cloth-making area.

From the middle of the sixteenth century, and for two hundred years or so, Norwich was probably the second largest city in England, rivalled only by Bristol and York. At the beginning of this period the weaving industry was in decline and Queen Elizabeth attempted to revive it by encouraging new immigration from the Low Countries. This coincided with a wave of religious persecution in that area, and by 1579 there were 6,000 Flemings and Walloons, known as 'Strangers', in the city's population of 16,000. The impact of these people, and their cohesion and influence as a group, can be gauged from the fact that an annual church service was held in Dutch in Norwich until the 1890s, and services in French continued until 1832 (Fowler, 1961). By the middle of the eighteenth century Norwich was one of the wealthiest cities in Britain, with the large population of 38,000. During the Napoleonic Wars, however, decline set in, and the city depended, throughout the nineteenth century, on its function as a market town for the surrounding agricultural districts. It lacked the fuel and power resources of the north of England and was therefore unable to participate fully in the industrial revolution, with the result that its place in the textile industry was taken over by the towns of Yorkshire and Lancashire. During the Victorian period the city gradually emerged, with the help of the development of the railways, as the mainly commercial and administrative centre that it is today.

The isolation which has affected Norwich particularly in the last 150 years has had unfortunate economic consequences. However, as a local writer has recently observed, 'it is possible for us who are living today to reflect that from an aesthetic point of view isolation had its

TABLE 1.3. *Population of Norwich county borough, 1921–67*

Year	Population	Year	Population
1921	120,661	1961	120,096
1931	126,236	1966	116,350
1939	121,700	1967	118,610
1951	121,236		

TABLE 1.4. *Population of five suburban parishes, 1951–61*

Parish	1951	1961
Thorpe St Andrew	8,281	10,788
Costessey	4,995	7,051
Catton	2,112	2,592
Hellesdon	6,359	9,744
Sprowston	5,485	9,609

TABLE 1.5. *Percentage of male work-force in selected categories*

	Employers, managers, professional	Junior non-manual, skilled manual
England and Wales	14.1	54.8
Norwich	10.7	62.6
Blofield and Flegg Rural District	17.0	45.9
Forehoe and Henstead Rural District	18.5	46.3
St Faiths and Aylsham Rural District	15.7	52.8

advantages' (Fowler, 1961). The centre of Norwich constitutes a considerable tourist attraction, and one estimate, based on current trends, has put the likely number of tourists to visit Norwich in the mid-1970s at about two million a year. The University of East Anglia is now situated in Norwich, as are also ITV and BBC television and radio stations. In 1961 Norwich was the thirty-fourth town in size in England and Wales.

1.3.1 Population. Since the First World War the population of Norwich has maintained a fairly steady level, as table 1.3 shows. The deline in population since 1931 has coincided with a large increase in the number of people living in the suburbs and suburban villages. Since

1921, the population of these areas has risen by over 300%. In 1961 an extra 21,500 people (equivalent to 18% of the resident population) came into Norwich to work each day. The increases in population of the five suburban parishes around Norwich between 1951 and 1961 are shown in table 1.4. During this same period, the largest population increases in Norfolk rural districts were in St Faiths and Aylsham (+8,374), Blofield and Flegg (+2,841) and Forehoe and Henstead (+2,484), all of which adjoin Norwich county borough. This represents increases of 26.5%, 8.9% and 10.00% respectively. The number of private dwellings in St Faiths and Aylsham Rural Districts rose by 49.3%. The importance of these areas to Norwich, and their social characteristics, as opposed to those of Norwich, are shown in the occupational statistics in table 1.5. This demonstrates that a large number of the Norwich professional and middle classes in fact live outside the city boundary, and that the social composition of the suburbs is biased towards the 'top' end of the occupational scale.

1.3.2 Social and economic character. Moser & Scott, in their study of British towns (1961), have placed Norwich, together with, for example, Bristol, Reading, York, Great Yarmouth and Ipswich, in a group of sixteen towns which are characterised as 'mainly commercial centres with some industry'. This group is added to those towns which are 'mainly seaside resorts' and those which are 'mainly spas, professional and administrative centres', and together these form Group A 'mainly resorts, administrative and commercial towns'. This group of thirty-six towns differs in its social and population characteristics from Group B, sixty-five 'mainly industrial towns' and Group C, fifty-four 'suburban and suburban type towns'.

For a total of 157 English and Welsh towns, Moser & Scott have made a comparison based on many different variables, mainly taken from 1951 Census data. As well as being allotted a percentage or index score, each town is arranged in rank order, from 1 to 157, for each variable. That is to say that a low number (high position) indicates a relatively high number or amount of each variable concerned. Variables for which Norwich was clearly above or below average for the country are listed in table 1.6, together with the rank position out of 157. Compared to other English and Welsh towns, Norwich has a high population. It has a high number of old people; illegitimate births; new houses (particularly local authority houses); local authority houses generally; and left-wing voters.

TABLE 1.6. *The position of Norwich relative to other centres*

Variable	Position
Population	43
Percentage of population aged 65 or over	34
Illegitimate births, 1950–2	26
Illegitimate births, 1955–7	31
Percentage of overcrowded households	128
Percentage of one-person households	48
Percentage of households in shared dwellings	132
New housing rate, 1945–58	27
New local authority housing rate, 1945–58	14
Local authority percentage of total houses built, 1945–58	47
Percentage employed in finance	3
Per capita retail sales, 1950	20
Percentage in 1955 voting Labour or other left wing	42
Percentage voting in contested local elections	24
Infant-mortality rate, 1955–7	150

It has a very high proportion of people working in finance, which underlines the previously mentioned important commercial function of the city. It also has a very high *per capita* retail sales figure, which is probably due to the large size of its rural hinterland, rather than to the general affluence of the region, which, as we have seen, is not very high. (The hinterland of Norwich, which has been defined as 'that area in which public transport carries passengers more conveniently to Norwich than to any other centre' (Thomas, 1961), had in 1961 an estimated population of 131,000, which is larger than that of the centre (Norwich county borough) itself. This gives a combined total of a quarter of a million people who look to Norwich as a commercial centre. Comparable centres have very much smaller hinterlands: Oxford (64,000); York (48,000); Plymouth (55,000). (Plymouth itself has a population almost twice that of Norwich.) The 1957 Census of distribution shows that Norwich is well above the national average both in its number of shops per head of population, and in turnover per shop. City stores have a very wide delivery area, and most deliver to the whole of Norfolk and parts of neighbouring counties.) Norwich also has a low number of overcrowded households and shared dwellings, and a low infant-mortality rate.

1.3.3   Internal differentiation. The only figures available for a discussion of the internal social and economic characteristics of the city of

Norwich are the 1961 Census figures concerning electoral wards. This is somewhat unfortunate, since ward boundaries are not necessarily economically or socially significant, and wards are usually larger in size than geographical neighbourhoods. However, an analysis of these figures can help to convey some picture of the changing social and geographical structure of the city, and of the characteristics of different areas.[1]

The pattern that emerges from this analysis indicates that Norwich falls into three main regions of population change (see map 1):

(a) a northern, central and eastern region where emigration has been at a high level;

(b) a western region, where emigration has been low; and

(c) a southern and south-western region which has had moderate-to-large increases in population.

Only Crome ward seems to fall outside this pattern, appearing as it does to drive a wedge of high immigration areas into the centre of the city. This is, in fact, a case of ward boundaries disguising what has actually occurred. Only the Heartsease Council housing estate, which did not exist in 1951, has had a significant increase in population. This estate occupies the rectangular area which juts out beyond the rest of the city in the east. It seems certain that the older area of Crome (left blank on map 1) has the same kind of emigration characteristics as the two wards on either side of it, Mousehold and Thorpe. (This is also likely to be true, of course, of the inner areas of Town Close and Lakenham). There is, in any case, a definite drift in population from the north, east and west of the city to the south.

This trend is also partly illustrated by the figures concerning the proportion of old age pensioners in each ward (see map 2), which show that older people are being left behind in the centre and north of the city. These figures are also helpful in demonstrating the character and age of each ward. The central areas of the city, particularly those with a predominance of pre-First World War terraced housing, have the highest proportion of old age pensioners, the outer areas a lower proportion, with the south-western areas of Eaton and Town Close having the lowest proportion of all (except for the two predominantly post-war council estate wards, Earlham and Crome).

---

[1] The figures in the following section are taken from J. H. Mabry, 'Norwich 1961 – an analysis of census returns', an unpublished study of 1961 Census returns for Norwich obtained from the General Register Office. I am grateful to Professor A. R. Emerson, University of East Anglia, for providing me with this study.

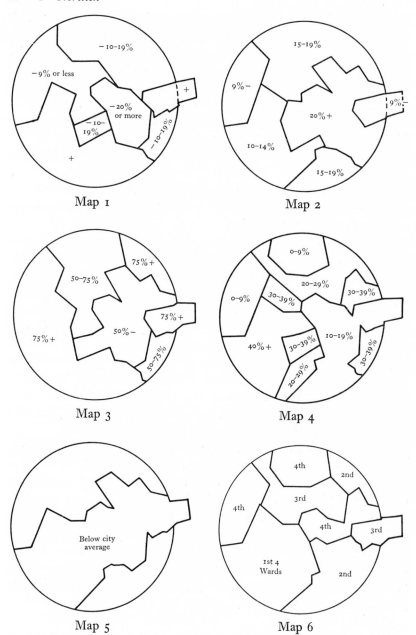

Map 1

Map 2

Map 3

Map 4

Map 5

Map 6

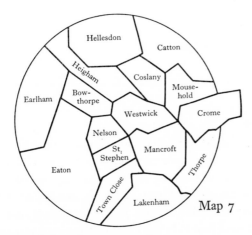

Map 7

Map 1   Population change, 1951–61
Map 2   Percentage of old age pensioners
Map 3   Percentage of households with four facilities
Map 4   Percentage of households owner occupied
Map 5   Percentage of persons living at more than 1.5 persons per room
Map 6   Social class index: four groups of four wards.
Map 7   City wards

These figures, combined with other indices of social characteristics (see maps 3–6), present a picture of the increasing economic and social dominance of the southern and south-western part of the city in general, and Eaton ward in particular. It is perhaps significant that this area lies on and around the approach roads from London, the A11 and the A140.[1] This bias to the south and south-west is to a certain extent counteracted by the more prosperous suburbs outside the city boundary to the north and east, such as Thorpe St Andrew and Catton. It is worth noting, however, that the most statusful of all the city suburbs, Cringleford, lies just over the city boundary immediately adjacent to Eaton.

[1] It is, however, true of many British towns that the south-western areas are generally more statusful than others. This may be ascribed to the prevailing south-westerly winds, which mean that these areas suffer less from air pollution.

2 The sample

2.1 Sampling

Many previous linguistic and dialectological surveys have been based on work carried out with informants who were chosen either because they were elderly natives of the area under survey and therefore likely to be 'pure' dialect speakers (cf. Orton & Dieth, 1962–), or simply because they were easily available. Other surveys, such as that reported in Kurath & McDavid (1961) in the U.S.A., have been of a more sophisticated type, but have relied basically on the same relatively haphazard methods. There are obvious and serious dangers in this type of approach, particularly when one is dealing with a large urban population, rather than with a small rural community. Typically, the urban population is heterogeneous, and both socially and geographically mobile; sociological factors are more important from the point of view of linguistic differentiation than geographical factors; and the social structure is of a complexity that makes close individual knowledge of the area impossible, and person-to-person contact as a means of selecting informants useless.

It is, of course, neither practicable nor desirable to interview the entire population of a city. That is to say that a survey of this kind must necessarily be incomplete. Obviously, a survey can only be complete if the population to be covered is small, as in a restricted rural area, or if the resources to be employed are very large. (Even if it were possible to interview every single individual in a survey, this would serve no useful purpose, since sample survey methods make the effort unnecessary, and the vast amount of detail obtained could well lead to confusion and inaccuracies.) On the other hand, one does want to ensure that the language one is describing is truly the language of the city, rather than that of a few hand-picked informants. (It is, of course, legitimate to rely on a few hand-picked informants if the object is, for example, to record older dialect forms before they become extinct. It is doubtful, however, if even this can be totally justified with any large, heterogeneous population.) Informants selected solely because they are available and willing to be interviewed are simply a part of the population of the city, not a representative sample, and no valid statements concerning the language of the city as a whole can be based on evidence obtained from informants selected in this way: 'It is entirely wrong to make an arbitrary selection of cases, to rely on volunteers or people who happen to be at hand, and then to claim that they are a proper sample of some particular population' (Moser, 1958, p. 51).

There is only one way to ensure that the results obtained in an incomplete survey of this kind can legitimately be said to apply to the population as a whole: the section of the population which is to be studied must be selected by 'accepted statistical methods' (p. 50). The informants, that is, must constitute a genuine representative sample of the city's population. This particular work is based on a series of interviews carried out with a sample of the population of the city of Norwich which was obtained by methods which are statistically acceptable. The sample is large enough and sufficiently scientifically devised to permit reasonably confident assertions to be made concerning the population as a whole, and small enough to permit accurate and intensive study over a limited period of time.

2.2 Sampling method

The sample, which is probably best described as a quasi-random sample, was taken from the local register of electors. A random sample is a sample where every member of the population has a calculable and non-zero chance of being selected. In a simple random sample every member has an equal chance of selection. The quasi-random sample method, which is described below, is often employed where the population in question is a large one, and when the sample is to be drawn from some kind of pre-arranged list, rather than by using some form of lottery method. Strictly speaking, this method is not equivalent to simple random sampling, since the number of possible samples is much smaller, but it is 'generally justified by the argument that the list [in this case the register of electors] can be regarded as arranged more or less at random, or that the feature by which it is arranged [streets and house numbers] is not related to the subject of the survey' (Moser, 1958, p. 77. Cf. Goode & Hatt, 1952, p. 217). It has one advantage for a linguistic survey, apart from the obvious advantages of speed and facility, in that there is a better chance of obtaining an overall geographical coverage of a particular area, and thus being able to investigate possible geographical variation. The method is to divide the number of the total population of the area in question by the number of informants desired, in order to obtain the sampling fraction. A number smaller than the sampling fraction is then randomly selected, and the person with that number on the list becomes the first member of the sample group. Then the remaining members of the sample group are obtained by adding the sampling fraction number to the number of the first member selected, and then to that of the second member, and so on, so that the selection of the first member automatically determines the selection of all the others. (All members of the population, in other words, do not have an equal chance of selection.) Thus, if the total population is 90, and the desired number of informants 9, the sampling fraction will be 10. If the first member randomly selected is number 4, then the remainder of the sample will consist of numbers 14, 24, 34, 44, 54, 64, 74, and 84, giving a total of 9 in all.

The sample for the Norwich survey was not drawn from the register of electors for the city as a whole. It was decided instead to sample four of the city's electoral wards only. This procedure has the approval of experts in the field of survey methods: 'Let us suppose that a sample of individuals is to be selected in a town with a population of 250,000. Most probably, one would decide to concentrate the interviews in a few areas, so the first step may be to pick some of the wards in the town' (Moser, 1958, p. 76). The advantages of this kind of approach in a survey of this type are that it opens up the possibility of investigating geographical variation within the city, and that it makes contacting informants and conducting interviews a much less laborious and time-consuming business, as the geographical area to be covered is much smaller. The four wards were not selected at random, but were chosen so that they had, between them, social and economic characteristics that were, on average, the same as those of the city as a whole.[1] They were, moreover,

---

[1] This method of selecting wards which are representative of the city as a whole, and of then taking an equal number of informants from each ward to ensure that this representativeness is maintained in the sample, would appear to be equivalent to selecting wards at random, and then taking informants from each ward in proportion to its population size. However, the advantage of the type of procedure adopted here is that all main types of social area are sure to be represented, which increases the chances of obtaining informants from all types of social background. With a sample of this size it would otherwise be quite possible to miss altogether professional workers and other probable RP speakers, who only constitute a very small percentage of the population. (For means of obtaining higher-than-representative proportions for comparative purposes see Martin (1954, p. 52).) In the present sample we have made certain of obtaining informants from the northern, central, southern and western parts of the city, which, as we saw in chapter 2, are socially and economically very

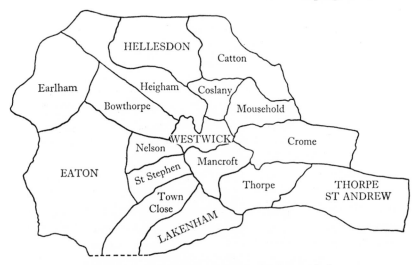

Map 8   Four wards and one suburb sampled

chosen so as to represent different types of area from the point of view of social, geographical and housing characteristics (see table 2.1, p. 24).[1] (This can be confirmed by checking with maps 1–6, p. 18.) The four wards were: Eaton (E); Lakenham (L); Hellesdon (H); and Westwick (W). The sampling fraction was adjusted so as to give an equal number of informants from each area. In addition, a sample was drawn from one of the suburban parishes outside the city boundary, Thorpe St Andrew (see map 8). It was important to do this because, as we saw in chapter 1, the suburban areas form an important part of the social structure of the urban area of Norwich. It means, too, that the eastern area of the city is also represented.

Each person listed in the register of electors also has a number, which is a useful aid in the selection of the sample. In each of the five areas, an initial sample of 25 persons was randomly selected from the register. A number smaller than the adjusted sampling fraction was taken from a table of random numbers. The person whose number this was became the first member of the sample in each area, and his selection automatically determined that of the remaining 24 members. The initial

different, and it is particularly useful to have both the economically dominant ward (Eaton) and one from the opposite end of the scale (Westwick) together in one sample.

1 The social class and socio-economic class and age indices are those developed by Mabry (unpublished), and the other figures are taken from the 1961 Census of England and Wales.

TABLE 2.1(*a*). *Economic and social characteristics of Norwich and four selected wards*

	Social class index	Socio-economic index	Pen-sioners (%)	Age index	Non-manual (%)	Foremen and skilled (%)	Semi-skilled and un-skilled (%)
E	71.50	62.00	14.00	57	50.00	33.00	17.00
L	47.50	50.70	17.00	52	26.00	45.00	30.00
H	40.00	45.00	18.00	50	14.00	53.00	32.00
W	38.00	43.00	26.00	37	15.00	53.00	32.00
Mean	49.25	50.10	18.75	49	26.25	46.00	27.75
Norwich	50.00	50.00	17.10	50	27.40	45.70	26.50

TABLE 2.1(*b*). *Type of occupation by ward*

	Pro-fessional (%)	Employers and managers (%)	Junior non-manual (%)	Foremen and skilled (%)	Service and semi-skilled (%)	Un-skilled (%)
E	11.00	15.00	24.00	33.00	10.00	7.00
L	1.00	5.00	20.00	45.00	18.00	12.00
H	0.00	4.00	10.00	53.00	12.00	20.00
W	1.00	4.00	10.00	53.00	18.00	14.00
Mean	3.25	7.00	16.00	46.00	14.50	14.25
Norwich	2.80	7.60	17.00	45.70	14.00	12.50

selection thus comprised 125 names and addresses, from five different areas of the urban region. It was decided on purely practical grounds that the maximum number of informants who could be interviewed in the time available was 50, 10 from each ward. Introductory letters were therefore sent out to 10 people randomly selected from each group of 25. The purpose of the letter was to secure the goodwill of the informant, to explain the purpose of the interview, to allay any suspicions concerning the integrity and honesty of the interviewer and the non-commercial nature of the study, and to warn the informant that he was to be called on. The letter was signed by myself, but the authenticity of the study was stressed by the fact that the letter was typewritten on University of Edinburgh notepaper, and mentioned both Professor

Lyons and the University of East Anglia. It also mentioned that I was a native of Norwich, which seemed to be of some help in counteracting the suspicions which some of the informants had for this kind of study.

2.3 Securing interviews

A day or two after the dispatch of each letter, I called on each potential informant to secure an interview, to explain further the purpose of the interview, and to give further details of the method (such as the use of the tape-recorder). On occasions the informant was willing to have the interview conducted straight away, but more frequently it was necessary to make an appointment for some future date. Some informants, of course, were less willing or more suspicious than others, and it was at this point that their reluctance had to be overcome. Often a certain amount of ingenuity had to be used in order to obtain co-operation, but more often people were very willing to help, and showed considerable interest at the prospect of talking about 'old Norfolk words' and other allied topics. Some, however, wanted to be assured about the complete anonymity of the study; and the tape-recorder had often to be justified as a time-saving device.

The success rate in securing interviews was not particularly high, for several reasons. It was decided, in the first place, not to interview anybody who had moved to Norwich from outside East Anglia in the last ten years. Strictly speaking, to obtain a realistic picture of the speech of the city, and particularly of attitudes to Norwich speech, it would have been necessary to interview everybody, irrespective of their origin. It was, however, felt that, in view of the short time available and the small size of the sample, time could not be spent on informants whose linguistic behaviour was radically different from other informants. Some of the initial selection, moreover, had moved away from Norwich since the compilation of the register, and others were blind or too senile or infirm to be interviewed. Difficulties of this kind cannot be overcome in a linguistic survey as readily as they can in an ordinary social survey: people who have left Norwich are no longer part of the Norwich speech community; blind people cannot take part in the reading tests; and so on. In addition, as with all social surveys, some people had died, and others refused to participate, or could not be contacted. In all such cases of failure, names of replacements were selected from among the remainder of the 25 in each ward. In all, to obtain the 50 informants, it was necessary to send letters to 95 of the original 125 people selected. Of these 95, 12 were not from Norwich, 5 had moved, 3 had died, and 3 were blind or infirm. (Those who had left their original address, but were still in Norwich, were located and interviewed if possible.) Of the remaining 72, 15 refused to be interviewed, and 7 were not contacted. This refusal and no-contact rate is high for a social survey. The standard approach in a social survey is to follow up a refusal with second, third and further visits, in order to secure an interview, because it is important to minimise the number of refusals, in order that the sample should remain truly representative. This is particularly so in ordinary social surveys, since, as can readily be imagined, the attitudes of people who refuse to be interviewed on, say, race relations, may well be significantly different from those of the rest of the population.

This approach, however, was not adopted in this survey, as it was thought that linguistic behaviour was unlikely to show significant differences of this type. Labov (1966a) has shown, in fact, that those informants who refused him interviews or could not be contacted, and whose linguistic behaviour was later studied by other means, were in no way different from the other informants in their language characteristics. It was therefore decided, for the purposes of the Norwich survey, that following up refusals in the usual way would be a time-consuming, unrewarding and unnecessary task. A further consideration was that, in order for an interview to be successful and as much conversation as possible to be recorded, the good-will of the informant was very necessary, and repeated attempts at persuasion were likely to jeopardise this. The number of refusals was probably also fairly high because the nature of the interview, which involved the use of a microphone and a tape-recorder, was rather more intimidating than the normal type of social survey interview (cf. Levine & Crockett, 1966, p. 78). (Reasons for refusal included: inability to afford the time; not feeling well enough to take part; failure to see the point of the study; unstated but obvious fear of the whole exercise; and one gentleman who did not 'believe in universities'.) 'No contact' means that several visits were made to the address in question, and that nobody could be found at home. This was often because of holidays, since the interviews were conducted during July. The policy of not following up refusals meant that very little time was wasted, and the 50 informants were written to, visited and interviewed in a little over three weeks.

2.4 Schoolchildren

The register of electors has one important defect as a sampling frame: at the time of the survey only people aged twenty-one or over were listed. To be of any significance, however, a linguistic survey of this nature needs to study the linguistic characteristics of all age-groups. This defect was therefore remedied by drawing a sample of 10 schoolchildren from two of the schools in Norwich. The children were all aged between 10 and 20, as there was not sufficient time available to obtain a sample of younger children as well. The schools were not selected at random; they were in fact two out of the three state-maintained grammar schools in the city. The sample was drawn from this type of school since they are the only local schools which have the entire city (but no areas outside the city) as their catchment area. This particular sample could for this reason act as a kind of control for the main sample in the investigation of geographical variation within the city, and could possibly also shed light on the speech of those areas of the city not covered in the main sample. It might be supposed that the fact that both schools were grammar schools would bias the sample towards the higher end of the social scale. This, however, was not the case.[1]

2.5 Characteristics of the sample

Thus, the final sample of informants who gave interviews on which this work is based consisted of 60 people. This sample is considerably smaller than those used both in New York City and in Detroit, but Labov has demonstrated that a sample even smaller than this is sufficient for the purposes of a linguistic survey, and concludes: 'the structure of social and stylistic variation of language can be studied through samples considerably smaller than those required for the study of other forms of social behaviour' (Labov, 1966a, p. 638).[2]

The different indices used for classifying each of these 60 informants

[1] One drawback which arises from taking a sample of schoolchildren is that we do not have in the sample any people aged under 21 who are working rather than still at school. This may have the effect of biasing results against standardizing tendencies due to the job situation. It will also be clear that the selection of the schoolchildren was slightly less scientific than that of the rest of the sample. This can be justified in terms of the time available for the survey, and in terms of the results obtained and discussed in later chapters.

[2] However, a rather larger sample would have been useful for those cases where it is desirable to classify informants according to sex, age and social class simultaneously.

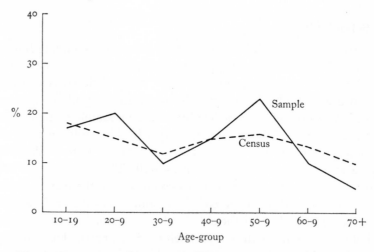

Fig. 1   Percentage of persons in different age-groups in Norwich, as reported in 1966 Sample Census and in Linguistic Survey Sample

individually, for the purposes of correlating their linguistic behaviour with sociological factors, will be described below. At this point, however, it will be useful briefly to illustrate the social characteristics of the sample as a whole, and to compare these with the characteristics of the population of the city as described in the Censuses of 1961 and 1966. This comparison will not, of course, constitute conclusive proof that the sample is truly representative of the city as a whole, and indeed no sample, however scientifically selected, can be free from inaccuracies. It will, however, underline the validity of using a sample for the purposes of a linguistic survey, rather than simply informants who happen to be available. It will also give some idea of the type of people who were interviewed during the course of the survey. It must be remembered, though, that the Census figures were respectively seven and two years out of date at the time when the sample was selected, and that 20% of the sample was drawn from Thorpe St Andrew, which is not included in the Census figures.

Figs. 1–3 show comparisons of the sample with the population of the city as a whole with respect to age-group; occupation; and educational characteristics. It can be seen that the general age-group structure of the city is reflected in the sample: both curves have the same kind of overall outline. Some groups, however, are slightly under-represented in the sample (probably, in the case of the over-sixties, because of the

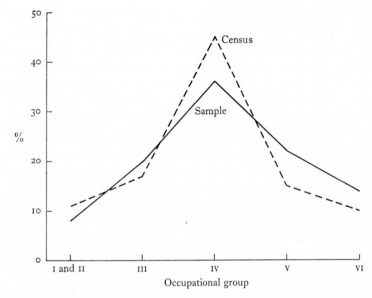

Fig. 2   Percentage of persons in different occupational groups in Norwich, as reported in 1966 Sample Census and in Linguistic Survey Sample

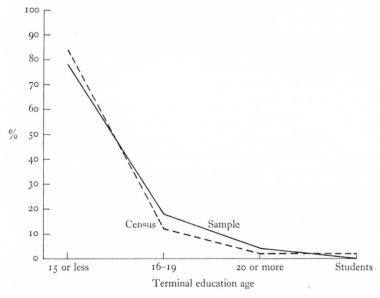

Fig. 3   Percentage of persons in different terminal education age-groups in Norwich, as reported in 1961 Census and in Linguistic Survey Sample

younger average age of those living in the more recently built areas of Thorpe). Other groups, notably the 50–59-year-old group, are over-represented. The two curves showing occupation structure also have the same overall outline. Most of the inconsistencies here, moreover, can be accounted for by the fact that the Census data is for males only, while the sample, of course, contains both males and females. The apparent over-representation of Group v, which includes personal-service workers, is therefore probably due to the large proportion of women who work in shops. The groups listed i to vi are based on classifications used in the 1966 Sample Census, which in turn are based on the Registrar General's Classification of Occupations (1966). Groups i and ii comprise professional workers, employers, and managers; Group iii other non-manual workers; Group iv foremen, skilled workers and self-employed persons; Group v semi-skilled and personal-service workers; and Group vi unskilled workers. (The Census figures also contain 2.1 % listed as armed forces or 'occupation inadequately described'.) The two curves showing educational status, here measured by the terminal education age of those aged over 15, are extremely close. The fact that there is a time-lag of eight years between the two sets of figures could well account for the apparent slight over-representation of the middle two groups, because of the steady increase in the proportion of the population who have remained longer at school. Sociological indices employed for characterising each informant individually are described in the following chapter.

3 *Social indices*

3.1 Measurement of social phenomena

One of the main purposes of this study is to investigate the nature and extent of the correlation between and co-variation of linguistic and sociological parameters in the city of Norwich. In this chapter, we shall discuss briefly those sociological parameters which can be subsumed under the heading of 'social stratification', together with the relationship between these parameters and language. Mainly, however, we shall be discussing the ways in which they can be associated with measurements of an individual's social status, in order that he can be ranked in the social scale and his linguistic behaviour compared with his social position. (The measurement of those sociological parameters associated with social context will be discussed in chapter 4, and the measurement of linguistic parameters in chapters 5 and 6.)

3.2 Social stratification

Social stratification is a complicated subject, and discussions and definitions associated with this topic in sociological literature are both varied and complex. At a simple level, however, social stratification can be described as one particular form of social differentiation (see Mayer, 1955, p. 4), and has been defined as 'any hierarchical ordering of social groups or strata in a society' (Bottomore, 1965, p. 15). In Britain, as in other Western societies, social stratification takes the form of the division of society into different social classes and status groups, rather than into, say, different castes. There is little point in attempting to evaluate or even enumerate the different approaches adopted by sociologists to the topic of social class and socio-economic class. There are very many different explanations and definitions of these terms in the sociological literature. And, as is the case with some linguistic terms, it is often necessary to define, in each individual study, exactly what is meant on each occasion by 'social class'. A simple and not particularly controversial definition of social class is the following: 'a major social group, members of which are of approximately [the] same economic position' (Reading, 1963, p. 27). An alternative definition is 'a major social group, members of which are of approximately [the] same economic position, prestige, occupational rank, power, value orientations, and characterised by interaction and class consciousness' (p. 27). Other sociologists introduce the concept of social evaluation, in addition to the concept of social differentiation, in order to define social class (see Barber, 1957, ch. 1). The type of attitude that is adopted to the term 'social class' in this study will emerge during the course of this chapter. But it is in any case widely accepted that social class stratification is based primarily on differences in wealth and income, and it is also true that most members of our society have some kind of idea, intuitive or otherwise, of what social class is.

Social classes, then, are not organised or sharply demarcated social groups, but are rather aggregates of people with similar economic characteristics. The differences between classes in income and wealth are expressed in different types of consumption, education, manners, dress, taste, speech and so on (Mayer, 1955, chs. 3 and 5). The exact nature of the mechanism leading to this differential expression of wealth is not clear. Obviously, it is partly due to the fact that more expensive clothes, consumer durables and so on are available only to those able to afford them. But it also seems certain that it is partly of the same nature as the mechanism associated with the spread of dialect features across geographical areas, so that dialect boundaries often coincide with troughs in the communications network (see chapter 1). In other words, social barriers are as effective as geographical barriers in halting or slowing down the diffusion of fashions, ideas, values and speech forms which have originated in a particular social group, from one section of the community to another. Hence different groups have different customs. These social barriers arise, in the first place, through differential access to socially desirable types of objects and activities, such as housing and education, because of differences in wealth and income. These two aspects of the mechanism of differentiation are, of course, interrelated, in that objects and activities initially available only to the wealthier members of the community come to be thought of as socially desirable by lower social groups. This type of downward diffusion, however, is by no means the only form of diffusion process.

These differences in consumption, manners, dress and so on give rise to different status groups, which are social groups whose members see themselves as equals, with common understandings, attitudes and behaviour, and who regard outsiders as social superiors or inferiors. There is thus a hierarchy of status groups, which is related to, but not identical with, the class hierarchy. This means that in a class society the stratificational structure is very complex, since objective factors, such as income, and subjective factors, such as status evaluation associated with, for example, consumption patterns, are interrelated and combined in a very complicated way. Moreover, in a society of this type, class boundaries and barriers are relatively fluid and flexible, and a relatively large amount of social mobility is possible, both up and down the social scale. There are also a relatively large number of anomalous individuals, and others whom it is difficult to place with any degree of assurance in a particular social class. There are those who, while objectively members of a particular class, assume, or attempt to assume, the status characteristics of another, usually higher, class. This anticipatory socialisation (when an individual takes as his reference group a status group to which he does not belong) is particularly important from a linguistic point of view.

In this kind of society, therefore, a study of the correlation of linguistic and sociological phenomena is much more complex and difficult than in, say, a caste society. The different social groups in a caste society are, relatively speaking, discrete units, there is little social mobility of individuals, and it is a relatively small distortion of the facts to discuss each caste dialect as a separate entity, in which contextual factors are the only relevant sociological parameters determining linguistic variation. This is just not possible in a class society, although some linguists have attempted it. For a linguistic study of any large community within a class society to be in any way significant the class continuum must be objectively measured against the linguistic continuum, and vice versa.[1]

It is, of course, an open question to what extent the 'class continuum' (and correspondingly the 'linguistic continuum') is, in fact, a continuum. We have already stated above that, in a class society, there is a relatively large amount of flexibility and social mobility. However, at least one fairly large barrier seems to remain. This is the gap between what are usually referred to as the 'middle classes' and the 'working classes', a distinction which is usually but not entirely related to the distinction

---

[1] 'The correlation of social status and linguistic performance first requires a careful delineation of each' (Shuy *et al.*, 1968, p. 11).

between those working in respectively non-manual and manual occupations. It has been shown, for example, that, in Britain, opportunities
for upward social mobility by working class people is relatively restricted
(Glass & Hall, 1954), and that their access to higher education is also
limited (Hall & Glass, 1954; Lawton, 1968, ch. 1). It has, moreover,
been shown that even the most affluent manual workers retain the
values, ideas, behaviour patterns and general culture of the working
class, and that there has been little *embourgeoisement* of the British
working class (Goldthorpe & Lockwood, 1963). This suggests that
occupation is in fact the main stratifying factor in our society, and that
difference in wealth and income, although obviously very closely related
to occupation, may not be the factor on which social class differentiation is primarily based. This of course relates to the subjective experience
of most members of our society, who know that to enquire about a
person's occupation is to enquire about his social position, and that
a car-factory worker who earns £2,000 a year has less social status than
a bank-clerk who earns much less. This split between 'working class'
and 'middle class' is therefore likely to be a very important factor in
a description of the linguistic characteristics of any British urban area,
particularly in so far as it acts as a barrier to the spreading of linguistic
changes. If the social barrier between the middle and the working
classes is a large or significant one, this will be reflected in the extent of
the diffusion of various linguistic innovations, and in differing norms
of linguistic behaviour generally (see Labov, 1966a, ch. 8).

3.3   Social class and linguistic studies

In linguistic work it has long been realised that language is in many
ways a form of social behaviour, and that social factors are as important
as geographical factors in determining linguistic variation. For this
reason linguists have attempted, in some previous studies, to classify
their informants sociologically, in order to relate their speech to their
social background. This has been done, in more or less sophisticated
ways, in an attempt to avoid making subjective and therefore possibly
unreliable and circular judgements of social status. In only a few studies,
however, have linguists actually been successful in achieving any kind
of non-linguistic and sociologically satisfactory measurement of their
informants' social class position. (Among these studies are the surveys
which have been carried out in New York City (Labov, 1966a), Detroit

(Shuy *et al.*, 1967), and the North Carolina Piedmont (Levine & Crockett, 1966).)

There is a large amount of sociological literature on this topic which is both readily available and extremely useful for linguists engaged in this type of work (see Warner *et al.*, 1959; Lundberg, 1940; Kornhauser, 1953; Hochbaum *et al.*, 1955). In spite of this, however, most attempted methods of measuring social class in linguistic studies, apart from the three just mentioned, have been unsatisfactory. One can cite, for example, the work of Kurath & McDavid in the U.S.A. (1961), which was one of the first large-scale attempts to measure social as well as regional variation. This attempt, as described by Kurath (1939), relies on a view of social class which regards class position as being more or less identical with level of educational attainment. This somewhat naïve position (together with the 'sampling' methods used in the survey) has been strongly criticised by Pickford (1956) for ignoring the great importance of other stratifying factors in American society. This means that the classification of speech forms in the survey as 'cultivated', 'middle class' and 'folk' can be neither objective nor consistent and is therefore of doubtful value. A similar study is that of DeCamp (1958–9) whose work is in many ways based on that of Kurath & McDavid. Here again the social classification of informants, which is if anything somewhat less sophisticated than that of Kurath & McDavid, is based only on education. DeCamp divides his informants into three educational groups. They consist of people who have, respectively, only elementary education; only secondary education; and some college education. (Informants are also classified according to ethnic group.) Both these studies represent a significant advance on, for example, the work of Orton & Dieth (1962–), and Sivertsen (1960), who pay very little or no attention to social differentiation. They are, however, still seriously deficient.

3.4 The social class index

In order to measure objectively the social class and status characteristics of the Norwich sample, an index of social class was devised, and an index score calculated for each informant. In this way, co-variation between linguistic behaviour and social status could be studied accurately, and statements concerning, for example, 'working-class speech' could be made with a reasonable degree of assurance and reliability. The advantage of using an index of the kind employed in this study, rather than some other measurement of social class, is that it provides an objective, standardised and easily calculated indicator of social class which is at the same time reliable and capable of ranking informants in a scale. The advantage of using an index constructed specifically for this particular study lies in the fact that 'there can be no such thing as a single index of socio-economic status for all purposes of social research in a modern, complex society' (Duncan, 1961, p. 139). It is also the case that different geographical areas may require different indices.

The index developed for the purpose of this particular work was a multiple-item index, rather than the simpler and more unreliable type of single-item index used, for instance, by DeCamp. A multiple-item index, by increasing the number of indicators of social class involved, is a much more refined and reliable means of measuring social class: 'several indicators in combination increase the validity of an index' (Barber, 1957, p. 176). It is also possible, with a multiple-item index, for individual indicators to be examined separately for correlations with linguistic behaviour, in order to gauge the relative importance of each one for linguistic variation. Many types of multiple-item indices for measuring social class have been devised by sociologists, and a large amount of work has been done on comparing these indices and assessing their validity (see Kahl & Davies, 1955; Finch & Hoehn, 1951). The problems of index construction for the purposes of non-sociological work are for this reason not too complex. The six indicators used in compiling this index, moreover, have all been employed previously by sociologists in constructing social class indices, although perhaps not in exactly this combination. It was felt that a six-item index would give a finer stratification of the informants than, for instance, Labov's three-item index. This was thought to be especially necessary since social differentiation is probably much greater in New York City than in Norwich, and a more sophisticated index is therefore essential in order to bring out the less obvious but equally important differences which are to be found in Norwich.

The six indicators used in constructing the index were: occupation; income; education; housing; locality; and father's occupation. We have already stated that occupation is probably the most important stratifying element in British society. This assumption has the support of sociologists: 'occupational position is the best single indicator of social stratificational position in contemporary American society... this is probably also true in any industrial society' (Barber, 1957, pp. 184–5). It therefore follows that 'in contemporary industrial society, the single item most commonly used for social class indices is occupational position' (p. 171). There is a considerable body of work on the social grading of occupations, which simplifies the task of devising this kind of index (see Moser & Hall, 1954; Hatt, 1950; Duncan, 1961; Davies, 1952). In many multiple-item indices the occupation indicator has been weighted relative to the other indicators in the calculation of the final index score, since it has been thought to be of prime importance (see Lenski, 1954). This was not done, however, in this particular work, since it was considered that weighting was implicitly present in the choice of the next two indicators, income and education. These two indicators are clearly closely correlated with occupation. They are also fairly obviously important stratifying factors in our society, in their own right, and have figured as such in many sociological indices. Housing and locality are less frequently used as indicators of social class, but are obviously of some significance, and by no means rare in indices devised by sociologists.[1] They are perhaps not so useful in wider studies, since they tend to be products of differences in the local community, and are therefore likely to vary in the nature and degree of their significance from place to place. They are, however, entirely suitable in a one-area study of this kind. Father's occupation is also clearly of some importance in assessing social class, since one is initially born into the particular social class group which is that of one's parents. This is particularly important from a linguistic point of view, since social mobility is known to have an effect on linguistic behaviour (Labov, 1966c). It is also known that father's occupation and class of origin are important factors from a purely sociological point of view (Martin, 1954). By including these last three indicators, housing, locality, and father's occupation, we hope to obtain a more precise subdivision of informants than would otherwise have been possible.

[1] See Mack (1951), who is more concerned with the condition and state of repair of the dwelling than the ownership or type, and Duncan & Duncan (1955). Cf. Barber (1957, p. 144), 'The type of dwelling place and its location within the local community are likely to be symbols of social class position in all societies.'

TABLE 3.1. *Index of occupation and father's occupation*

	Index score
I　Groups 3, 4	5
II　Groups 1, 2, 13	4
III　Groups 5, 6	3
IV　Groups 8, 9, 12, 14	2
V　Groups 7, 10, 15	1
VI　Group 11	0

(General Register Office, Classification of Occupations, 1966)

3.5　Index score calculation

We can now proceed to a description of exactly how the index is calculated. We have already stated that the social class index is composed of six separate indicators. For each of these indicators a six-point scale was developed, and a score ranging from 0 to 5 allotted to each informant. Possible social class index scores therefore ranged from 0 to 30.

3.5.1　Occupation. The six point scale developed for the calculation of scores for occupation and father's occupation is shown in table 3.1.

The groups used in the scale are those of the Registrar General's Classification of Occupations (1966). The arrangement of the groups is based on, but not identical with, the arrangement used in certain of the tables in the 1966 Sample Census. The composition of the groups is as follows: Groups 3 and 4 consist of professional workers; Groups 1, 2 and 13 of employers and managers; Groups 5 and 6 of other non-manual workers; Groups 8, 9, 12 and 14 of foremen, skilled manual workers, and own account workers; Groups 7, 10 and 15 of personal service, semi-skilled and agricultural workers; and Group 11 of unskilled workers. More detailed explanation of exactly what those terms imply can be found in the Classification.

Married women and widows were rated on their husbands' occupation, and unmarried women on their fathers'. This was done because 'with the still limited employment opportunities for women – that is, especially in professional and administrative roles – occupation is not a satisfactory index of social status for women in our society' (Glass & Hall, 1954, p. 83). It also seems clear that the social class position of the bread-winner determines the social class position of the family. However, in those cases where working women had occupational status

TABLE 3.2. *Index of income*

				Index score
G	£2,000+	⎫		⎧ 5
F	£1,000–£1,999	⎬ (annual salary)		⎨ 4
E	£999 –	⎭		⎩ 3
D	£20+	⎫		⎧ 3
C	£15–£19	⎬ (usual weekly wage)		⎨ 2
B	£10–£14	⎭		⎩ 1
A	£9 –			0

higher than that of their husband or father, the informant's own occupation was used, since it seemed probable that her higher status would in many ways be recognised as such by society as a whole, and that her linguistic behaviour would accordingly differ from that of her husband or father. Schoolchildren, like unmarried women, were ranked according to their father's occupation, both for occupation and for father's occupation. Father's occupation was scored according to the father's present occupation, or, if he was no longer working, his last occupation (cf. Glass & Hall, 1954, p. 83).

3.5.2 Income. The scale for ranking informants according to their income is shown in table 3.2. Women and schoolchildren were ranked as for occupation. Information concerning income was obtained by presenting the informant with a card showing the scale illustrated in table 3.2, and asking him to state which of the groups A to G he came into. This was done in order to overcome the reluctance which most people feel about discussing their financial circumstances, and in fact no informant refused to give this information. There was, on the other hand, no means of knowing how true the information given was. In two cases, married women did not know how much their husbands earned. In these cases, and in the cases of the schoolchildren, who could not be expected to know the details of their father's income, a reasonable assessment was made based on knowledge of the husband or father's occupation.

3.5.3 Education. The education-index scale is shown in table 3.3. The educational level was in all cases that of the informant. Schoolchildren

TABLE 3.3.   *Index of Education*

		Index score
I	Some university or college education	5
II	A-level or equivalent	4
III	O-level, C.S.E. or equivalent	3
IV	15 + ⎫	⎧ 2
V	14 ⎬ Terminal education age	⎨ 1
VI	13 − ⎭	⎩ 0

who had not yet taken any external examinations were given a score of 3, since, as grammar school pupils, they could reasonably be expected to take either O-level or CSE examinations in the future.

3.5.4   Locality. The social status of different localities within a city can to some extent be measured objectively (see Shuy *et al.*, 1968, p. 13). In this work, however, no attempt was made to achieve this kind of measurement. Instead, the different areas investigated in the survey were ranked subjectively – a much quicker and simpler process. This ranking was based on knowledge, acquired during many years' residence in the city, of the status significance of different neighbourhoods. It is likely that this ranking would, to a large extent, be agreed upon by most inhabitants of the city.[1] The justification for the inclusion of this indicator in the index is that the city neighbourhood in which a person lives is an important component of his social status (Barber, 1957, p. 145), and that neighbourhood can sometimes be the only differentiating feature between two people of otherwise equal status characteristics. The importance of locality is underlined by the well-known fact that a house in a statusful neighbourhood can command a higher price than an equally good house elsewhere. Details of the ranking of localities are shown in table 3.4.

3.5.5   Housing. The housing scale was based on three different parameters: house ownership; age of house; and house type. It was considered, first, that, other things being equal, an owner-occupied house is associated with higher social status than a rented house, and that

---

[1] A comparison of table 3.4 with the information given in chapter 1 concerning the social and economic characteristics of the city will show that this subjective ranking is perfectly consonant with the facts and figures illustrated there.

TABLE 3.4. *Index of locality*

		Index score
I	Eaton, except council estates, and north-east Lakenham	5
II	Thorpe	4
III	South Lakenham, Eaton council estates	3
IV	Central Lakenham	2
V	Hellesdon	1
VI	Westwick	0

a house rented from a local authority carries less status than one rented privately. Secondly, it was thought that, other things again being equal, the newer the house, the higher the status. The age of each house was measured as 'pre-1914', 'pre-1939' or 'post-war', since the two major wars represent significant gaps in house-building programmes. This means that, because of changes in building styles and materials, houses fall into three main recognisable and relatively discrete groups, with associated status connotations. Thirdly, it was considered that a detached house has higher status than a semi-detached house, which in turn has higher status than a terraced house or flat, at least in Norwich. Each of these three features (ownership, age and type) can easily be ascertained and measured. The matrix combining these three parameters, from which the housing score was read, is shown in table 3.5. Only those scores which are in italics in the table actually occurred in the sample, partly for obvious reasons. (No local authority houses, for example, were built before 1914.)

3.6 Characteristics of the sample

The informant's scores for each of the six indicators were combined, and the total was taken as his social class index. The social class characteristics of the sample as a whole, as measured by the index, are shown in fig. 4. This shows the distribution of informants obtained in the sample by social class level, and demonstrates that the sample adequately represents the whole range of class differences, from the lowest to the highest. This remains true in spite of the fact that both extremes, as one would expect from their proportion in the actual population, are not as well represented as the middle ranges. The graph shows some

TABLE 3.5. *Index of housing: index scores*

	Council rented			Privately rented			Owner-occupied		
	T/F	S-D	D	T/F	S-D	D	T/F	S-D	D
Pre-1914	0	0	1	0	1	2	1	2	3
Pre-1939	0	1	2	1	2	3	2	3	4
Post-war	1	2	3	2	3	4	3	4	5

T, Terrace; F, Flat; S-D, Semi-detached; D, Detached.

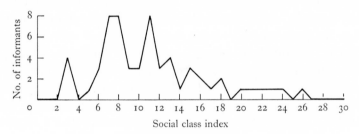

Fig. 4   Social class characteristics of sample

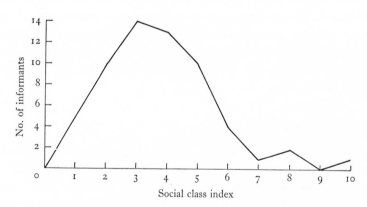

Fig. 5   Social class characteristics of sample,
measured by occupation and education

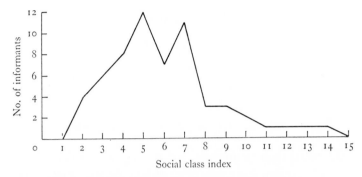

Fig. 6   Social class characteristics of sample, measured
by occupation, education and income

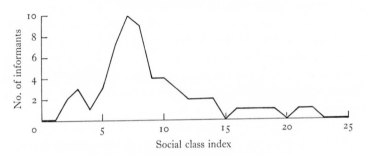

Fig. 7   Social class characteristics of sample, measured by
social class index minus locality indicator

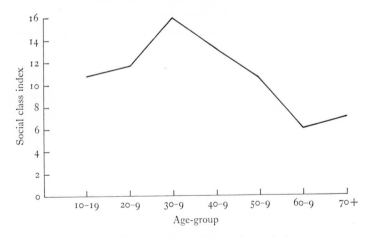

Fig. 8   Social class characteristics of sample by age group

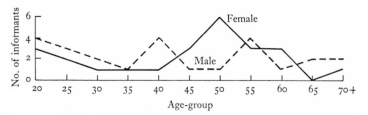

Fig. 9   Sex characteristics of sample by age group

breaks in the social class continuum, and is suggestive of how the continuum might be broken down into more or less discrete units or classes
(see ch. 5). Natural breaks which occur around clusters of informants
may justify the social class divisions used in subsequent chapters. Figs. 5
and 6 show that an index based on only two or three indicators would
have given a much more obscure picture of the social class differences
between informants and of the clusters and breaks in the class continuum. Fig. 7, when compared to fig. 4, shows that the inclusion of the
locality indicator has a significant effect in further stratifying the sample.
Fig. 8 shows the social class characteristics of the sample by age-group.
This demonstrates that the sample of schoolchildren, although taken
from grammar schools, is not biased towards the higher end of the scale
(see chapter 2). If anything, the reverse is true. It also appears that older
informants tend to be, on average, of a lower social class than younger
informants, as one would expect from the general social and educational
characteristics of the population as a whole. Some supplementary information is given in fig. 9, which shows the sex distribution of the adult
sample, by age-group. (Age characteristics of the sample as a whole were
given in chapter 2.)

4 Social context and the questionnaire

4.1 Language and social context

The co-variation of linguistic and sociological phenomena can be thought of as taking place along two main dimensions. The two dimensions are: (a) the dimension of social differentiation, and the social class, age and sex of the individual; and (b) the dimension of social context, and the social situation in which the individual is involved in social interaction. In chapter 3 we examined the first of these dimensions of co-variation, and discussed the relationship between language and social class. We also demonstrated the methods developed for measuring social class position. In this chapter we shall briefly discuss the relationship between language and social context, and examine ways in which social context can be measured and controlled.

Linguists have always been aware that different styles of language occur in different social contexts, and some theoretical work, such as that of Crystal & Davy (1969) has appeared on the subject of stylistic variation.[1] It is still the case, however, that very little work has actually been carried out on comparing the speech of individuals in different social contexts, or on specifying the particular social contexts in which certain forms occur. In this work an attempt has been made, following Labov (1966a), to control social context accurately and to correlate context with linguistic forms. The purposes of this are: first, to secure accurate statements about the way in which language varies with social context; second, to discover the linguistic norms of the speech community, as they are revealed in the direction of stylistic variation, from informal to formal contexts; and third, to permit an accurate study to be made of the effects of stylistic variation on linguistic change, and of the mechanism of linguistic change as it is revealed in the interplay of stylistic variation with social class and age variation.

[1] See also Halliday et al. (1964, ch. 4); Spencer et al. (1964); and Joos (1967).

4.2   Social context and the interview

The problem is, therefore, one of actually obtaining information on this type of variation and on the connection between social class and social context in language. At the time when this survey was carried out, a fairly formal interview situation seemed unavoidable in securing information from a large number of informants in a study of this kind. (Subsequently, Labov, in particular, has developed more sophisticated techniques for obtaining language samples from groups of speakers and individuals – see p. 52 below.) Labov (1966a, ch. 4) has shown, however (and much of his methodology has been adopted in the Detroit survey) that the interview situation can be structured so as to ensure that information concerning different contextual styles of speech is obtained, and that all informants are placed in a series of 'contexts' which are, relatively speaking, the same for each of them. In this way, accurate information can be obtained on stylistic variation of the type discussed above.

4.3   Formal speech

The structuring of the interview is reflected in the structure of the questionnaire. The questionnaire used in this survey was designed specifically for work in Norwich, but the assumptions that underlie its construction are the same as those upon which Labov based his New York City questionnaire. It was assumed, for example, that the contextual style of speech elicited from the informants in the bulk of the interview would be that style of speech most appropriate to a tape-recorded interview with a stranger. This type of speech is defined as *ormal speech*. Some informants, of course, feel more constrained and inhibited than others, and are therefore more 'formal'. But the position of this particular style on the style continuum is the same, relative to the other styles, for all speakers. The formality of the context, too, is relative. There are obviously contexts which are much more formal than this particular type of interview situation, and an attempt is made in certain sections of the questionnaire to increase the formality of the situation, in order to elicit forms which are likely to occur in these contexts (see pp. 47–50). Formal speech is likely to be elicited in response to the questions in sections I, III, V and VIII of the questionnaire (see Appendix, p. 195). Sections I, III, and VIII are included, not only to elicit formal speech, but also to obtain information which is necessary for the survey. Section V is included mainly to elicit formal speech, but also to provide a suitable context for question V. 4(iii) (see p. 51 below) which is designed to elicit casual speech. This section is also useful in that it provides for a comparison between attitudes to Norwich English (section VIII) and attitudes towards Norwich itself.

4.4 The reading passage

Once we have achieved the setting up of one contextual style within the interview, that of formal speech, it is a relatively easy task to extend the spectrum of contexts in a more formal direction. The object of this is to gain insight into styles that are more formal than formal speech as here defined; to obtain information on a wider range of stylistic variation; and to discover more precisely what are the norms of the speech community. Section IV, which consists of the reading passage, is designed to elicit the next most formal style in the interview, which is defined as *reading style*. Here we attempt, in the context of the interview, to simulate a change along the continuum of style of discourse by switching the mode of discourse (see Halliday *et al.*, 1964, p. 90). The informant was asked to read the passage, which includes many examples of phonological variables (see chapter 6), as naturally as possible, 'just like you'd normally say it'. The effect of this instruction is probably not very considerable, but the result is to standardise the style for all speakers towards the informal end of the range of possible styles in this context. The actual material and nature of the reading passage is also important in this respect: the passage is written in a colloquial style on an informal topic, and as if spoken by a young man, in order to produce a performance that is as relaxed and natural as possible. (Here we are making use of the interconnection between style of discourse and field of discourse.) The advantage of standardising in this direction is that it avoids certain characteristics of formal, slow reading style, which would make the results difficult to compare with speech.[1]

[1] Characteristics of formal, slow reading style we wish to avoid are the lack of reduced forms and the absence of juncture features such as the 'intrusive *r*'.

4.5　The word list

The next stage in the extension of contextual style in a more formal direction is to be found in the responses elicited in section II, the word list, which are said to be in *word list style*. The informants were asked to read aloud, at a normal speed and as naturally as they could, a list of 212 lexical items.[1] This means that, for three or four minutes, the informant's attention is directed at a single item at a time, and at his pronunciation of that particular item. The effect of this is to produce a style of pronunciation more formal than that of the reading passage, and thereby to introduce a further degree of sophistication into the examination of contextual styles. In addition to this, the list is designed to provide information concerning all segments of Norwich English, and the phonological variables in particular. The list, moreover, includes all the items in the reading passage which contain phonological variables. This makes comparison of individual items in different styles possible, and means that overall scores for the two tests are reasonably comparable. It is also worth noting that a test of this form ensures that a large amount of necessary phonological information can be gathered which one could not otherwise be certain of eliciting during an entirely conversational interview. (This is also true of the reading passage.)

The word list test is of course an artificial one, in that informants are not likely to use their 'normal everyday pronunciation' when reading out a list of single words. It should be stressed, however, that we are concerned here to produce a formal (rather than a 'normal') style of pronunciation, in order to obtain information about the community's linguistic norms, and to extend the range of stylistic variation studied, and that we are not specifically interested in the pronunciation of individual items in this context, but rather in scores produced for different phonological variables. The word list method is therefore perfectly adequate for our purposes and there is no need to adopt the more time-consuming 'sentence frame' type of question employed, for instance, by Houck (1966; 1967). Houck believes that, by using this kind of technique, he will obtain 'isolated approximations of casual speech', because the informant's attention is concentrated on obtaining the correct answer, rather than on pronunciation. This would appear, in the absence of evidence to the contrary, to be a rather vain hope,

---

[1] The items were presented to informants on cards which contained 18 items each. The items were hand-written in large block capitals to make for easy reading.

especially in an admittedly linguistic interview. The response, however obtained, is a single item pronounced in isolation (in the presence of a tape-recorder) and is therefore likely to have at least some of the phonological features characteristic of this type of unusual utterance. The only way to obtain examples of casual speech is actually to record *speech*. It is much more satisfactory to recognise that a list of single items will provide a style of pronunciation much more formal than casual speech and to take advantage of this fact. Houck's intention is also presumably to avoid 'spelling pronunciations'. It was found in the Norwich survey, however, that the effects of this type of pronunciation are minimal, and at the same time interesting and informative. It must be said in favour of Houck's method that in its original use in the Survey of English Dialects (Orton & Dieth, 1962–) and other similar surveys it serves a definite and useful purpose. The rural dialect survey is concerned to discover what different objects and activities are actually called in different areas of the country, and there is therefore a need to avoid prejudicing the informant towards any particular variant. There is also likely to be a problem of illiteracy in this type of survey. By extending this technique to a large urban survey, however, and by his excessive preoccupation with 'minimal pairs', Houck appears to have expended a great deal of unnecessary effort, particularly in the development of suitable sentence frames for items like 'pud' and 'gill'. In Norwich, on the other hand, a very large amount of information was obtained in a very short period of time, without irritating the informant with such questions as 'A little flying creature with feathers is called a ....'. A small number of mistakes occurred in the reading of the word list, naturally enough, but since the total number of items elicited for this test in the survey was almost 13,000, the effect of mistakes was totally negligible.

4.5.1   The rapid word list. It was thought possible that differences in scores between the reading passage and the word list might be partially due to speed of utterance, rather than to formality of context. This possibility was checked by the material elicited in section vi, the rapid word list. Informants were asked to read a list of 44 items, and to say aloud 27 others (numerals from 1 to 20, and the days of the week) as quickly as possible, but without being incomprehensible. It was found that scores for this test were not significantly different from scores for the word list test. It was therefore considered that differences between reading passage and word list scores could be accounted for solely in terms of stylistic variation, and rapid word list scores have therefore been treated as word list style.

4.6   The pairs test

The final stage in the extension of formality of context is contained in section VII, the pairs test. In this test, pairs of items which are often homophonous in Norwich English, but not in RP, (or vice versa), have to be read together. In this way, a maximum amount of attention is focussed on a particular phonological variable, and the expectation is that pronunciations will be produced that are even more formal than those elicited by the word list test. In a similar test in New York City, Labov found that by contrasting normally homophonous pairs such as *dock* and *dark*, a higher number of post-vocalic *r*'s in *dark* was elicited than in other contexts (1966a, p. 98). (Post-vocalic *r* is a prestige marker in New York City English.) The Norwich results, however, are often more complex than this. For instance, the juxtaposition of a normally homophonous pair such as *boot* : *boat* [buːt] might produce a corrected (towards RP) form of *boat* as [bout]. It might also, however, particularly with lower-class speakers, produce instead a 'discorrected' (lower-status) form of *boot* as [bʉːt]. This test has also been used to investigate the Norwich vowel system more accurately, and to study the nature of phonetic differentiation within the system.

4.7   Casual speech

The spectrum of contexts has now been extended as far as possible in the formal direction. The next problem is therefore one of extending the spectrum in the informal direction. It is obvious that, during most of the interview, the informant will be using formal speech, and will not speak to the interviewer as he would to his family or to his friends. How then do we obtain examples of this more natural and typical casual style of speech? Labov has shown that, although it is almost by definition impossible to elicit casual speech of this kind within the context of the interview, it *is* possible to obtain examples of spontaneous speech. Spontaneous speech is 'the counterpart of casual speech which does occur in formal contexts, not in response to the formal situation, but in spite of it' (1966a, p. 98). It is also possible to tape-record examples of casual speech outside the formal context of the interview. (Spontaneous and casual speech are in effect identical from the point of view of stylistic variation, and will be referred to simply as casual speech in the rest of this work.) Labov has, in addition, set up a schema for the identification of casual speech: he defines a series of contexts where casual speech may occur, and lists a series of channel cues which are characteristic of casual speech. This schema has been adopted with slight modification here.

The contexts where casual speech may occur are as follows:

(1) Speech outside the context of the formal interview. This can occur before the interview starts, after it has finished, or during the interview in breaks, for instance, for a cup of tea.

(2) Speech addressed to a third person.

(3) Speech not in direct response to questions. Many speakers, particularly older informants, digressed considerably from the subject at hand, and were of course encouraged to continue with their reminiscences, stories and favourite topics. In many cases it was therefore possible to dispense altogether with section v. (There is, incidentally, a slight danger of a bias occurring in the casual speech material, since older informants tended to provide more examples of this type of speech. This means that speech forms characteristic of older people may be over-represented in the results calculated for casual speech.)

(4) Speech in response to questions in section III, on East Anglian dialect words. Most speakers found this section amusing; humorous and nostalgic reminiscences were frequent; and the constraints of the formal interview situation were often forgotten.

(5) Speech in response to the question 'Have you ever been in a situation, recently or some time ago, where you had a good laugh, or something funny or humorous happened to you, or you saw it happen to someone else?' This question, which was adopted from Houck's (1967) Leeds questionnaire, comes at the end of a series of questions on Norwich, and on whether it is possible to enjoy oneself in the city. In this kind of context, most informants found the question quite natural and acceptable, and responded readily with an amusing incident. The informant is under some compulsion to make the story seem amusing, and usually becomes involved in the story-telling and the comedy of the situation to an extent that overrides the formal constraints of the interview. The result is casual

(in fact spontaneous) speech. This question was used rather than Labov's 'danger of death'[1] question, as most Norwich people seemed to have lived rather more peaceful and uneventful lives from this point of view than the inhabitants of New York City. Labov's question was used, however, if the informant was unable to recall any amusing incident. The interviewer was able to use the 'danger of death' question most often in connection with war-time experiences, a favourite topic for digressions.

The channel cues involved in the identification of casual speech are 'modulations of the voice production which affect speech as a whole' (Labov, 1966a, p. 104). The cues are: a change in the tempo of speech; a change in the pitch range; a change in volume; and a change in the rate of breathing (including the occurrence of laughter). These changes 'form socially significant signs of a shift towards a more spontaneous or more casual style of speech' (Labov, 1966a, p. 110). When one or more of these channel cues occur in conjunction with one of the five contexts listed above, the utterance which contains them is considered to be casual speech.[2]

Winford (1972) has demonstrated the extent to which spontaneous speech in interviews actually falls short of genuine casual speech by comparing informants' spontaneous speech with their casual speech in 'peer group interaction'. His results show that in those cases, such as the present study, where no 'peer group interaction' speech has been obtained, it is possible to predict, by extrapolation from information concerning the nature of stylistic shifts between formal speech and casual speech, what is the exact relationship between spontaneous interview speech and genuine casual speech. Labov has also now developed, as mentioned above, more refined techniques for recording samples of casual speech which are considerably superior to the interview technique (see Labov 1969; 1970).

4.8   Interviews

Of the 60 interviews, 50 were carried out by myself and 10 by a second interviewer, Adrian Hannah. Both he and I have lived most of our lives

---

[1] 'Have you ever been in a situation where you thought there was a serious danger of your being killed? That you thought to yourself "This is it"?' (1966a, p. 595.)

[2] These channel cues have been attacked as unreliable by Wolfram (1969, p. 58), but it seems quite likely that this may be due to the fact that little casual speech was obtained in the Detroit survey (see Shuy *et al.*, 1967).

in Norwich, we are the same age, and attended the same school. We were, moreover, both likely to appear to informants as university students, and we both attempted to conduct all the interviews in the same fashion. There are slight phonological differences in our speech, but this seems to have been of no consequence. There appears to be no significant difference between the two sets of interviews with respect to either the degree or the nature of the stylistic variation elicited. This demonstrates the usefulness of a scientifically structured interview procedure which permits objective comparison between one interview and another. Interviews were kept as informal as possible, and most were conducted sitting in armchairs in the informant's living room. The informant's family and friends were in most cases encouraged to remain present, if the informant wished them to do so. This increased the possibility of obtaining examples of casual speech of the type mentioned under (2) above.

4.9   The questionnaire

The structure of the questionnaire itself is also designed to put the informant at ease. (The questions themselves were not read out in the form in which they appear on the questionnaire. These were rather guides as to what information the interviewer should obtain, in as informal and conversational a way as possible.) The first section of questions keeps the informant on his home ground, as it were, and allows him plenty of scope for anecdotes and descriptions of personal experiences. This section is then followed by the word list, which, although the longest of the reading tests, is also the simplest, which gives the informant confidence for the later reading tests. Note, moreover, that there is no danger here, because of the length of the list, of the informant's attention being drawn to the phonological variables, as there was with Labov's questionnaire. The relatively relaxing section III, which is intended to elicit information concerning knowledge and use of local dialect words, follows the word list, and allows the informant time to recover before the reading passage, section IV. Then comes another relatively relaxing section, section V, which contains the questions on Norwich itself, and gives the informant a breathing space before the final reading tests. The pairs test comes last of all the reading tests, since in this test attention *is* drawn, to a certain extent, to the phonological variables. The questions on Norwich speech are also placed at the end, since these too are likely to draw attention to particular aspects of the informant's own speech. Finally, sections IX and X are designed to test the extent to which informants accurately perceive their own speech, and the extent to which they hear themselves using the community's linguistic norms, even when this is not the case. They are also designed to test the extent to which informants are insecure about their own speech in so far as they characterise their speech as incorrect.

5 The social differentiation of a grammatical feature

5.1 Measurement of linguistic phenomena

In the last two chapters we have been discussing methods of measuring social class and social context which will permit a study to be made of the relationships that obtain between these sociological parameters and linguistic material. We shall now turn, in this and the following chapter, to a discussion of methods of measuring the linguistic material itself. The main purpose of this work is to investigate and draw conclusions from phonological material. However, the investigation of the co-variation of phonological features with sociological parameters is a complex matter, and some reasonably sophisticated techniques are required for this purpose. Before we begin this investigation, it is useful at this point to give a simple, preliminary demonstration of the fact that it is indeed possible to measure linguistic material and to investigate the co-variation which it undergoes with sociological features. This will be done by taking one non-phonological and easily quantifiable linguistic feature and examining the way in which it correlates with social class and social context.

5.2 The present tense marker

The non-phonological feature which we will take for this purpose is the form of the third-person singular, non-past tense, non-continuous aspect of the verb in Norwich English, as in 'he loves', 'she has', 'it goes'. It is a characteristic of East Anglian dialects that this particular form for all verbs other than the copula 'be' is identical with the form for all other persons in the same paradigm (see Orton & Tilling, 1969, p. 296). That is to say that forms such as 'he love', 'she have', 'it go' are usual. It is likely that this feature was at one time more widespread geographically in the south of England than it is at present (see McDavid, 1969, p. 87), but it has recently gained some recognition from linguists as a typically East Anglian feature (see Bright, 1966, p. 112; McDavid, 1967). Nelson Francis has stated, for instance, that the lack of the third-person singular marker is standard even for the youngest speakers in certain of the areas of Norfolk which he investigated.[1] This feature is also one of the characteristics of American non-standard Negro English, and of other American dialects (see McDavid, 1966; Labov, 1966*b*; Wolfram, 1969).

In Norwich itself this particular linguistic feature is very common. It appears to have, however, all the characteristics associated with a linguistic variable: it does not occur consistently in the speech of most individuals; it is not used equally by all speakers; and its incidence varies from verb to verb. This particular aspect of the heterogeneity of the speech community can be ascribed historically to the influence of standard English, through the presence of standard speakers in the community, the normative influence of the educational institutions and possibly the mass media, and to the influence of the dialects of those areas adjoining East Anglia which do not have this feature, through diffusion and immigration processes. The hypothesis underlying the work described in this chapter is that the proportion of verb forms without the third-person singular marker in a given amount of speech will show a direct relationship to the social class of the speaker and to the social context.

5.3   Method

To test this hypothesis is relatively simple, especially compared to the problem of investigating phonological variation. The method is as follows. For each informant, in both formal speech (FS) and casual speech (CS) styles, a count was taken of the total number of marker-less forms used, together with the total number of possible marker-less forms, i.e. third-person singular present forms. One complication here is that several verbs, for example, *come, give, see,* have past tense forms that are identical with non-past forms: 'You give it to me yesterday', 'I see him last week'. In these cases it is often not possible to distinguish between past tense forms and marker-less non-past forms in the third person. Forms of this type were therefore omitted from the calculations.

[1] In his Norfolk field-notes for the *Survey of English Dialects*, Francis states that in the Blickling locality the third-person marker is completely lacking, and quotes 'That have been' and 'She wear' as examples. He also states: 'This is standard in youngest speakers.' I am very grateful to S. F. Sanderson for permission to consult these records, and to P. M. Tilling, S. Ellis and W. N. Francis himself for their help and advice.

The next step was to calculate for each group of informants with a particular social class index score (index scores ranged from 3 to 26) a third-person singular present marker score. This score was calculated as the percentage of all third-person singular present tense verb forms which were marker-less. The higher the score, in other words, the higher the number of non-standard forms. The score in each case is a percentage score for each group as a whole, and not the mean of the percentage scores obtained by each individual in the group.[1] Results were developed initially for the adult sample only. This was because the sample of schoolchildren was not drawn by means of the same method as the rest of the sample, and it was therefore thought possible that results for this section of the sample might not be strictly comparable with those obtained for the majority of the informants. To avoid the possibility of introducing a bias into the figures at this preliminary stage, figures for the under-twenties were not introduced until later.

5.4   Scores

The third-person singular present tense marker scores obtained by adults are shown in fig. 10 (CS) and fig. 11 (FS). No informant with a social class index of 19 or over used marker-less forms, in either style, and so these do not appear. Note also that no relevant forms were recorded in CS for those informants with social class index scores of 10, 14 or 16. A comparison of figs. 10 and 11 reveals immediately that the hypothesis is at least partly confirmed. Scores for CS are on the whole higher than those for FS, with six groups of informants showing scores of over 90% in CS, and only two in FS. The percentage of marker-less forms, that is to say, falls as the formality of social context increases. This linguistic variable is therefore an indicator of social context. The other part of the hypothesis, that this linguistic variable will show correlation with social class, is not so readily demonstrated. There is, it is true, a definite tendency for marker scores, in both styles, to decrease as social class rises, particularly when one includes the higher class groups not shown on the graphs. This tendency, however, is not a clearly defined one, and there are several somewhat anomalous scores.

---

[1] Only relatively few instances of relevant verb forms were obtained from each informant, and taking a mean of individual percentages would have introduced a bias for this variable in favour of those informants who provided only one or two instances and whose percentage scores were therefore less reliable. An overall group percentage score in this case gives a much more accurate reflection of group behaviour.

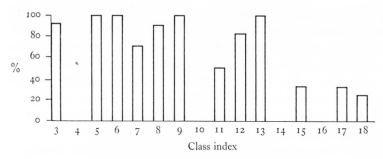

Fig. 10   Percentage of marker-less forms by
class groups – CS, adults only

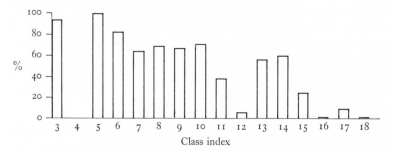

Fig. 11   Percentage of marker-less forms by
class groups – FS, adults only

Tentatively we may say that the linguistic variable appears to vary with social class, but the exact nature of the co-variance is unclear. The problem is that, because of the fine social differentiation which we have been employing here, each of the twenty-one cells (or groups of informants with a particular social class index) contains a small number of individuals. The small numbers reduce the reliability of the scores and also mean that any overall social class norms are obscured. The solution is to group the informants into a smaller number of larger social class groups. In this way, overall class differentiation of the linguistic variable will be clearly illustrated, and the linguistic norms and linguistic behaviour of the different social classes will be more plainly revealed.

5.5   Social class groups

The next problem is therefore one of splitting up the class continuum which we have obtained by means of the social class index into larger, more discrete groups which are relatively unified in their linguistic behaviour, and which reflect the class structure of society as a whole. There is no reason, incidentally, why a particular class grouping should be relevant for all linguistic variables, since different variables will have differing degrees of social significance, and will also be capable of reflecting breaks in the class continuum at differing points. For the purposes of the linguistic variable in question here, however, the first step is to look for clusters of scores, or for breaks in the continuum of scores which may well reflect breaks in the social class continuum itself, and to make tentative class divisions at these points. (Calculations show that the divisions made here are also generally the most suitable for analysis of the phonological variables. They also correlate well with breaks illustrated on the graph in fig. 4, p. 42.)

An obvious first move in this direction is to group together all those informants with social class scores of 19 or over, who have 0% markerless forms in both FS and CS. This, the highest social class group, will be called Class I. If we now look at fig. 10, the CS scores, the composition of the second highest group also suggests itself. The CS scores for all the groups shown in fig. 10 range between 70% and 100%, with the exception of the anomalous group with the social class index score of 11 and those groups with index scores of 15 and over. This latter series of groups has much lower scores, of below 40%. There is, moreover, a large break in the continuum between the 100% at index 13 and 33% at 15. We will therefore set up Class II as consisting of all the informants from the four cells 15 to 18. The decision to divide at 15, rather than at 14, for which no CS scores were obtained, is supported by the FS scores (fig. 11) which show a large drop from 60% to 25% between 14 and 15. FS figures also show that Class II groups have the lowest scores of all the groups (with the exception of the anomalous cell at 12), and that two of these groups have 0%, including the cell at 16, which did not figure in the CS scores.

In the selection of further class groups, CS scores are not especially helpful, since they are not very significantly differentiated. We therefore turn to the FS scores (fig. 11). Here, what stands out most clearly is the composition of the lowest social class group. Groups 3–6 have scores of above 80%, whereas all the other groups have scores of around 70% or below. There is also a significant break in the continuum of scores between 83% at social class index score 6 and 64% at 7. We will therefore set up the lowest class as consisting of the Groups 3–6. There thus

TABLE 5.1. *Composition of the five classes*

Class	Class index	Number
I	19+	6
II	15–18	8
III	11–14	16
IV	7–10	22
V	3–6	8

remains a so far undifferentiated central series of eight groups, 7–14. Within this series, there is one really significant break in scores, between 71 % at 10 and 38 % at 11. If we divide here, we have two classes consisting of four cells each: Class III, 11–14, with FS scores of under 60 %; and Class IV, 7–10, with FS scores of 60 % or more. This is in fact the only cut which will produce such a satisfactory division. (A cut between 11 and 12, for instance, where there is also a large break in scores, produces two classes of differing size with considerable overlap in scores and little significant clustering.)

We have thus established five major social class groups whose composition with respect to the social class index is as shown in table 5.1 (see also fig. 4, p. 42).

The relatively sophisticated and comprehensive nature of the social class index means that occupation is by itself not especially significant with respect to social class composition. It is, however, interesting to illustrate the nature of the five above classes by listing briefly their main occupational characteristics. Class I, for example, is a middle-class group of informants consisting mainly of professional people, including school-teachers, managers, employers, bank clerks and insurance workers. Class II is a lower middle-class group consisting almost entirely of non-manual workers and including typists, commercial travellers and office workers. Class III is an upper working-class group of foremen and skilled workers, and a few non-manual workers of low status and working-class background.[1] Class IV is a working-class group consisting entirely of manual workers, while Class V is a lower working-class group consisting mainly of labourers and other unskilled workers. (To avoid confusion, Class I will be referred to as 'MMC' = 'middle middle-

---

[1] This classification of non-manual workers as working class stresses the usefulness of a multiple-item social class index. The linguistic data obtained from these informants has definite working-class characteristics.

class', and Class IV as 'MWC' = 'middle working-class'. The term 'middle-class' can then be used to apply to both Class I and Class II, and 'working-class' to Classes III, IV and V.)

5.6 Social class scores

It is now possible to calculate percentage scores for each of the five classes as a whole for both contextual styles of speech, and to investigate the exact nature of the variation exhibited by this particular linguistic feature. The class scores are illustrated in fig. 12. This demonstrates extremely clearly that the linguistic variable we are concerned with here is involved in a very wide range of social class differentiation; that there is very marked social stratification of this variable, with scores rising progressively from Class I to Class V, and with clearly defined differences in the norms for each class; and that the variable is also involved in a considerable amount of stylistic variation.

In their everyday speech, lower working-class (LWC) (Class V) speakers use a very high percentage, almost 100%, of marker-less forms. The type 'she love' is clearly the norm for this class. For them, moreover, this form is not heavily stigmatised, and has little social significance, since the score for FS is only slightly lower than that for CS (87% as opposed to 97%). The LWC, this suggests, are relatively isolated from the normative influences operating within the speech community.

Middle middle-class (MMC) (Class I) speakers, on the other hand, use no marker-less forms, in either contextual style, so that for them this linguistic variable can have no stylistic significance at all. Both upper working-class (UWC) (Class III) and middle working-class (MWC) (Class IV) speakers also use a high percentage of marker-less forms, around 80%, in their everyday speech. These two classes are mainly distinguished from each other by the much greater awareness that UWC speakers have of the social significance of this variable, so that in a more formal context they use considerably less than half (38%) the possible number of marker-less forms, whereas the MWC score stays relatively high at 64%. Lower middle-class (LMC) (Class II) speakers use hardly any marker-less forms in their FS, at 5%, but a fairly considerable and much larger amount, 29%, in their CS.

We can say, therefore, that there is an overall norm for the working-class (LWC, MWC and UWC) of over 70% marker-less forms in every-

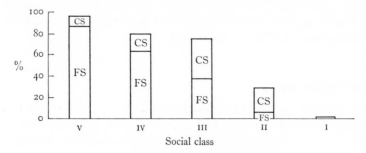

Fig. 12   Percentage of marker-less forms by
social class – adults only

day speech, and that, while each of the three classes is clearly differentiated by the use of this variable in their everyday speech, the most
striking difference is due to the adjustment made by the UWC in FS.
The middle-class (LMC and MMC), on the other hand, use very few
marker-less forms, or none at all, in FS, and a relatively small amount,
less than 30 %, in CS. Use of marker-less forms in CS distinguishes the
LMC from the MMC. The very large gap between the UWC and LMC
scores of respectively 75 % and 29 % in CS supports the hypothesis
developed in chapter 3 that the biggest class division in modern British
society is that which exists between the working and the middle classes.
Further support for the great social importance of this division is given
by the fact that the two classes which show the greatest awareness of the
social significance of this linguistic variable, that is to say the two
classes which show the greatest amount of stylistic variation between
FS and CS, are those two classes which have greatest cause to be aware
of this major social class division, the two 'border-line' classes, the LMC
and the UWC. One can propose, as one of the mechanisms behind this
phenomenon, the social need for the LMC to dissociate themselves
from the working-classes, and the desire of the UWC to acquire some
of the attributes of middle-class status.

Fig. 13 now shows that, if we also include the scores for those
informants aged nineteen or less, no significant change in the social
stratification of this variable occurs. The only change that does occur
has the effect of increasing the differentiation between the UWC and
the MWC, and slightly decreasing the differentiation between the MWC
and LWC. We can therefore conclude that the incorporation of the
sample of schoolchildren into the main sample introduces no serious

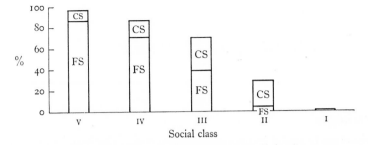

Fig. 13   Percentage of marker-less forms by social class – full sample

bias into the figures for this linguistic variable. (These figures, together with the social class characteristics of the schoolchildren illustrated in chapter 3, suggest that it is possible to consider that the sample of schoolchildren forms a natural extension of the adult sample.)

It has thus been demonstrated that it is possible to measure linguistic material sufficiently well to permit an examination to be carried out of the social class and social context variation that occurs in language. The particular linguistic variable on which an examination of this type has been carried out in this chapter has emerged as a significant marker of social class. It is also involved in stylistic variation, and is, at least subconsciously, recognised by the speech community as a stigmatised feature.

6 The phonological variables

6.1 Variables

We have already stated in preceding chapters that the main purpose of this work is to investigate and draw conclusions from the co-variation of sociological parameters with phonological material. The linguistic variables dealt with in the rest of this work, therefore, will be phonological variables. A phonological variable can be defined as a phonological unit which is involved in co-variation with sociological parameters or with other linguistic variables. It can be thought of as consisting of the pronunciation of a particular segment in a particular set of lexical items, and does not necessarily have specific phonological implications (although it may be employed to investigate possible phonological contrasts). Lexical sets will be left undefined here, but a few examples, together with comparisons with RP and some historical notes, will leave no doubt as to what items are involved.

6.2 East Anglian phonology

Before we go on to list and describe the various phonological variables, it will be useful to describe briefly the most salient features of Norwich, Norfolk and East Anglian phonology generally, so that the Norwich phonological variables can be seen as part of a complex but coherent system, rather than in isolation. The pronunciation of East Anglian English is clearly that of a variety of the English of the south, rather than the north, of England. This is to say, for example, that [ʌ] or some variant of this vowel occurs in items such as *cup*, *hut*, rather than [ʊ], and that a distinction is made between items from the lexical classes of *put* and *putt*.

It also means that a long vowel [aː], or some variant of this, occurs before [f], [θ] and [s], as well as in items such as *chance*, *dance*, *plant*, rather than a short vowel [a]. East Anglian speech also clearly belongs to the south-east rather than to the south-west or south central England. Post-vocalic /r/, for example, does not occur in items such as *cart, port, beard, fur* (except as a very rare relic form in the speech of some elderly people).

This very brief characterisation of East Anglian phonology leaves it undifferentiated, as yet, from the accents of the Home Counties. East Anglian speech, however, and particularly that of Norfolk and east Suffolk, is quite strikingly different from that of the counties nearer to London. What, then, are the differences? We can first of all give some idea of the distinctive characteristics by listing some of the points at which the phonology of Norwich English differs from that of the Home Counties and from RP. (We can subsequently outline some of the points at which Norwich speech differs from that of rural East Anglia.) The following is a short list.

1. Reflexes of ME ǭ and ME ou are kept distinct in Norwich English, as /uː/ and /ɒu/. (Under ME ou we must include late ME ou from ŏ+l, but not, necessarily, late ME ou from OE ŏ+h(t), where Norwich generally follows RP.) This means that, in contrast to Home Counties speech and RP, Norwich distinguishes pairs of items such as the following:

$$\begin{array}{ll} \text{moan} & : \text{mown} \\ \text{sole} & : \text{soul} \\ \text{nose} & : \text{knows} \\ \text{toe} & : \text{tow} \end{array}$$

Items in the first column are pronounced with a [ʊu ~ ʉː ~ uː] vowel, those in the second column with [ʌu ~ ɐ̈u ~ ɒu]. Final unstressed open syllables generally have /uː/ whatever their source, as in *billow, window, follow*. The item *no* has /ɒu/ as the negative particle, /uː/ as the adverb: e.g. 'No, that's no good' [nʌu ðæs nʊu gʊd].

2. Reflexes of ME ọ̄ have two alternative pronunciations. Some items, such as *do, loose, soon, who*, have [ʉː ~ əʉ ~ ɵʉ ~ ɜʉ] = /ʉː/ in the speech of all non-RP speakers. Others, such as *boot, moon, fool*, can have either /ʉː/ or /uː/. This means that in many varieties of Norwich speech pairs such as the following are homophonous:

$$\begin{array}{ll} \text{boot} & : \text{boat} \\ \text{moon} & : \text{moan} \\ \text{soup} & : \text{soap} \\ \text{tomb} & : \text{tome} \end{array}$$

3. Items such as *tune, news, music, queue*, which have [ju: ~ jü:] in RP, have no palatal glide in Norwich, and are pronounced with a vowel

identical with the /ʉ:/ described above. This means that in many varieties of Norwich English pairs such as the following are homophonous:

Hugh : who
cute : coot
mute : moot
Bute : boot

Items such as *sure* are pronounced with /ɜ:/, which means that pairs such as the following are homophonous:

pure : purr
cure : cur
surely : Shirley

Note that /j/ is generally retained in *use, ewe, value* (but not *curlew*).

4. In some varieties of Norwich English, items such as *boat, sole*, which are listed under 1 with /u:/, are subject to shortening, to /ʊ/. This means, for example, that items such as *road* and *hood* are perfect rhymes. This 'East Anglian short *o*' would appear to be linked historically to the perhaps more widely known 'New England short *o*', with which it seems to have many characteristics in common (see Avis, 1961; Kurath & McDavid, 1961, p. 12). Both features, for instance, appear to be recessive, and vary widely in their incidence from word to word, context to context, and speaker to speaker. Neither of them, moreover, occurs in final open syllables, as in *go*. The New England short *o*, on the other hand, contrasts with the vowel of *put, pull*, whereas the East Anglian short *o* does not. The East Anglian shortening also occurs (to a limited extent only in Norwich), with the /u:/ items listed under 2, such as *boot, spoon*. This is usual in the context __ /f/, as in *hoof*, *roof, proof*, and is common in the context __ /m/, as in *room, broom*, where /ʊ/ alternates with /ʉ:/ *and* /u:/.

It should be clear from the above that a complex system of phonological contrasts involving /u:/, /ʉ:/, /ʊ/, and /ɒu/ operates in Norwich English (especially when correction towards RP and hyper-correction are also taken into account), which distinguishes it both from RP and from Home Counties speech. The latter two varieties have only a three-way system of phonological contrasts at this point, compared to the four-way Norwich system outlined above.

5. Items such as *here* and *there*, which are distinguished in RP and Home Counties speech as /ɪə/ and /ɛə/ respectively, are generally not

distinguished in Norwich.[1] This means that pairs such as the following are homophonous:

> fear : fair
>
> here : hair
>
> beer : bare

These items are pronounced with a vowel of the type [ẹ: ~ ɛ:], with the possibility of a schwa off-glide.

At a lower phonetic level there are very many other differences that could be mentioned. Notable are: the hyperlength of stressed long vowels, and the corresponding reduction and disappearance of unstressed vowels: e.g. *thirty-two* [ˈθə̰::ʔˈtɜʉ]; the tendency to centralisation of short vowels; the marked nucleus-glide differentiation of the diphthongs, with second elements approaching [i] and [u] rather than [ɪ ~ ë] and [ʊ ~ ö], e.g. *day* [dæ̈·i]; the very front [a:] vowel in *after, cart*; and the unrounded nature of the vowel in *hot, top*.

The speech of Norwich differs in some interesting ways from that of rural East Anglia as a whole. To complete this brief characterisation of East Anglian phonology, we shall list some of these differences below. Information on the rural speech of East Anglia has been taken from three main sources: Kökeritz's (1932) study of the Suffolk dialect, for which field-work was carried out between 1926 and 1930; Lowman's records of field-work carried out in Norfolk and Suffolk in 1936 for the *Linguistic Atlas of the Eastern United States*;[2] and the records so far published by the *Survey of English Dialects* (*SED*) for Norfolk, Suffolk and Essex (Orton & Tilling, 1969), and the as yet unpublished field-records of work carried out for the *SED* by W. Nelson Francis in three Norfolk localities. *SED* work was carried out in 1956–7 for Norfolk, 1958–9 for Suffolk, and 1952–62 for Essex. Map 9 shows the various localities investigated by the various surveys. Most of the features typical of rural speech listed

---

[1] This merger, which has also taken place in New York City (Labov, 1966a), South Carolina (Kurath & McDavid, 1961), and in some New Zealand accents, amongst others, is not surprising in view of the small functional load carried by the distinction. Fry (1947) has calculated that /ɛə/ and /ɪə/ are respectively seventeenth and eighteenth in order of frequency of occurrence of the 20 RP vowel phonemes, and between them account for only 0.55 % of the total number of phonemes occurring.

[2] Lowman's records are a part of those he made in a survey of a large area of the south of England in connection with work on the *Linguistic Atlas of the United States*. The records are as yet unpublished, apart from a number of maps in Kurath & McDavid (1961), and are in the custody of the University of Chicago. I am extremely grateful to Professor R. I. McDavid who took a great deal of trouble to permit me to see these records.

Map 9   Rural dialect surveys

below are also found to a limited extent in the speech of some, mostly elderly, people in Norwich.

1. Of the Norwich characteristics listed above, the distinction /uː/ – /ɒu/ appears to be or have been usual throughout Norfolk, in most of Suffolk, and probably also in Essex, although the phonetic nature of the distinction is not in all cases the same.

(i) Kökeritz has [ʊ:] in *alone, coal, clothes, loaves, soap, toe*, etc., and [ɑʊ ~ ɒʊ ~ oʊ] in *blow, crow, grow, know, though*, etc. Items such as *bought, thought*, which generally have /ɔ:/ in Norwich, as in RP, also always have /ɒu/ in this dialect.

(ii) Lowman's records also show a clear distinction for all three Norfolk and four Suffolk localities. He writes, for example:[1]

Necton	clothes	⌄o·ə	though	(<ɔUᵛ
Stiffkey	clothes	⌄o·ə	growing	(⌄ɔUᵛ
South Walsham	clothes	oᵁ	low	⌄ou⌄
Ilketshall	clothes	^o·ᵊ	though	(⌄ɔU
Martlesham	clothes	^o·	growing	⌄ɔU
Honington	clothes	⌄o·	though	ᵛʌUᴧ
Buxhall	clothes	⌄o·ᵊ	though	⌄ʌUᵛ

Some localities have a closer vowel, in some items, of the Norwich /u:/ type: e.g. *go* [g⌄u:].

(iii) The position, twenty years later, as portrayed by the *SED* material, is less clear. In the published material, all the Norfolk localities have an [ʌu] type vowel in *mow, colt*, or *colts-foot*, and /u:/ as [ou ~ oʊ ~ o:ʊ etc.] in *load, unload, over* or *foal*. None of the Suffolk or Essex localities, however, appears to have preserved the distinction, except that some Suffolk localities have a high vowel [ü: ~ əʊ] in *foal*, as opposed to [ʌʊ] in all other cases. It can therefore be assumed, in the absence of further evidence, that the East Anglian /u:/ – /ɒu/ distinction has been lost, or almost so, in Essex and in most of Suffolk,[2] and now survives mainly in Norfolk, including Norwich. The amount of phonetic differentiation would appear to be greater in Norwich than in the rural areas, since Lowman writes [o·ə ~ oᵘ] and Francis [ou ~ oʊ] for Norwich [ʊu ~ u̟:], although some examples of higher vowels do occur. For instance, Francis writes *road* and *toad* with [u̟:] in Grimston, and *coal* with [u̟:] in Ludham. Under Ludham he writes: 'ME ǭ > [ou], not as high as Cardinal [u] usually...This is a feature of the lower-class dialect of Norwich, where ME ǭ is commonly [u̟:].' Under Ashwellthorpe he writes: 'ME ǭ > [ou] but sometimes very high [o̟:] or even [u̟:].'

---

[1] Lowman's records employ the transcription system used by the *Linguistic Atlas of the Eastern United States*. Details of this can be found in Kurath (1939, pp. 122–46), and in Kurath & McDavid (1961, p. 1). Note that Lowman uses the symbol (to indicate unrounding, and that the symbols [U] and [ʉ] indicate vowels more open than [u] and [ʉ] respectively.

[2] One qualification must be that, as map 1 shows, the *SED* Suffolk localities are further south than the northernmost localities studied by Kökeritz and Lowman.

2. In rural East Anglia reflexes of ME ǭ, generally speaking, occur with /ʉ:/ or /ʊ/, and only rarely with /u:/. Forms with /ʊ/ appear to be particularly common in Suffolk.

(i) In Kökeritz, reflexes of ME ǭ are most commonly written with the sign [ʉ:], which appears, from his description, to be a close rounded front or central vowel approaching [ʉ:], with a certain amount of diphthongisation. A number of items of this type also occur with /ʊ/, which is much more frequent than in Norwich and probably than in Norfolk as a whole. Some items also occur with some type of RP-imitative /u:/. Kökeritz comments: 'The children use [ʉ:]...and also a kind of hyper-correct rising diphthong [ŏu:] in *moon* and *soon*...I have heard the Standard English vowel [u:] for instance in *boot, do, food*...' (p. 46). Also noteworthy are a number of items with /ʌ/, such as *broom, roof, spoon*. The shortening [u:] > [u] appears to have been much more widely applied in Suffolk than in those varieties of English from which RP is descended, and these forms can be accounted for by this development having occurred, in these items, before the sound-change [u] > [ʌ], (as in RP *blood, flood*). The merger of *boot* and *boat* items, as in Norwich, would appear not to have taken place, as the few instances of the RP /u:/ in *boot*, contrast, if only minimally, with the [ʊ:] in *boat*. The small amount of phonetic distinction, however, would suggest that the merger is imminent. This is confirmed by Lowman's records. Kökeritz does mention, moreover, a diphthongised variant of [ʊ:] with a first element 'equivalent to short [o:]', which would make for a merger with the [ŏu:] diphthong of the children mentioned above. (The Norwich merger, this suggests, is due to the influence of RP forms, in the case of *boot* items, and a closer vowel than elsewhere in East Anglia in *boat* items.) Examples from Kökeritz include:

/ʊ/:*bloom, hoof, root, tooth*
/ʉ:/:*fool, loose, shoe*
/ʊ ~ ʌ/:*broom, roof*
/ʉ: ~ ʊ/:*noon, soon, afternoon*
/ʉ: ~ u:/:*cool, do, food, moon, school*
/ʉ: ~ u: ~ ʊ/:*shoot, boot, goose*
/ʉ: ~ ʊ ~ ʌ/:*spoon*

(ii) Lowman's records show a position very similar to that illustrated by Kökeritz: /u:/, /ʊ/, /ʌ/ and /ʉ:/ all occur. /ʉ:/ is written as [Ʉ̈ ~ (ə̈)] in Norfolk, [Ʉ̈ ~ Ɨʉ] in Suffolk. /u:/ is generally written [o·], a clear

Map 10   Distribution of forms for *broom, root* and *stool* (after *SED*)

● /ʉː/

○ /uː/

× /ʊ/

— No response

indication of at least a partial merger with *boat* items, which are also written in this way[1] (see p. 69 above), although /uː/ forms are not especially common for this lexical class, and some items have [Uˑ] which is not so frequent with *boat* items. The merger appears to be more frequent in Norfolk than in Suffolk, and more frequent in east than in west Suffolk; /uː/ forms are *most* common in west Norfolk, where they may be the result of Midlands as well as RP influence. Otherwise the tendency is to /ʉː/ in north and east Norfolk, /ʊ/ in Suffolk and south Norfolk. Some items, such as *two*, have /ʉː/ throughout.

[1] A good example of this is *toadstools*, which Lowman writes [toˑdstʌoˑɫz].

(iii) The *SED* records show a similar alternation between /ʉ:/, /u:/ and /ʊ/ forms, although /u:/ forms seem to be on the increase. For example, *stool*, which has only /ʉ:/ in Kökeritz, has only /u:/ in Suffolk and south Norfolk here (see map 10). Map 10 shows the distribution of forms for *broom*, *root* and *stool*. Generally speaking, /ʉ:/ forms occur in north Norfolk, /ʊ/ in south Norfolk and Suffolk, and /u:/ in west Norfolk, but sporadic /u:/ forms (mostly in *stool*) occur in all but two of the Norfolk and Suffolk localities.

The position with respect to the *boat*:*boot* merger is not clear. Francis writes [ou~oʊ] for Norwich /u:/ in *boat* (occasionally [ʉ:]), whereas *boot* items, when they do not have /ʉ:/ or /ʊ/, are written [ʊu~əu:~ ʊ:~u:]. There is thus no evidence of a complete merger in Norfolk. (We can expect none from the Suffolk localities, as here the /u:/ – /ʌu/ distinction appears to be lost – see p. 69 above.)

3. (i) The absence of the palatal glide [j] in *tune*, *music*, etc. and the merger of *who*:*Hugh* etc. as /hʉ:/ appears to be universal in the areas studied by Kökeritz, who states: 'The Suffolk dialect has levelled ME ǭ with ME eu, the common sound being [ʉ:]' (p. 159). He points out, in addition, that this is also true of Norfolk and Essex.

(ii) The same state of affairs emerges from Lowman's records for the whole of Norfolk and Suffolk. He writes, for example:

	two	*music*
Necton	<ʉ̈ᵘ>	ʉ̈ᵘ>
Stiffkey	<ʉ̈ᵘ	ʉᵘ>
South Walsham	(ʌ̞θ⁽ʉ>	(ᴧθ⁽ᵘ<
Ilketshall	ʉ̈·ᵘ·<ᴧ	ᴧʉ̈ᵘ>
Martlesham	<ʉ̈ᵘᴧ	>Iʉ>
Honington	ᴧIʉ>	Ĭu<
Buxhall	>Iu <	Iʉ>

(The forms from Martlesham, which is very close to Ipswich, may indicate a distinction.)

(iii) In Francis' records we find the same picture confirmed in responses such as: *knew* [nʉ:]; *huge* [hɜʉ·dʒ].

4. We have already seen above that the East Anglian short *o*, as it affects reflexes of ME ǭ, is more prevalent in the rural dialects of East Anglia, and especially in Suffolk, than in Norwich. This is also true, and to a larger degree, of reflexes of ME ǭ.

(i) Kökeritz lists, amongst others, the following items with /ʊ/, and indicates that the vowel in these words is identical with that in *pull*, *hood*, etc.: *boast*, *boat*, *bone*, *choke*, *cloak*, *clover*, *coach*, *coast*, *coat*, *don't*, *folk*, *goat*, *hole*, *home*, *hope*, *load*, *loaf*, *moat*, *most*, *oak*, *oath*, *oats*, *over*, *poach*, *pole*, *post*, *road*, *rope*, *smoke*, *stone*, *toad*, *whole*, *wholly*.

(ii) Lowman's records also show a large number of examples of the short *o*, and in fact the short vowel [U ~ ^o ~ ^oᵊ] etc. seems to be more common than the long [˃̬o· ~ ˅̠u·]. Examples like *stone* [ston] make it clear that the short *o* does not in all cases (usually in Norfolk) represent a merger with the vowel of *pull*, *hood* (which always have [U]), as is the case in Suffolk and present-day Norwich.

In the records we find the following examples:

/ʊ/ in all localities – *froze*, *posts*, *comb*, *bone*, *oats*, *whole*, *home*.
/u:/ in all localities – *clothes*, *pole*, *coal*, *road*, *goal*.
/ʊ ~ u:/ – *boat* (in one locality shown as 'quick' v. 'slow'), *stone*, *yolk*, *poached*, *hotel*, *ghosts*, *don't*, *won't*, *woke*, *wrote*, *over*, *toad* (/ʊ/ in Suffolk, /u:/ in Norfolk).

(iii) In so far as it is possible to estimate, the proportion of short *o*'s seems to have decreased by the 1950s. In the published *SED* material, for instance, *comb* has short [o] in three Norfolk localities and [ʊ] in one Norfolk and two Suffolk localities. All the others, however, have a long vowel, except for one Suffolk locality which has [ʌ]. In the unpublished material, *yolk*, *toad*, *oak*, *loaf*, *don't*, all of which had the short *o* in the pre-war records, have only the long vowel. The long vowel also occurs in *toes* and *spoke*, while *stone*, *road*, *both*, *broke* have both variants. *Whole* has only [o]. In his notes, Francis mentions shortened forms at Blickling, Ludham, Ashwellthorpe and Grimston, and writes, under Pulham (south Norfolk): 'Evidence of shortened lax forms, apparently much more prevalent in the dialect 50–75 years ago, was rather plentiful in the speech of...the oldest informant; thus [ɹʊd, stʊn, kʊm, spʊ·k, tɹ̤ʊt] [=*road*, *stone*, *comb*, *spoke*, *throat*]. The prevalence of [ou] in the speech of younger persons seems to be a result of Standard English influence.'

5. The tendency to merge /ɪə/ and /ɛə/ appears to be prevalent throughout East Anglia, but not to be so fully carried out, particularly in Suffolk, as in Norwich. The merger would appear to be undergoing a set-back in the south of the region.

(i) Kökeritz states: 'While the diphthong [ɪə] hardly ever occurs as a substitute for Standard English [ɛə], the use of the latter phoneme on the other hand is extended to nearly all the words pronounced with [ɪə] in

Standard English, which consequently exhibit double pronunciations in the Suffolk dialect' (p. 71). There is thus a tendency to merge these two classes in this area, with a considerable amount of 'phonemic overlapping'.

(ii) The table opposite shows some of the evidence concerning this point from Lowman's records. This suggests that the merger has been completed, more or less, in Norfolk, with South Walsham, the nearest point to Norwich, having the more open vowel characteristic of the city. The position in Suffolk is not so clear. Ilketshall is perhaps nearest to a complete merger, Buxhall and Martlesham furthest from it, but the position can be interpreted as indicating the type of situation described by Kökeritz, or as suggesting that these localities have a surface contrast, with an incidence differing from that of RP. Note that Martlesham also has [ᵛɛə ~ ᴧɛə] with *here, ear, beard*, labelled as 'older form'.

(iii) In the unpublished *SED* records we find:

	hear	year	clear	hare	pears	chair
Blickling	ɛ·ə	ɪə	ɛ·ə	ɛ:ə	ɛ·ə	ɛ·ə
Ludham	ɛ:ə	ɪ·ə		ɛə	ɛ·ə	ɛ:
Ashwellthorpe	ɛ:ə	ɪ·ə		ɛ:ə	ɛ·ə	ɛ·ə

The forms for *hear* and *clear* suggest a complete merger; the forms for *year* cast some doubt on this. Francis has stated that he regards the merger as being usual at least in Ashwellthorpe (personal communication). Note that the schwa off-glide is usual in the rural dialects; this is not the case, except with older speakers, in Norwich. The position concerning the above forms is further complicated in the rural dialects by the phenomena discussed under 6 and 7 below.

6. The older rural dialects of Norfolk and Suffolk (but not, it seems, of Essex) retain the distinction between ME ā as [e: ~ ɛ: ~ e·ə] and ME ai as [æɪ ~ æi ~ ɛɪ].

(i) Kökeritz states that the Suffolk dialect, 'as spoken by elderly people, clearly distinguishes between such words as *name* (pronounced with [ẹ:]) and *nail* (pronounced with [æɪ] or [ɛɪ]) which in Standard English are pronounced alike' (p. 55). He also points out that this distinction, under the influence of RP and 'Cockney', is dying out, with younger people generalising the [æɪ ~ ɛɪ] or a compromise/RP-imitative [eɪ] to both groups of items.

(ii) In Lowman's records we find some type of [æɪ] for all localities in *eight, pail, they, way*, and some form of [e·ə ~ ɛə ~ ɛe] in *April, paper, lane, apron, bracelet, relations* and *make*. The distinction between the two

	hear	here	ear	beard	queer	there	chair	where	parents	careless
Necton	˅eˑə	˅eˑə	˅eˑə	eˑˀ	˄eˑˀ	eˑɜ˅	˅iˑə	eˑə	˅eˑə˄	eˑˀ
Stiffkey	˄˅eˑə	˄eˑə˄	˄eˑə˄	˄˅eˑˀ	eˑə˄	˅eə	eˑə	eˑə	eˑə	˄eˑˀ
South Walsham	˅ɛə˄	eɜ˄	˄ə˅ɜ˄	eˑɜ˄	eə	eˑɜ˄	˄eə˅	eɜ˄	˄ə˅ɜˀ	eə˄
Ilketshall	˅Iˑə	˅eˑə	eˑə	eˀɜ	eə	eˑɜ˄	eI˅	eɜ˅	˅eˑˀ	˄eˑə
Martlesham	eI	ˑie	˅ieˑ	eˑiˑ	eˑə	eˑɜ˅	eɜ˅	eˑə	eˑɜ˄	eˑiˑ˄
Honington	eI	˅iˑɪ˄	eˀeˑɜ˅	eˀeˑɜ˅	eˑə˄	eˑɜ˅	eˑə	eɜ˅	eˑɜ	˅iˑˀ˄
Buxhall	eI	˅iˑɪ˄	eiɜ	eˑiˑ˄	eˑə˄	eˑɜ˄	eə˄	eˑə˄	eˑɜ˄	˅iˑɪ˄

sets is clear enough. However, in five out of six examples *chamber* has [æɪ], and Martlesham has [æɪ ~ ɛɪ] alternating with [e·ə], significantly labelled 'older form', in *bracelet, relations, make,* and *apron*. A further point that emerges from these records is that a great many of the [e·ə] < ME ā forms represent a merger with the vowel of *here, hair,* discussed under 5 above. South Walsham, for instance, has [ᴧɛ·ə] in both *beard* and *April,* and this tendency would also appear to be particularly common in Necton and Stiffkey.

(iii) The *SED* records show many examples of the distinction preserved, but also many more [æɪ] < ME ā than in the pre-war records. In some cases a distinction appears to be preserved as [ɛɪ] – [æɪ], as in *make, break, take – pay, tail*. Under Ludham, Francis writes: 'ME ā – several different variants, perhaps indicative of change – [ɛ ~ e] no longer than half-long with lax high off-glide – forms with [æɪ] may show phonemic shift with reflex of ME ai, ei, which is [æɪ] or [ɛɪ].' We can say, then, that this distinction is generally on the decline in rural East Anglia. The distinction can, it is true, still be heard in Norwich, but this is generally in the speech of elderly people, in casual WC speech, or in humorous or facetious conversation. In these cases, the vowel of *name* etc. generally does not have the schwa off-glide in Norwich, so that *fierce, face* are both [fɛ̝:s].

7. There are traces, quite substantial in the pre-war records, of a distinction between reflexes of ME ę̄ as [ɹi ~ i:] and ME ẹ̄ as [e: ~ e·ɪ]. Reflexes of ẹ̄ appear in some cases to have fallen in with reflexes of ME ā, and in others to have remained distinct.

(i) In the localities studied by Kökeritz, items of this type have either the [ę̝:] of *name* or the [i:] of RP *see*. It is also striking that Kökeritz records several instances of [ę̝:] derived from ME ę̄. Thus, *deep,* for example, has [ę̝: ~ i:].

(ii) Lowman writes a number of reflexes of ę̄ with an open vowel. Thus Necton has *beans* as [bᴧe·ənz]. What is striking here is that this indicates a vowel that is identical with that of the classes *here, there,* and *name,* in many cases. Thus, Necton, in addition to *beans* [bᴧe·ənz], has *bairns* [be·ənz], *ear* [ᴧe·ə], and *relations* [rəlᴧe·ᵊʃənz]. (This apparently does not apply to the areas studied by Kökeritz, since [e:] in *deep, name,* without the schwa off-glide, contrast with *here* and *there* items with the off-glide [ɪə ~ eə ~ ɛə].) Lowman has the [e·ə] vowel in *grease* in four localities, including all three Norfolk localities; in *beast* in one Norfolk locality; in *wheat* in both Norfolk localities which gave this item and in two out of three Suffolk localities, in one of which it is labelled 'older form' and occurs alongside [ˆɪj]. It also occurs in *bread* in Stiffkey and *meat* in Necton.

(iii) Francis states that ME ẹ̄ and ẹ̄ have fallen together in Ashwell-thorpe, but that informants were aware of older forms with [e:] < ME ẹ̄ and occasionally used them. The older form of the dialect, he says, appears to have had a three-way contrast:

$$\text{ME } \bar{a} > [\varepsilon: \sim \varepsilon:^{\text{I}} \sim \varepsilon:^{\text{ə}}]$$
$$\text{ME } ai > [æi \sim \varepsilon i]$$
$$\text{ME } \bar{ẹ} > [e: \sim e·ɪ]$$

There is probably no trace of this feature in Norwich, except perhaps in the tendency of some informants to pronounce *St Stephens* with [e: ∼ e·ɪ].

8. Some traces of post-vocalic /r/ are found in all three sets of rural dialect records. It is obviously very much a relic form, and tends to occur only in items which have RP /ɜ:/. One Norwich informant, moreover, consistently had [ɹ] after [ɜ:]. It is not clear whether this, too, is a form of relic pronunciation, or a personal idiosyncrasy.

9. (i) Kökeritz writes: 'The principal modern Suffolk equivalents of ME ĕr, ĭr and ŭr...are [a: ∼ ʌ ∼ ɜ:], and the circumstance that the comparatively rare [ɜ:]...is almost exclusively recorded as an alternative pronunciation of [a:] and [ʌ] warrants the conclusion that [ɜ:] is a late importation from Standard English.' He shows that [a:] occurs mostly as a reflex of ĕr, and [ʌ] mostly as a reflex of ĭr, ŭr, although this is not consistent. According to Kökeritz, [a:] occurs with: *certain, concern, earn, learn, service*, but also with: *bird, burn, nurse, work*; [ʌ] occurs with *bird, church, burst, worse, turn* etc. Under [ʌ] Kökeritz includes the variants [ä ∼ ɜ ∼ a]. The [a], however, may equally well represent a shortening of [a:], which is also fairly frequent in items such as *partner*.

(ii) Lowman's records show a situation that is considerably more complex than Kökeritz's fairly neat distribution of RP /ɜ:/ items over [ʌ ∼ ɜ: ∼ a:]. For example, Lowman writes RP /ʌ/ items such as *up, worry*, with some form of [ʌ], but also with some form of [ɜ] or [ɐ]; RP /ɑ:/ items, on the other hand, always have some form of [a:], usually [a·] itself, but occasionally modified, e.g. [ᶺ₂a· ∼ ₂ᶺa·]. RP /ɜ:/ items, on the contrary, show a very wide range of variation. Table 6.1 gives a complete list, which shows that some items, notably *sermon, learnt, vermin*, together with *thirteen, Thursday, hers*, in a few localities, probably have

TABLE 6.1. RP /ɜ:/ in Lowman's records

	thirteen	thirty	first	Thursday	furthest	hers
Necton	ᵛɐ	ɐ	ʌᵊ ~ ᵛᶹ⁻ ~ ᵛᴧ	ᵛɐ·	ᴧᴧ	ᵛɐ·
Stiffkey	3ʳ ~ ɐ	ɐ	ᵛɐ· ~ ᵛᴧ	ᴧᴧa·ʳ ~ ᴧᴧa·	ᵛᴧ·	ɐ·
South Walsham	ᴧᴧa	ᴧᴧa	ᴧᴧa ~ ᶜᶹ	ᴧᴧa·	ᴧ	ᴧᴧa·
Ilketshall	ᴧᴧa· ~ ᵛɐ·ʳ	ɐ·	ɐ ~ ᵛᴧ	ɐ·	ᴧ	ᵛɐ·
Martlesham	ᵛᴧr ~ ᵛᴧ·	ᵛᴧ·	ᵛᴧ	ᵛᴧ·	ᶜᴧ·	ᵛᴧ·
Honington	ᵛᴧ	ᵛᴧ	ᵛᴧ	ᴧᴧa	ᶜᴧ	ᴧᴧa·
Buxhall	ɐᵊ~ ᵛᶹ	ɐᵃ	ᵛᴧ	ɐ ~ ᵛᶹ ~ ᴧᴧa·	3	ᴧᴧa·

	vermin	learnt	church	nurse	sermon	purpose
Necton	ᴧᴧa·	ᴧᴧa·	ᶜɐ	ᵛᴧ	a·	ᵛɐ· ~ ᴧᶹʳ
Stiffkey	a·	ᴧᴧa·	ᵛ3	ᴧ·	ᴧᴧa·	ɐ·
South Walsham	ᴧᴧa·	ᴧᴧa	ᴧᴧ	ᶜᶹ	ᴧᴧa·	ᵛɐ·
Ilketshall	a·	a·	ᴧɐ	ɐ·	a·	ᴧɐʳ
Martlesham	ᴧa·	ᴧa·	ᵛᴧ	ᵛᴧ·	ᴧa·	ᵛᴧ·ʳ
Honington	ᴧa·	a·	ᶜᴧ	ᵛᴧ ~ ᵛ3ə	ᵛᴧ· ~ 3ə	3ə ~ ᵛ3
Buxhall	ᵛa·	ᴧᴧa·	ᵛɐ· ~ ᴧæ	ᵛᴧ· ~ ᵛ3ə	ᵛᴧə ~ ᴧa·	ᵛ3r

the same vowel as *barn, basket,* etc. It also shows that some items, notably *furthest,* together with *nurse, church, thirteen, thirty,* in some localities, probably have the same vowel as *up, mug,* etc. For the most part, however, there occurs an intermediate vowel of the type [ɐ ~ ɐ· ~ ʌ· ~ 3 ~ a ~ ᴧæ] etc. (The [ɐ] variant seems to be more prevalent in Norfolk, the [a· ~ ʌ] variants, as Kökeritz's evidence suggests, in Suffolk.) This (and other similar phenomena discussed above) poses many problems for a taxonomic phonemic type of phonology, which, together with terms like 'phonemic overlapping', 'variance analysis', and 'phonemic indeterminacy', will be discussed in later chapters.

(iii) Francis writes in his Norfolk field-notes:

work	[ɐ: ~ ɑ: ~ ɜ:]
Thursday	[ɐ: ~ ɑ:]
third	[ɜ: ~ ä ~ ạ]
thirty	[ɜ· ~ ǣ ~ ə]
thirteen	[ɜ ~ ë: ~ ɛ̈]
thirsty	[ɐ· ~ ä ~ ɜ]
fern	[ɜ: ~ ä: ~ ɐ·]

This reveals an equally large amount of variation. There appears to be some evidence, although less than in Lowman's records, of a merger of these items with RP /ɑ:/ items: thus, Francis also writes [ɑ:~ä:] in, for instance, *darning*. In spite of this he states, in the phonetic notes for Ashwellthorpe, that [ɜ~ə~ɛ̈~ɐ] occur, short and long, in these items, and that these are all apparently allophones which are distinct from [a:~ɑ:]<ME ăr. In Norwich there are fairly frequent traces of this phenomenon, although most, especially younger speakers, have /ɜ:/, which tends to be rather open [ɜ̞:]. Note that WC speakers tend to have /ɜ:/ also in *clerk*, *Derby*.

10. The [a:] in *cart*, *partner* is, in the speech of a few older informants, distinct from the vowel of *half*, *path*, *glass*, *dance* which is [æ:]. There are traces of this in all three sets of rural records, but very little in Norwich.

11. Just as Norwich [ɛ:] in *here*, *hair* is [ɛ:ə~e:ə] etc. in rural areas and with older speakers, so older rural dialects distinguish *poor*, *pore*/*paw* as [oə~ɔə]/[ɔ:]. Norwich generally has [ɔ:] in all cases.

12. We have already seen that /h/ is retained throughout rural East Anglia, including Essex, but that in Norwich it is usually lost. Kökeritz states that, in the areas he investigated, only the urban areas of Southwold and Halesworth (1968 populations 2,180 and 2,440 respectively) showed any tendency to 'h-dropping'.

13. There is a notable tendency for front vowels to be raised in some words: e.g. *head*, *get* with [ɪ]; *sat*, *catch* with [ɛ]. Kökeritz states that 'the substitution of [ɪ] for [e] is extremely common in the Suffolk dialect' (p. 13).

14. RP /kw-/ often corresponds to /k-/ or [k̯-] in Norfolk and Suffolk rural dialects amongst older speakers: e.g. *quarter* [kǫ:tə].

15. RP /ʃr-/ and /θr-/ correspond to /sr-/ and /tr-/ with older speakers: e.g. Lowman has *three* [tɹ̩͜ɪj] in Necton.

16. /l/ is usually 'clear' in all positions: e.g. *hill* [hɪl]. This corresponds to Norwich [hɪɫ~ḁ̈ɫ] etc.

17. Final *-ed* is often /-ət/: e.g. *hundred* [hʌndɹəʔ].

6.3 Phonological variables

The majority of segmental phonological elements in Norwich English are involved in variation of some social significance. The variables involved in this study were initially selected from among these on the grounds of:

(a) the amount of apparent social significance in the pronunciation of the segment or segments involved; and

(b) the amount of phonetic differentiation involved.

This selection was made (and different values allotted to various phonetic realisations – see p. 82 below) on the basis of:

(i)   native knowledge of the speech of the area;

(ii) results obtained in a small pilot survey conducted in December 1967; and

(iii) the records made by Kökeritz, Lowman and Francis (see p. 67 above).

The *consonantal* phonological variables – variables are symbolised by enclosure in parentheses – are: (h), (ng) and (t). We have already stated that, in order for this type of study to be significant, the linguistic data must be rendered quantifiable, (just as the sociological data is), and that phonological variables provide a method of achieving this aim (see Labov, 1966 d). We can first of all illustrate how phonological variables can be used to make linguistic material susceptible to this kind of measurement, and thus facilitate the study of co-variation, by examining the variable (t).

6.3.1   This variable is concerned with the realisation of /t/ in Norwich English where it occurs inter-vocalically and finally, as in *better, bet,* but not where it occurs in stressed syllable initial position, as in *tea, return* (or where it occurs in the context /n—/, as in *went, wanted* or in the context /l—/, as in *felt, melted*). It is a well-known fact that, in many varieties of English, /t/ is realised as a glottal stop in items like *better* and *bet,* particularly but by no means exclusively in urban areas. It is not so widely recognised that a second type of glottalised pronunciation, [t?], also occurs. Map 11 indicates those areas of England where these two types of pronunciation are found at the level of conservative rural dialects. It will be seen that Norfolk is clearly one of the areas in question (see also Gregg, 1958, for another area). In most phonetic environments, glottalisation of the precise types described above is a feature of non-standard (in England, non-RP) type of pronunciation. It was therefore assumed that, in Norwich, there would be a correlation of the following type between the social class of the speaker, the social context, and the amount of glottalisation:

(a) Style FORMAL, class HIGH: glottalisation LOW.

(b) Style INFORMAL, class LOW: glottalisation HIGH.

● [ʔ] in *water*

✕ [tʔ] in *water*

Map 11   Areas of England where two types of glottalised
pronunciation are found (after *SED*)

In investigations concerning the realisations of (t), four phonetically
distinct types were distinguished:

[tʰ]   (aspirated)
[t]   (unaspirated)
[tʔ]   (glottalised)
[ʔ]   (glottal stop)

On the basis of the assumptions concerning class and style discussed above, these types were then allotted values as follows:

$$(t)\text{-}1 \quad [t^h \sim t]$$
$$(t)\text{-}2 \quad [t\widetilde{?}]$$
$$(t)\text{-}3 \quad [\widetilde{?}]$$

Using these values for the phonological variable (t), each informant can be assigned a (t) index for each of the contextual styles obtained by means of the questionnaire. The index, which indicates the extent to which each informant deviates from an idealised RP type of pronunciation, is computed in the following way. Each occurrence of the variable in each style is recorded, its value on the above scale noted, and the *average* score for the style calculated. For example, in WLS, an informant may have the following types of (t):

3	instances of (t)–1	$3 \times 1 =$	3
3	instances of (t)–2	$3 \times 2 =$	6
6	instances of (t)–3	$6 \times 3 =$	18
12			27

$$\text{Average score: } \frac{27}{12} = 2.25$$

From this average score, an index is obtained by subtracting 1 and multiplying by 100. This gives the informant an index for this style of 125. This method of computing indices gives a score of 000 for consistent use of (t)–1 and 200 for consistent use of (t)–3. The score of 125 in this case indicates a norm[1] for this contextual style nearer to (t)–2 than to (t)–3. (Since, in the case of this variable, medial (t) scores, as in *better*, may well differ significantly from final (t) scores, as in *bet*, scores for the two types are also computed separately.)

It is this method of computing indices for individuals, and, subsequently, for groups, which renders the phonological material quantifiable, and which therefore makes this kind of study possible. Much more reliable and significant conclusions can be drawn from the information

---

[1] This method of computing indices was initially developed by Labov in his New York study. The term *norm* is perhaps not accurate here. The *mode*, it could be argued, might be a better indication of the pronunciation norm than the *mean*. Another flaw in this system of calculating indices is that the range of variable-types employed is concealed in the mean score. This fault could be rectified by some measure of consistency of performance such as the standard deviation or mean deviation (see Trudgill, 1971, p. 203).

● (h) in *hammer*

Map 12   *h*-pronouncing areas in England (after *SED*)

that an informant has a (t) index of 125 in WL style and an index of, say, 230 in CS than from an impressionistic statement to the effect that the informant uses a higher number of glottal stops in CS than in WL style.

Some phonetic difficulties arise in connection with this variable, in that it is not always possible to determine whether, for example, a final unreleased voiceless stop is glottalised or not. It is difficult, too, to know how to classify ejective [t']. Doubtful cases such as these are omitted from the index calculations.

6.3.2   The variable (h). This variable is the initial consonant of *happy*, *home*, etc., and is well-known as a linguistic variable throughout England. In most parts of England, and particularly in urban areas, (h) indices are likely to be in direct and straightforward relation to the education and social class of the speaker. In Norwich, however, the position is likely to be more complex. This is because Norwich is surrounded by what is, at least amongst older speakers, an h-pronouncing area even at the level of rural dialects, as map 12 shows. This suggests that older people in Norwich as well as immigrants from the surrounding rural areas are likely to have lower (= more 'RP-like') (h)-indices than younger people. The value scale for (h) is:

(h)–1   [h]
(h)–2   ø

An index score of (h) 000 therefore indicates a consistent 'h-ful' pronunciation. Note that weak forms of items like *have*, *him*, which are normally [əv], [əm], etc. in most varieties of English are excluded from the calculations of index scores for (h).

6.3.3   The variable (ng). The variable (ng) is the final consonant in *walking*, *running*, etc., which is a well-known variable in many parts of the English-speaking world (see Fischer, 1958; Sivertsen, 1960, p. 129; Gimson, 1962, p. 194; Labov, 1966a, pp. 394–9). The usual non-RP pronunciation of the *-ing* suffix in Norwich, and throughout East Anglia, is [ən~ŋ] rather than [ɪn]. The value scale is:

(ng)–1   [ŋ]
(ng)–2   [n]

The variable is therefore concerned with the proportion of [n] to [ŋ] found in this suffix in a given body of speech material.

6.4   Vocalic variables

The remaining phonological variables are concerned with the pronunciation of vowels. They are: (a), (ā), (a:), (e), (er), (ɛr), (ī), (ir), (o), (ou), (ō), (ū), (yu). The method of handling these will necessarily be more complex than that used so far. In the case of the consonantal variables we are dealing simply with the presence or absence of a particular consonant, or with variant pronunciations that are auditorily quite distinct. The index value scales, that is to say, are well motivated. In the case of the vocalic variables, on the other hand, there are no, or very few, auditorily distinct variants. The range of pronunciation of any given vocalic variable is likely, on the contrary, to take the form of a certain undifferentiated area within the vowel trapezium. This means that each variable has a series of infinitely graded realisations that can fall at any point along the appropriate phonetic continuum, which can only be divided up for the purposes of the index value scale in a manner that is rather arbitrary. It also means that there will be, as it were, border-line pronunciations, to which the transcriber will have difficulty in allotting a particular value.

The solution to this problem is to divide up the continuum using cardinal vowels and other points of reference as a guide, and to base the number of values for each scale on the amount of phonetic differentiation involved and the number of different types that the transcriber can perceive without difficulty. Each instance of a variable then has to be allotted a particular value, according to which idealised pronunciation-type it approaches most closely. It is not important, for the purposes of this study, that the continuum is divided up in a relatively arbitrary fashion, since the division is the same for all informants, which is all we require to make the results strictly comparable. (It may, however, obscure details that might be important for other purposes.) It is also, for reasons of comparability, important that the transcriber be consistent in his allocation of border-line cases to particular values. In the present study it is felt with some confidence that this consistency has been achieved. Moreover, any mistakes that do occur are likely to be insignificant in view of the large amount of material involved. We can illustrate the above points by taking as an example the variable (a).

6.4.1 The variable (a). The variable (a) is the vowel in *bad, cap, matter*, etc. In Lowman's records we find the following phonetic types in items of this kind: [æ ~ ᵛæ ~ ᐟæ ~ ^æ ~ ^æ· ~ ^æ·ᵊ ~ æᶠᵛ ~ ɛ ~ ɛ· ~ ᐟɛᵊ]. Francis' transcriptions are similar, and include the variant [ɛ̞]. The different Norwich variants are mainly differentiated by length, height, and diphthongisation, of which vowel height is socially the most distinctive. We can distinguish in Norwich English the following pronunciation types: [æ̞ ~ æ ~ æ̞ ~ æ̈ ~ æ· ~ æ̃ ~ æ: ~ æ:ᵉ ~ æ̞: ~ ɛ̞: ~ ɛ ~ ɛ: ~

ɛːᵊ ~ ɛːᵉ], etc. The number of possible symbols here, however, does not reflect the number of discrete pronunciation types that it does, for example, in the case of (t). It merely reflects the limitations of the transcription system in representing an infinitely varied number of pronunciations.

According to the principles described above, therefore, we set up the index value scale consisting of the following idealised phonetic types or approximate vowel qualities:

(a)–1   [æ]
(a)–2   [æː]
(a)–3   [æːᵋ]
(a)–4   [ɛː]
(a)–5   [ɛːᵉ]

Under (a)–1 [æ] we subsume all pronunciations of the type [æ ~ æ̞ ~ æ̝ ~ æ̃ ~ æ·], but not examples of [ɛ], etc., and so on. There are, of course, some cases where it is doubtful whether a particular instance of a vowel should be considered long or short, or whether it more closely resembles [æ] or [ɛ]. This is inevitable, since the phonetic symbols can only be approximate, and the transcriber is fallible. This, however, is by no means an insuperable problem, and the results are felt in all cases to be as accurate and, more important, as consistent as possible.

In the above value scale, (a)–1 represents the typical short [æ] sound of most varieties of RP; (a)–2 represents a sound, typical of many varieties of Norwich English, which, although identical or similar in quality, is longer, allowing for phonetic context, than the RP vowel. Variants (a)–3 to (a)–5 indicate closer and more diphthongised varieties of this vowel. Index scores, which can in this case range from 000 to 400, are calculated in the same way as the consonantal index scores.

6.4.2   The variable (ā). The variable (ā) is the vowel sound in items such as *name, nail, day, acre*. In his records, Lowman writes items of this kind, where they do not have the monophthongal [eː]-type pronunciation, with: [v̩ɛɪ˃ ~ ˃æ·ɪˆ ~ æɪˆ ~ v̩æɪˆ ~ v̩æɪᵛ], etc. Francis has similar transcriptions. It can be seen that there is variation in the quality of both elements of the diphthong, as well as in the quantity of the first element. The value scale for Norwich reflects these facts. The different types are:

(ā)–1   [eɪ ~ ɛɪ]
(ā)–2   [ɛɪ ~ æɪ]

(ā)–3   [æi]

(ā)–4   [æ:i ~ ǣ:i ~ ǽ:i]

(ā)–1 is intended to indicate an RP type of pronunciation, (ā)–2 a very common MC Norwich pronunciation with a more open first element, (ā)–4 the most 'extreme' Norwich pronunciation with a more open first element and a closer second element, and (ā)–3 a pronunciation intermediate between these two.

6.4.3   The variable (a:). The variable (a:) is concerned with the quality of the vowel in *after, cart, path*, which varies in Norwich from (a:)–1 = RP type [ɑ:], through (a:)–2 [ä: ~ ä:] to (a:)–3, a very front [a: ~ ã:] (cf. Lowman's [ʌ̞a·]).

6.4.4   The variable (e). The variable (e) is the vowel in *tell, bell, well, healthy*, where /e/ occurs in the context __/l/; and *better, metal*, where /e/ occurs in the context: [bilabial C]´_[ʔ] [V̆]#, i.e. in stressed penultimate syllables after a bilabial consonant and before /t/ where /t/ is [ʔ] – (not before [t] or [tʔ]). The value scale is as follows:

(e)–1   [e ~ ɛ]

(e)–2   [ɛ̈ ~ ä ~ ɜ]

(e)–3   [ɐ ~ ʌ̈ ~ ʌ̞]

(The centralisation of /e/ may also occur in some other contexts, such as:

$$´ \begin{cases} /ð/ \\ /v/ \end{cases} + /ə/$$

as in *never, leather*, but the details are not clear.) Kökeritz observed a similar tendency in Suffolk in the 1920s and 1930s, where it appears to have taken the form of opening to [ɛ] or [æ], and to have occurred in a wider range of environments. He also observed *better*, for instance, with [ʌ]. Lowman, too, writes *twelve* [twˁʌlv] in Necton, South Walsham, Ilketshall and Honington. Francis writes [ɛ̈] in this item. In Norwich, the extreme centralisation to [ʌ] etc. would seem, as a widespread feature, to be a recent development.

6.4.5   The variables (er) and (ɛr). The variables (er) and (ɛr) are concerned with the nature of the vowel in items of the classes *here* and *hair* respectively. The index value scales are:

(er)–1   (ɛr)–1   [ɪə]

(er)–2a   (ɛr)–2a   [e: ~ ë:]

(er)–2b   (ɛr)–2b   [eə ~ ëə]

(er)–3a   (ɛr)–3a   [ɛː ~ ɛ̈ː]
(er)–3b   (ɛr)–3b   [ɛə ~ ɛ̈ə]

The common scale means that the amount of differentiation, if any, between the two lexical classes can be measured, and that cases of hypercorrection can be noted. By means of the subdivision 2a–2b, 3a–3b, calculations can be made concerning the schwa off-glide. One can investigate, for example, its frequency of occurrence, and study whether or not it is used to differentiate the two sets of items.

6.4.6   The variable (ī). The variable (ī) is the diphthong in *ride, right, rhyme, riper*. Kökeritz has this diphthong as [ɑɪ ~ ɒɪ ~ ʌɪ] with [əɪ ~ ɜɪ] as variants. Lowman writes [˃ʌʊɪ ~ ˃ʊɪ ~ ˃ʌ·ɪ^], etc., and Francis [ʌɪ ~ ʌi ~ ʌɪ]. The index value scale is:

(ī)–1   [ɑɪ ~ ä ɪ]
(ī)–2   [ʊɪ ~ ʌ̈ɪ]
(ī)–3   [ʊi ~ ʌ̈i]
(ī)–4   [ɔi ~ ʌɪ]

6.4.7   The variable (ir). This variable is the vowel in items such as *bird, further, fern*, i.e. reflexes of ME ĕr, ŭr, and ĭr, as discussed above (6.2, p. 77). The scale is as follows:

(ir)–1   [ɜː]
(ir)–2   [ɐː]
(ir)–3   [aː ~ ʌ]

6.4.8   The variable (o). The variable (o) deals with the degree of rounding or unrounding of the vowel in *top, cod, box*. The unrounding of this vowel appears to be a feature only of Norfolk speech within East Anglia. Lowman writes [˃ʌɑ ~ ɒ], etc., and Francis [ɑ· ~ ɑː ~ ɒ]. The value for Norwich is:

(o)–1   [ɒ]
(o)–2   [ɑ ~ ä ~ ä]

6.4.9   The variables (ou), (ō) and (ū). These three variables are the vowels in *know, boat* and *boot* items respectively, as discussed above (6.2, p. 65). The common index scale for all three variables means that the amount and nature of the phonetic differentiation of these three lexical sets can be investigated, and hyper-correct pronunciations closely

TABLE 6.2   *Index value scales of the phonological variables*

Variable	Value 1	2	3	4	5
(a)	æ	æ:	æ:ɛ	ɛ:	ɛ:ᵉ
(ā)	eɪ	æɪ	æi	æ:i	
(a:)	ɑ:	ä:	a:		
(e)	ɛ	ǽ	ʌ		
(er)	ɪə	e:(ə)	ɛ:(ə)		
(ɛr)	ɪə	e:(ə)	ɛ:(ə)		
(h)	h	—			
(i)	aɪ	ɐɪ	ɐi	ɔi	
(ir)	ɜ:	ɐ:	a:		
(ng)	ŋ	n			
(o)	ɒ	ɑ			
(ou)	ʌu	ɵu	u:	ʊ	
(ō)	ʌu	ɵu	u:	ʊ	
(t)	t	tʔ	ʔ		
(ū)	ʌu	ɵu	u:	ʉ:	ʊ
(yu)	ju:	ʉ:			

studied. Note that (ū)–4 is not equivalent to (ou)–4 or (ō)–4, but that (ū)–5 *is* identical with (ou)–4 and (ō)–4. The index value scales are:

(ou)–1   (ō)–1   (ū)–1   [ʌu ~ ɔu ~ ɒu]
(ou)–2   (ō)–2   (ū)–2   [ǫʊ ~ ɵʊ]
(ou)–3   (ō)–3   (ū)–3   [u: ~ ʉ: ~ ʊu]
(ou)–4   (ō)–4   (ū)–5   [ʊ ~ ɤ]
                  (ū)–4   [ʉ: ~ ʝʉ ~ ɜʉ]

(ou)–1, (ō)–1, (ū)–1 represent East Anglian /ou/; (ou)–2, (ō)–2, (ū)–2 represent RP /ou/; (ou)–3, (ō)–3, (ū)–3 represent East Anglian /u:/; (ū)–4 represents East Anglian /ʉ:/; and (ou)–4, (ō)–4, (ū)–5 represent /ʊ/.

6.4.10   The variable (yu). The variable (yu) is the vowel in *Hugh, tune, music*, and is concerned with the presence or absence of the glide [j]. The scale is:

(yu)–1   [ju: ~ jʉ:]
(yu)–2   [ʉ: ~ ɜʉ]

Note that for most variables, the lowest score 000 represents a consistent idealised RP pronunciation; highest scores, ranging from 100 to 400, represent consistent use of the most extreme form of Norwich pronunciation.

7 The co-variation of the phonological variables with sociological parameters

7.1 Measurement of co-variation

One of the chief aims of this work is to investigate the co-variation of phonological and sociological variables. In order to measure this type of correlation, a record was first taken of each occurrence of all the variables in the four contextual styles for each informant. Index scores for each informant in each style could then be developed, and, subsequently, the mean index score for each social group calculated. By means of these scores we are able: (i) to investigate the nature of the correlation between realisations of phonological variables and social class, social context, and sex; (ii) to discover which variables are subject to social class differentiation and which to stylistic variation; and (iii) to find out which variables are most important in signalling the social context of some linguistic interaction, or the social class of a speaker.

The methods we are using of calculating and portraying individual and group phonological indices were initially developed by Labov (1966a). In some respects, however, the present work represents a development of Labov's techniques in that use is made of phonological indices for investigating problems of surface phonemic contrast, and for studying aspects of what is usually termed 'phonological space'. (For reasons that will be given later the term 'phonetic space' will be preferred in this work.) Some variables are also investigated in this work which do not produce evidence of social and stylistic differentiation that is so clear-cut or conclusive as that discussed by Labov. This increase in complexity means that it is possible to gain some additional insight into the linguistic behaviour of different social groups, and to learn more about the mechanisms of stylistic variation and linguistic change.

We can begin by taking as an example the phonological variable (ng), the pronunciation of the suffix -ing. This is well-known as a variable in many different types of English, and seems likely to provide a good example of social class and stylistic differentiation. We can tell, by means of information developed for this variable, whether the Norwich questionnaire has or has not been successful in eliciting different contextual styles, and whether the social class index has or has not been successful in distinguishing between groups of informants who have significantly different phonological characteristics.

7.2 The variable (ng)

Table 7.1 shows the average (ng) index scores for the five social classes established in chapter 5, in each of the four contextual styles: Word List Style (WLS), Reading Passage Style (RPS), Formal Speech (FS), and Casual Speech (CS). Tests of significance have not been carried out on this, or on the data for the other variables. As Labov (1970) has said concerning other sociolinguistic data: 'It is immediately obvious to the sophisticated statistician that tests of significance are irrelevant...even if a particular case were below the level of significance, the convergence of so many independent events carries us to a level of confidence which is unknown in most social or psychological research.' Table 7.1 demonstrates that:

(i) the Norwich questionnaire has in fact been successful in eliciting four hierarchically ordered and discrete contextual styles, since, for each class, the scores rise consistently from WLS to CS;

(ii) the social class index has provided a successful basis for the establishment of discrete social classes as these classes are reflected in their linguistic behaviour, since, for each style, the scores rise consistently from MMC to LWC;

(iii) the method of calculating index scores for phonological variables is a successful one and is likely to be useful in the study of Norwich English; and

(iv) the phonological variable (ng) is involved in a considerable amount of social class and contextual variation, with scores ranging over the whole scale from 000 to 100.

The information given in table 7.1 is more clearly portrayed in Fig. 14. Index scores, from 000 representing consistent use of [n], to 100 representing consistent use of [ŋ], are plotted along the ordinate. The four contextual styles, from WLS, the most formal, to CS, the most informal, are shown along the abscissa. The lines on the graph connect scores obtained by each of the five social classes in the four contextual styles.

TABLE 7.1. *(ng) index scores by class and style*

Class		Style			
		WLS	RPS	FS	CS
I	MMC	000	000	003	028
II	LMC	000	010	015	042
III	UWC	005	015	074	087
IV	MWC	023	044	088	095
V	LWC	029	066	098	100

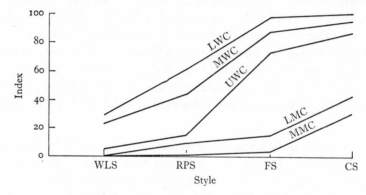

Fig. 14   Variable (ng) by class and style

The stylistic variation of this variable is portrayed in the consistent downward slope of the lines from right to left across the graph, representing an increase in [ŋ] endings as we move from everyday speech to more formal styles. The variable (ng), it can be seen, is a very good indicator of social context, with scores ranging, as we have already noted, from 000 (MMC and LMC in WLS; MMC in RPS) to 100 (LWC in CS). Note that stylistic variation is greatest in the case of the UWC, whose range is from 005 to 087, and whose line on the graph consequently has the steepest gradient. We have already discussed (see chapter 5) the greater awareness the UWC and LMC have of the social significance of linguistic variables, because of the 'border-line' nature of their social class position. The linguistic insecurity revealed here in the large amount of UWC stylistic variation for (ng) is clearly part of the same tendency.

The social class differentiation of (ng) is, of course, shown on the graph by the clear separation of the lines connecting the scores for each class, and by the hierarchical ordering of these lines, LWC–MMC. The amount of differentiation can be gauged from the spatial separation of the lines on the graph. Thus the greatest amount of differentiation occurs in FS, where the two MC groups appear to have the ability to control (ng) forms to a level nearer that of the more formal styles, whereas the three WC groups have scores which more closely approach their CS level. Note that in CS, which we can assume to be reasonably representa- tive of normal, everyday speech in familiar social environments, the three WC groups show only a small amount of differentiation one from the other, 087–100. This is also true of the two MC groups, 028–042. There is, on the other hand, a very significant difference between the (ng) level of the WC as a whole and that of the MC. This underlines once again the importance of this particular social division in the social structure.

We have shown, then, that the proportion of [n] to [ŋ] suffixes that occurs in speech is a function of the social class of the speaker and of the social context in which he is speaking. Moreover, although (ng) quite clearly differentiates between all five social groups, it is most important in distinguishing MC from WC speakers. UWC speakers have the greatest amount of stylistic variation, and MMC speakers the smallest, although it is instructive to note that even this class uses an average of 28% forms with [n] in CS.

7.2.1   Sex differentiation of (ng). Fischer, in his study of this variable in an American locality (1958), found that males used a higher percentage of [n] forms than females. Generally speaking, this is also the case in Norwich, as table 7.2 shows. In seventeen cases out of twenty, male scores are greater than or equal to corresponding female scores.[1] We can therefore say that a high (ng) index is typical of male speakers as well as of WC speakers. This link between the linguistic characteristics of WC speakers and male speakers is a common one. Almost all the Norwich variables have the same kind of pattern as that shown in table 7.2, with women having lower index scores than men. This is a fact which is not, on the face of it, particularly surprising, but one that is at the same time

---

[1] The low score obtained by male LMC speakers in CS requires some comment. The score is clearly unrepresentative, being lower than both the RPS and FS scores and the male MMC score, and is due to the fact that only a very small number of instances of this variable happened to be obtained for this group in CS.

TABLE 7.2. (*ng*) *indices by class, style and sex*

Class		WLS	RPS	FS	CS
		\multicolumn{4}{c}{Style}			
MMC	M	000	000	004	031
	F	000	000	000	000
LMC	M	000	020	027	017
	F	000	000	003	067
UWC	M	000	018	081	095
	F	011	013	068	077
MWC	M	024	043	091	097
	F	020	046	081	088
LWC	M	066	100	100	100
	F	017	054	097	100

in need of some explanation. There would appear to be two inter-connected explanatory factors:

1. Women in our society are more status-conscious than men, generally speaking, and are therefore more aware of the social signifi-cance of linguistic variables. There are probably two main reasons for this:

(i) The social position of women in our society is less secure than that of men, and, generally speaking, subordinate to that of men. It is therefore more necessary for women to secure and signal their social status linguistically and in other ways, and they are more aware of the importance of this type of signal.

(ii) Men in our society can be rated socially by their occupation, their earning power, and perhaps by their other abilities: in other words, by what they *do*. For the most part, however, this is not possible for women, who have generally to be rated on how they *appear*. Since they cannot be rated socially by their occupation, by what other people know about what they do in life, other signals of status, including speech, are corre-spondingly more important. This last point is perhaps the most important.

2. The second, related, factor is that WC speech, like many other aspects of WC culture, has, in our society, connotations of masculinity, since it is associated with the roughness and toughness supposedly characteristic of WC life, which are, to a certain extent, considered to be desirable masculine attributes. They are not, on the other hand,

TABLE 7.3. *Sample of 10 informants: average scores,*
word-internal and word-final (t) by style

(t)	WLS	RPS	FS	CS
Word-internal, e.g. *better*	029	052	113	134
Word-final, e.g. *bet*	028	089	151	161

considered to be desirable feminine characteristics. On the contrary, refinement and sophistication are much preferred.

This discussion is of course necessarily at a rather simple level, but it is clear that we have reflected in these phonological indices part of the value system of our culture as a whole. From the point of view of linguistic theory, this means that, as far as linguistic change 'from below' is concerned, we can expect men to be in the vanguard. Changes 'from above', on the other hand, are more likely to be led by women.[1] The type of sex differentiation shown in table 7.2 is, in any case, usual. Only a reversal of this pattern, or a large increase in the normal type of male/female differentiation can be considered to be significantly unusual in any way.

7.3 The variable (t)

The pattern of class, sex and style differentiation illustrated in the case of (ng) is the typical pattern associated with a normal linguistic variable. This can be confirmed briefly by a further illustration of another well-known variable in British English: (t), the amount of glottalisation in the pronunciation of syllable-final /t/. The class and style differentiation of (t) is shown in fig. 15. The style differentiation follows the normal pattern seen in the case of (ng), with all classes decreasing the frequency of (t)–2 and (t)–3 as formality of context increases. Class differentiation also follows the usual pattern, although there is no differentiation of LWC and MWC scores. Moreover, UWC scores closely approach those of the LWC and MWC in CS. We can see, in fact, that the WC as a whole has almost 100% 'extreme' forms, (t)–3 ($=$ [ʔ]) in CS.

[1] Labov's terms 'change from below' and 'change from above' refer respectively to changes from below and above the level of conscious awareness. Usually, however, changes from above involve the downward dissemination of prestige features, i.e. they are social changes 'from above' as well. Changes from below, moreover, very often start among lower class groups (see Trudgill, 1972).

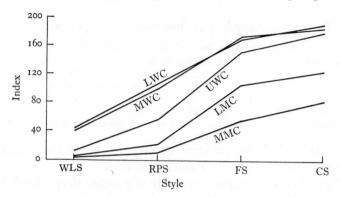

Fig. 15   Variable (t) by class and style

Index scores also show that glottalisation is more frequent in the case of word-final (t) than it is word internally. A comparison of (t) indices for a random sample of 10 of the 60 informants gives the average scores shown in table 7.3. (Only WLS provides an exception.) We can therefore claim that glottalisation (usage of [tʔ] and [ʔ]) of /t/ is inversely proportional to social class and social context, and is more frequent word finally than word internally.

7.4   The variable (ā)

Another variable which has the same kind of normal differentiation pattern is (ā). This is the vowel in *name, nail, plate*. Fig. 16 shows that (ā) is subject both to class and style differentiation, although the stylistic variation is not especially great, and the UWC and MWC scores are more or less undifferentiated except in WLS. We can interpret this pattern as indicating that there is a CS norm for LWC speakers between [æi] and [æːi]; for the MWC and UWC [æi]; for the LMC between [æi] and [æɪ]; and for the MMC [æɪ]. Surprisingly, the MMC approaches [eɪ] or [ɛɪ] only in WLS.

7.5   Stylistic variation

We shall proceed now to a discussion of those Norwich variables which do not exhibit, in all respects, the regular kind of style and class differentiation demonstrated by (ng), (t) and (ā). The point of investigating the following 'irregular' variables is that, through an examination of the

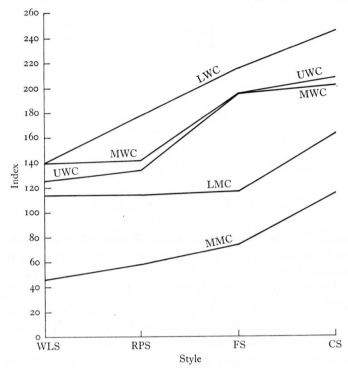

Fig. 16   Variable (ā) by class and style

points at which they deviate from the normal pattern, they can provide us with information about the nature of stylistic variation, linguistic change, and a number of other topics which may be of some theoretical interest. The first group of variables that we shall study in this way are those that throw some light on the nature and causes of the stylistic variation we saw exemplified in the case of (ng), (t) and (ā).

7.5.1   The variable (a:). The first variable which is of some value in this respect is (a:). Indices for this variable measure the vowel quality in items of the lexical set of *cart, path*. Scores range from 000 for consistent use of [ɑ:] to 200 for consistent use of [a:]. Fig. 17 shows the class and style differentiation of (a:) in the Norwich sample.

It is immediately apparent from fig. 17 that the two lowest WC groups use a very high number of very front vowels in everyday speech – almost 100 %. The UWC also has a CS index which is only slightly lower.

4

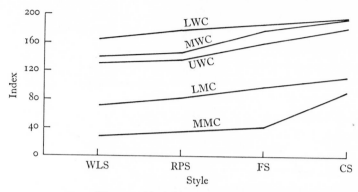

Fig. 17   Variable (a:) by class and style

MC scores, on the other hand, are considerably lower than WC scores, and in fact the overall WC/MC division seems from the graph to be the most significant. We can state, on the basis of these scores, that the typical WC pronunciation of (a:) is [a:], the LMC pronunciation [ä:], and the MMC pronunciation [ɐ:].

We can also see in fig. 17, however, that, for the WC as a whole, there is only a small amount of stylistic variation of (a:), especially in the case of the LWC. We can interpret this as indicating that although WC speech is characterised by a pronunciation of this variable that is significantly different from that of the MC, little attention is directed towards this difference within the Norwich speech community. (This interpretation is supported by the fact that (a:) was not the subject of overt comment or criticism in any of the discussions of Norwich English recorded during the interviews.) It is interesting to speculate as to why some variables, although demonstrating marked class differentiation, are subject to little or no stylistic variation (are 'irregular' in the above sense), while others are involved in a great deal. It is of course true that there is a small amount of regular stylistic variation of (a:) amongst the WC, but the relative insignificance of this can be gauged from a comparison of fig. 17 with figs. 14 and 15. If it were not for these (a:) scores, one could have supposed that stylistic variation was a function of class differentiation: members of lower class groups attempt to reproduce forms more characteristic of higher social groups in more formal contexts. We are clearly not able to do this, however. The question we must answer is: how is it that for some variables speakers are relatively unaware of the social implications of the forms they use, and therefore carry out little or no stylistic shifting? We can guess, on the basis of (a:) and the three other variables discussed below, that there might be two explanations:

1. Speakers are more aware of the social significance of forms which are overtly stigmatised. These consist of (i) forms which may be the stereotyped object of humour or ridicule, such as (h)–2, and (ii) forms which are actively discouraged by the educational institutions, such as (t)–3 or (ng)–2. We could speculate further as to why some variables are more liable to overt criticism of this kind than others. One of the principal reasons would seem to be orthographical: (t)–3, (h)–2 and (ng)–2 can be characterised as 'dropping your '*t*'s', '*h*'s', and '*g*'s', respectively.

2. Speakers are more aware of the social significance of forms which are currently involved in linguistic change. The fact that conflicting forms can be heard from people of different ages within the same social group means that attention, conscious or subconscious, is directed towards these differences.

The variable (a:) does not come under either of these headings: it is not overtly stigmatised; and it is not involved in any kind of linguistic change. This explains the general lack of stylistic differentiation. On the other hand, though, we should note that there *is* stylistic differentiation to some degree in the MMC scores. These speakers *are* aware of the social significance of (a:) (although the awareness is probably sub-conscious, since no overt comments were noted). It therefore seems that there is a third factor that we have to take into account: the amount of difference between a local linguistic variable and its RP counterpart, in the case of those speakers who are familiar with RP forms. If the difference is large enough, it may result in awareness of the significance of a variable on the part of these speakers, and hence in stylistic shifting. We can investigate further the validity of the three factors by studying other variables which are not involved in stylistic variation in the 'regular' way. These variables are (ō), (yu) and (ɛr).

7.5.2 The variable (ō). This variable deals with the vowel of *road, home, go*, etc. An index of 100 would be given for consistent use of RP-type /əʊ/ and 200 for consistent use of Norwich /u:/. Scores over 200 indicate some use of East Anglian short *o*, as in *home* [hʊm]. Class and style differentiation are shown in fig. 18. It can be seen that it is only the WC for whom the 'short o' is to any great extent a characteristic feature. It is also noteworthy that there is a big contrast between MC

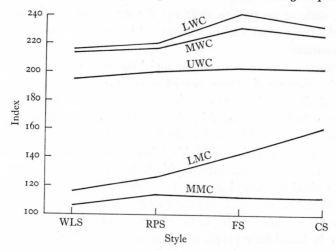

Fig. 18   Variable (ō) by class and style

and WC speakers, but that not even the MMC consistently *quite* achieves the RP norm in any style.

There is very little evidence of style differentiation of (ō), except in the speech of the LMC, which has a marked fall in scores from CS to WLS. Now, the variable (ō) is not subject to any overt criticism in Norwich (although it is one of the very first features noticed by speakers from the Home Counties: the contrast between [ruːd] and [ræ̈ʊd] *road* is quite striking). Neither is it involved in any linguistic change. These two factors are probably sufficient to explain the general lack of stylistic variation. What, however, of the LMC? The stylistic variation of this group can probably best be explained in terms of the third factor discussed above. While other classes make little attempt to 'correct' their pronunciation towards RP-type forms in more formal contexts, LMC speakers *are* aware of the social significance of (ō) variants. This is because of their rather tenuous border-line social class position, and their greater contacts with RP speakers in the MMC, which, combined with the fairly large amount of phonetic difference between WC [uː] and MC [ɐʊ], is sufficient to produce stylistic variation.

7.5.3 The variable (εr). This variable is the vowel in *there, chair, care.* The pattern of variation is illustrated in fig. 19. We can see that there is a certain amount of class variation of (εr), with the MMC clearly separated from the rest. (200 indicates consistent [εː], lower scores

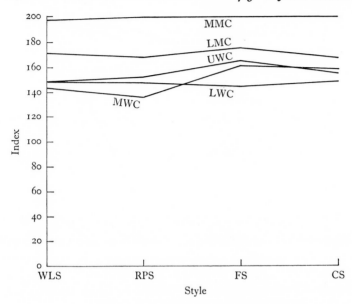

Fig. 19   Variable (εr) by class and style

a higher vowel.) There is, however, *no* stylistic variation of this variable. We therefore expect that none of the three factors suggested above as leading to stylistic shift will be present in the case of (εr). This is certainly the case for two of them: the phonetic differences involved in class differentiation are not very great; and (εr) is not the object of any overt criticism in Norwich. It *is*, however, involved in a certain amount of linguistic change – an apparent counter-example. We shall see below (7.8.2), though, that this change involves the merger of (er) vowels with (εr) vowels, rather than vice versa, and that social consciousness is therefore directed towards (er) rather than (εr). The variable (εr), then, is only passively involved in linguistic change and is not itself under- going change. It is this factor that would appear to be crucial in bringing about stylistic differentiation.

7.5.4   The variable (yu). This variable is the presence or absence of the glide [j] in the lexical set of *tune, music, queue*. Fig. 20 shows that there is marked class differentiation of this variable (although the LWC and MWC are undifferentiated, and the UWC has an index consider- ably lower than the LMC in CS). The stylistic variation – which we are concentrating on here – is rather unusual and generally slight. The

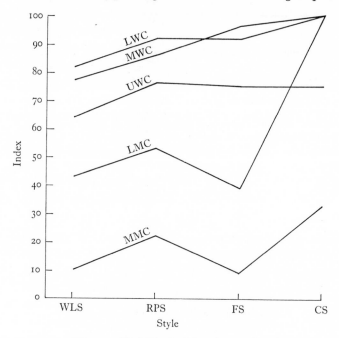

Fig. 20   Variable (yu) by class and style

unusual nature of this variation appears to be due to the fact that [j] does not depend for its frequency of occurrence in this lexical set simply on social class and social context. It also depends on the initial consonant of the item involved (and to some extent on the lexical item itself). For example, although [j] never occurs after /r/ and /l/, as in *rule* and *lute*, it occurs more frequently after the initial consonants of those items nearer the end of the following list than after those at the beginning: *suit, news, dune, tune, view, few, music, beauty, pew, queue* (i.e. [j] is much more frequent in *queue* than in *suit*).

This means that, while WLS and RPS scores are comparable, since they include the same items, FS and CS scores are not. Neither are the WLS and FS scores. This factor explains the otherwise strange overlapping of UWC and LMC scores in CS. There are, that is to say, certain complicating factors that have to be taken into consideration when conversational material for some variables is compared with material based on prepared reading tests (see also 7.7.3 below).

RPS and WLS scores, then, are strictly comparable, and there is some evidence of normal stylistic differentiation at this point. We would therefore expect that at least one of the three factors discussed above would be involved in the case of (yu). This, however, does not appear to be the case: there is no overt stigmatisation of (yu); no linguistic change; and no large phonetic difference between Norwich and RP leading to stylistic variation by the MC. How, then, can we explain the fact that this variable is involved in stylistic differentiation? The answer is that attention is focussed on (yu) because of the importance this variable has for the phonological system as a whole. Variation of (yu) is not the purely phonetic variation of, say, (t): the presence of [j] is crucial for establishing a contrast between items of the type:

> Hugh : who
> dew : do
> cure : curr

In other words, because of this surface contrast, the two different variants of (yu) are of more systematic linguistic significance than variants of those variables which are subject to purely phonetic variation. Now, it might be argued that both (ō) and (ɛr), discussed above, are also involved in similar types of oppositions: (ō) and (ou) are not distinguished in RP, while (er) and (ɛr) are often not distinguished in Norwich. However, consciousness appears to be directed in both cases to the other member of the pair, (ou) and (er), both of which are subject to style variation. We can suggest, then, that we have in fact discovered, through an examination of (yu), a fourth factor which can lead to the stylistic differentiation of variables.

Our investigation into the co-variation of phonological and sociological phenomena has thus provided us with certain insights into the nature of stylistic variation. Although related to social class differentiation, it is not an automatic consequence of class differentiation. Stylistic variation takes place in the case of variables subject to class differentiation only when social consciousness is directed towards these variables by reason of the fact that they are:

(i) undergoing linguistic change; or
(ii) subject to overt corrective pressures; or
(iii) involved in surface phonological contrasts; or
(iv) markedly different from prestige accent equivalents (in the case of those speakers who have some contact with the prestige accent).

7.6 Linguistic change

Analysis of the co-variation of linguistic and sociological parameters can also throw light on another important linguistic problem: linguistic change (in this case phonetic and phonological change). For a thorough study of linguistic changes in progress, and of the mechanisms and processes by means of which these changes take place, we need a careful correlation of variable index scores with age-group membership. (I propose to do this in some detail in a forthcoming volume.) For present purposes, it will be sufficient, in our study of class and style variation, to outline the way in which 'irregularities' of class and style variation can indicate that linguistic changes are in progress, and provide us with information about the actual nature of the processes involved. We can illustrate this point by an examination of a number of the Norwich variables, and we can begin by studying the variable (e).

7.6.1   The variable (e). This variable is the vowel of *tell, well, better* (see 6.4.4). Fig. 21 shows that the pattern of class differentiation for (e) is an unusual one. The UWC has an index score that is significantly higher than that of the MWC in CS, and both the UWC and MWC have scores that are higher than those of the LWC in all contextual styles. For the WC as a whole, that is, the regular pattern of class differentiation is completely reversed. Note, also, that in CS the LWC score approaches those of the MC very closely. We can attempt to explain this in the following way. We can suppose that the LWC, as a relatively 'under-privileged' group, is isolated from innovating tendencies. If this is the case, since the LWC is differentiated from the rest of the WC in an unusual way, we can hypothesize that high scores for this variable (a large amount of centralisation) represent an innovation in Norwich English. The phonological variable (e) is involved in linguistic change, in that centralisation of this vowel is increasing. In the vanguard of this change, we can hypothesize further, are the upper members of the WC. The LWC and LMC are also participating in the change, but at a lower level, and the MMC are not participating at all, or very little.

This hypothesis is confirmed by the pattern of age differentiation in table 7.4, which shows (e) indices for CS for seven different age-groups. This shows that there is in fact a very marked amount of age-differentiation of (e). Younger people under 30 have much higher (e) scores than older people. This is particularly clear in the case of informants aged

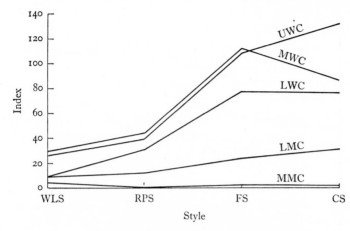

Fig. 21   Variable (e) by class and style

TABLE 7.4. *Age-differentiation of (e) in CS*

Age-group	Index score
10–19	173
20–19	100
30–39	067
40–49	088
50–59	046
60–69	058
70+	081

10–19 (and is in fact especially evident in the speech of the male members of this group, whose average score is the maximum, 200). Centralisation of (e) is more prevalent among younger speakers, and is becoming increasingly so. (See Labov, forthcoming, for further discussion of Norwich (e).) Our conclusion is, therefore, that linguistic changes in progress may be reflected in unusual patterns of class differentiation of the type seen in fig. 21. This conclusion is confirmed by a number of other variables studied below.

7.6.2   The variable (i). This variable is the pronunciation of the vowel in *right, ride, rye.* Fig. 22 shows that (i) differentiates between the social classes in the usual way, except that the MWC has higher scores than the LWC in three of the four contextual styles. We have just seen that

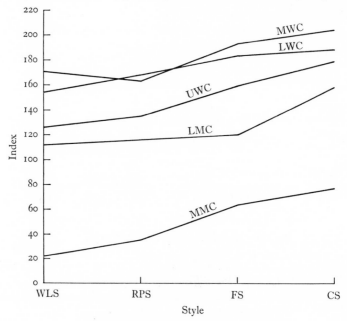

Fig. 22   Variable (ī) by class and style

this kind of overlapping pattern may be a sign of a linguistic change in progress, and this is, therefore, a possibility worth investigating here.

We can see from fig. 22 that the MWC is the only class which has an index score of over 200, which indicates a fairly consistent use of some (ī)–4 forms. The index scale for (ī) is as follows:

$$(ī)–1 = [aɪ]$$
$$(ī)–2 = [ɐɪ]$$
$$(ī)–3 = [ɐi]$$
$$(ī)–4 = [ɔi]$$

The rural dialect records discussed in chapter 6 indicate that the older East Anglian form of this variable was [ɐi] = (ī)–3. As (ī)–1 and –2 represent RP-influenced forms, it may therefore be the case that [ɔi] is a fairly new development in Norwich. If this is the case, then the MWC, because of its high scores, must have been instrumental in introducing this particular form into the speech community.

We can investigate this possibility further by a more detailed break-down. Table 7.5, for instance, shows the extent to which (ī)–4 is a MWC characteristic. 95 % of this class use some (ī)–4, and 50 % of the MWC use 10 % or more (ī)–4 compared, say, to only 37 % of the LWC.

TABLE 7.5. *Percentage of informants of each class using* (ī)–4

(%)	Any (ī)–4	50%+	20%+	10%+	5%+
MMC	17	17	17	17	17
LMC	25	12	12	12	12
UWC	37	0	12	19	37
MWC	95	18	36	50	82
LWC	62	0	0	37	50

TABLE 7.6. *Informants using* (ī)–4

	No.	50%+	20%+	10%+	5%+
Male	27	6	12	16	24
Female	8	0	0	3	6
Total	35	6	12	19	20

TABLE 7.7. *Percentage of informants in two age-groups using* (ī)–4

Age	Any (ī)–4	50%+	20%+	10%+	5%+
10–39	61	11	18	43	61
40+	56	9	12	22	41

(Note that the MMC 17% and LMC 12% scores represent one informant each only. These two informants are both men who have been upwardly socially mobile.) Table 7.6 shows the numbers of male and female informants who use any (ī)–4, together with, again, those who use more than certain percentages of (ī)–4 as opposed to other (ī) variants. It shows that over half the informants use some (ī)–4, but that only eight of these are women. No woman, moreover, uses more than 20% (ī)–4. The sex differentiation of this feature is therefore very marked indeed. The variant [ɔi], that is, is a characteristically male MWC form. We can also show that it is, in fact, a linguistic innovation in Norwich English. Table 7.7 demonstrates that a higher percentage of those aged 39 or under have (ī)–4 forms than those aged over 40. This, then is a second example of an unusual class differentiation pattern revealing that a change is in progress. (It is also another example of a change which is being led by the male members of the upper WC.)

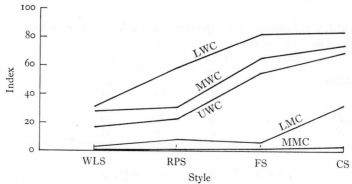

Fig. 23   Variable (o) by class and style

TABLE 7.8. (*o*) *indices by class, style and sex*

Class		Style			
		WLS	RPS	FS	CS
MMC	M	000	000	001	003
	F	000	000	000	000
LMC	M	004	014	011	055
	F	000	002	001	008
UWC	M	011	019	044	060
	F	023	027	068	077
MWC	M	029	026	064	078
	F	025	045	071	066
LWC	M	014	050	080	069
	F	037	062	083	090

7.6.3   The variable (o). Indices for this variable measure the degree of lip-rounding in the pronunciation of the vowel in the lexical set of *top, fog, lorry*. Fig. 23 shows that there is a large amount of class differentiation, with the biggest division again being between the MC and the WC: unrounded vowels are predominantly a WC feature. The style variation that is clearly illustrated suggests further that (o) should meet at least one of the four criteria established in the previous section (see 7.5.4). This it does not at first appear to do. The class differentiation pattern, moreover, is quite regular, and shows no sign of any linguistic change. Table 7.8, however, throws some light on this problem. We saw in table 7.2 that there is a regular sex differentiation of (ng) such that male speakers have consistently higher scores than female speakers. The figures in table 7.8 show that, although MC men once again have higher scores than women, for the WC this pattern is more or less completely reversed. In 10 cases out of 12, WC women have higher scores than men. This is the only case of such a complete reversal of the pattern of sex differentiation among all the Norwich variables.

In view of the discovery made above about the relationship between unusual class differentiation patterns and linguistic change, it is not unreasonable to suppose that unusual structures of sex differentiation may have the same cause. This is in fact the case – (o) is undergoing change in Norwich English (see Trudgill, 1972) – and this accounts for the stylistic variation shown in fig. 23. The actual configuration of the sex differentiation pattern can be explained by the rather unusual nature of the linguistic change involved. Male WC speakers are introducing into Norwich English, as an innovation, the [ɒ] vowel which, as well as being the RP pronunciation, also happens to be the form used in the local accents of Suffolk. (Lowman writes *bog* [bɑg] in the three Norfolk localities, but [bɒg] in the four Suffolk localities.) We therefore have here an interesting case of a change 'from below', due to the influence of neighbouring accents, led by WC men, coinciding with the RP form which is predominantly a female MC characteristic.

7.6.4 The variable (a). This variable is the vowel in *bat, bad, carry,* etc. Fig. 24 shows that there is an overall tendency to the regular kind of class and style differentiation noted in 7.2. On the other hand, however, there is a considerable amount of overlap in the scores of the WC, and stylistic differentiation between RPS and WLS is, for four of the five social classes, in the 'wrong' direction. One explanation for this can perhaps be adduced from the fact that the overlapping of different social class scores is largely due to the LWC. We have already noted that this class is to a certain extent isolated from innovating tendencies. It is therefore possible that the overlapping of scores is due to some kind of linguistic change in Norwich English which index scores for this variable may have obscured.

In fact information from the rural dialect surveys discussed in chapter 6 leads us to suppose that two somewhat conflicting diachronic tendencies are at work here. The Norwich (a) index has the following variants:

(a)–3 = [æ:ᵉ], etc.
(a)–4 = [ɛ ~ ɛ:], etc.
(a)–5 = [ɛ:ᵉ], etc.

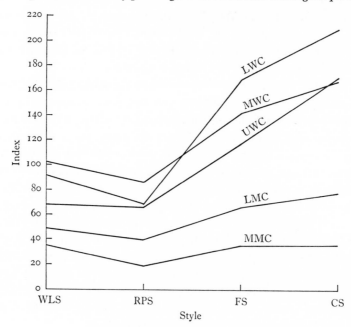

Fig. 24   Variable (a) by class and style

Kökeritz (1932, p. 10) states that his informants used vowels of the quality [æ~æ:~ɛ~ɛ:] for this variable. He considers that [ɛ] forms may be partly due to 'Cockney' influence. However, the fact that the Suffolk children had only [æ~æ:] suggests rather that [ɛ~ɛ:] is the older East Anglian form, and that it is in the process, at the time when Kökeritz is writing, of being replaced by RP-type [æ]. This hypothesis is partly confirmed by Forby's (1830) statement (and he is writing of the first half of the last century) that *bad, man*, etc., are often pronounced '*bed*', '*men*', etc. in Norfolk (especially in the region of King's Lynn). We can therefore hypothesize further that older Norwich speakers will tend to have a higher number of (a)–4 [ɛ~ɛ:] forms, and that middle-aged speakers will tend to have the newer RP-like forms of (a)–1 or (a)–2. This in turn will mean that the diphthongised (a)–3 and (a)–5 forms must occur in predominantly the speech of younger informants. If this is the case, then, within the WC, age-group differences will be more important than class differentiation, and the overlapping shown in fig. 24 will occur.

This hypothesis is confirmed by the facts shown in table 7.9, which

TABLE 7.9. *Percentage of (a) variants*

Age-group	(a)–1 (%)	(a)–2 (%)	(a)–3 (%)	(a)–4 (%)	(a)–5 (%)	Total (%)
10–19	5	40	44	6	4	99
20–29	26	31	26	10	6	99
30–39	22	45	25	5	5	102
40–49	21	37	14	12	14	98
50–59	32	35	25	8	0	100
60–69	26	34	27	8	4	99
70+	18	28	26	25	3	100

demonstrates that the older East Anglian form of [ε~ε:] is more commonly retained in the speech of older Norwich people, but that the more typical modern Norwich pronunciation is [æ:~æ], which in the speech of many, particularly the young, is diphthongised to [æ:^{ε}~æ:^{1}~ ε:^{e}]. This suggests further that for some, particularly older or LWC speakers, (a)–4 represents a more formal pronunciation than (a)–3. For them, [ε] functions just as the more modern [æ] does for younger speakers. Diphthongisation and vowel height must therefore be regarded as independent variables which cannot successfully be incorporated into a single index, as we have tried to do here. Table 7.9 gives the percentage of each particular variant of (a) used by each age-group in FS and CS combined. It shows that both 10–19 and 70+ age-groups use a small percentage of (a)–1, but for different reasons: the 10–19 group uses instead a high percentage of diphthongised (a)–3, whereas the 70+ group uses a high percentage of (a)–4 [ε~ε:]. (a)–4 is employed to a large extent only by the 70+ group, and is therefore clearly dying out. It has largely been replaced by the more RP-like (a)–1, but this too is clearly ceding ground to (a)–2 [æ:], which is the most common Norwich variant at the moment. (The demise of (a)–1 is most clearly indicated by the very low score, 5%, among the 10–19 group.) Even (a)–2, however, would appear to be ceding ground to the diphthongised forms, (a)–3 and (a)–5, which between them are the most common form of (a) for speakers aged 29 and under. We can therefore postulate a diachronic progression: [ε > æ > æ: > æ:^{ε} (> ε:^{e})]. The increase in diphthongisation is more clearly revealed in table 7.10, which shows the percentage of total monophthongal and total diphthongal pronunciations of each age-group. The scores that stand out as exceptional are the

TABLE 7.10. (a): *Monophthongs and diphthongs*

Age-group	Total monophthongs (%)	Total diphthongs (%)
10–19	51	48
20–29	67	32
30–39	72	30
40–49	70	28
50–59	75	25
60–69	68	31
70+	71	29

51 % only total monophthongs and the 48 % total diphthongs of the 10–19 group.

All groups show some usage of all (a) variants, but no group except the 70+ group has above 12 % (a)–4. All groups use at least 68 % total monophthongs, except the under-thirties. No group uses more than 31 % total diphthongs, except, once more, the under-thirties. Again, an overlapping in the social class differentiation diagram reveals that a linguistic change is in progress, and also that, because of this change, the index scale initially developed for (a) was not sufficiently sensitive to handle this variable satisfactorily.

7.7   Relic forms

We have seen in the previous section that a number of phonological variables in Norwich English are currently involved in linguistic change, and that this is reflected in an unusual pattern of class or sex differentiation. Another class of variables that we can usefully discuss at this point are those which, although they have been involved in linguistic change, are not any longer involved in changes of any significance. This fact can also often be read out from the class differentiation diagrams for these variables. The variable (ir), for example, was set up in the first instance partly because of the variable forms recorded in the rural dialect surveys (see 6.2). Fig. 25, however, shows that the older rural type of pronunciation is now very much a relic form in Norwich English.

7.7.1   **The variable (ir).** This variable is the vowel of *bird, hurt, fern.*
We saw in chapter 6 that the typical rural East Anglian pronunciation

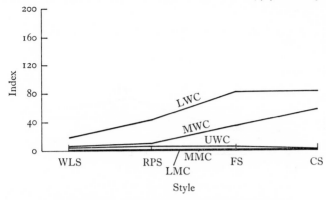

Fig. 25   Variable (ir) by class and style

of (ir), although subject to complex variation, was markedly different from RP: forms with [ɐ: ~ a: ~ ʌ] were usual. These forms are now obviously dying out. Fig. 25 shows that the highest score of all is 082 out of a possible high of 200. Moreover, non-RP forms are more or less entirely confined to the two lowest class groups. The two MC groups have 000 throughout, and the UWC has a high of only 003 (and note too that even the LWC uses only 10% non-RP forms in WLS). We can conclude, then, that (ir)–2 and (ir)–3 are heavily stigmatised in Norwich, and are in the process of dying out in favour of RP [ɜ:]. Only the LWC uses more than 25% non-RP forms in any style – a further indication of the social class barriers to the diffusion of normative and innovating influences as they affect this relatively isolated group.

7.7.2   The variable (ō). We saw above (7.5.2), in the class differentiation of (ō), that only the WC had a significant proportion of the typical East Anglian short *o*. Fig. 26 now shows in more detail the social distribution of the short *o*: it gives the percentage of (ō) which were (ō)–4 in each style for each class. We should note that even the LWC uses no more than 42% forms with short *o*. This suggests that the short *o* is also something of a relic form in Norwich. This fact can be emphasised by noting that the 42% is composed of a relatively small number of common lexical items. Details are given below in table 7.11, which shows the number of instances of (ō)–4 recorded in the Norwich survey per item. In addition to these items, *aerodrome, comb, alone* and *combed* were recorded with (ō)–4 in WLS and RPS. It can be seen from table 7.11 that *don't, only, suppose* and *home* account for the vast majority

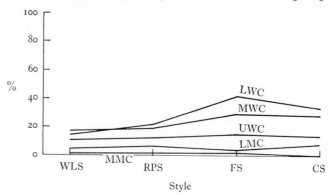

Fig. 26   Variable (ō): percentage of (ō)-4 by class and style

TABLE 7.11. *Number of occurrences of (ō)-4*

	FS	CS
don't	156	44
only	51	8
suppose	28	9
home	22	11
Road	8	0
won't	8	6
both	7	6
broke	4	2
supposed	4	3
whole	4	1
Holme	4	0
over	4	0
Holmes	2	0
bloke	2	2
post	2	0
stone	2	1
going to	1	4
homework	1	1
most	1	1
spoke	1	0
photo	1	0
notice	1	0
coats	1	0
road	1	1
roads	1	0
blokes	1	0
rollerdrome	1	0
Close	1	0
drove	0	1
Hippodrome	0	1
woke	0	3

of short *o* forms in the material recorded here: 80 % in the FS material and 72 % in the CS material (including *supposed, homework*). Note that *aerodrome, Hippodrome* and *rollerdrome* are almost universally pronounced with (ō)-4 in Norwich, but are not of especially frequent occurrence.

Table 7.11 shows further that phonetic environment is not the only factor which determines the presence or absence of [ʊ] in a given word, although the word-final consonants are all alveolars or nasals, with the exception of [v], [θ] and [k]. Other factors are *sentence stress, speed of utterance*, and *social connotation*: short *o* is more likely to occur in lightly stressed words, in rapid speech, and in words most current in popular speech or within the family. (These are all factors mentioned by Avis (1961) in connection with the New England short *o*.)

7.7.3 The variable (ū). This variable is the vowel in *boot, spoon, roof*. One variant of this vowel is /ʊ/ – the East Anglian short *o* also occurs with lexical items of this class. Fig. 27 shows the percentage of (ū) items that had /ʊ/ by class and style. It can be seen that there is a certain amount of class differentiation of this feature, although this is very small. What *stylistic* variation there is, moreover, appears to be, with the exception of the LWC shift between CS and FS (which should probably be interpreted as a genuine stylistic shift of the normal type), in the *wrong* direction. This, however, is quite easily explained: short *o* in (ū) items occurs in Norwich most often in the case of a relatively small number of lexical items which are well represented in the WL, less well in the RP, and which occur even less frequently in speech. The best illustration of *class* differentiation, therefore, can be obtained from the WLS figures, where all informants pronounced the same (relatively large number) of (ū) items. This shows that the MC is distinct from the WC in its use of short *o* forms. The bunching together of lines at the bottom of the graph indicates the extent to which this, too, is now a relic form.

7.8 Phonetic space

A study of the class and style differentiation of variables can also be helpful in the study of certain theoretical problems. There are, for example, three pairs of variables in Norwich English which are involved in 'phonemic mergers' in some way: (ou) *knows* and (ō) *nose* are distinct in much Norwich speech but not in RP; (er) *beer* and (ɛr) *bear* are

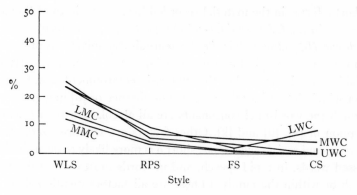

Fig. 27   Variable (ū): percentage of (ū)–5 by class and style

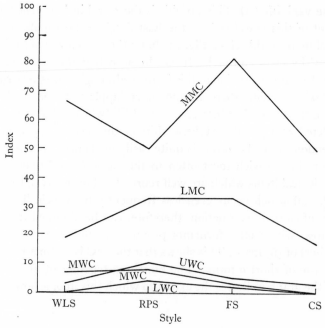

Fig. 28   Variable (ou) by class and style

distinct in RP but not in many varieties of Norwich English; and (ō)
boat and (ū) *boot* are also often not distinguished in Norwich. These
oppositions and mergers make for a complex situation of variation
which, under analysis, can provide us with information about certain
aspects of phonological theory; about the nature of phonological or

phonetic space; and about the nature of linguistic variation (in particular whether this is due to 'inherent variability' or 'dialect mixture').

7.8.1 The variables (ou) and (ō). We have already discussed the class and style differentiation of (ō) above (7.5.2; 7.7.2). The other variable, (ou), is the vowel in *know, old, throw*. In order to facilitate a comparison of (ou) and (ō) the index scales for the two variables have been made identical. This means that an (ou) score of 100 is given for a consistent RP-type pronunciation, and 000 for a consistent pronunciation of East Anglian [ɒu]. Fig. 28 shows that there is a clear differentiation of (ou) scores between the MMC and the LMC, and between the LMC and the WC. Within the WC, however, differentiation is minimal: this class as a whole is more or less consistent in its use of Norwich /ɒu/. There is also a very small amount of stylistic variation of (ou), at least amongst the WC. (In this case the class lines slope from left to right across the graph, since lower scores indicate vowels further removed from the RP norm, because of the common (ō)/(ou) scale.) The wide fluctuation in the MMC scores suggests random variation over a relatively large phonetic area [ɵʊ ~ ɔʊ], and perhaps reflects the large amount of variation in RP in the pronunciation of this vowel (see Gimson, 1962, p. 128).

We can now use the combined index scale to measure the amount of differentiation between (ō) and (ou) made by different classes in different styles. Figs. 29, 30 and 31 combine (ō) and (ou) scores for the MMC, LMC and UWC respectively (graphs for the MWC and LWC would be very similar to the UWC). These figures portray graphically the average amount of phonetic space differentiating the two sets of items (*nose* and *knows*) for the three classes. Fig. 29 shows that the MMC is quite close to actually merging the two sets, as in RP, around the RP norm of 100, but that it does not in fact, on average, do so. This poses an interesting question for phonological theory. The MMC as a whole, on average, preserves the distinction between (ō) and (ou) quite clearly. At its smallest, however, the amount of distinction shown here is 31 index points (compared with around 200 for the WC). Is this distinction large enough to be consistent with the type of distinction normally considered to be 'phonemic'? The amount of phonetic distinction is in fact so small (perhaps of the order of [ɵʊ] vs. [ɔʊ]) as to suggest that a linguist unfamiliar with East Anglian phonology might not notice the difference. These figures also mean, of course, that there is a very large amount

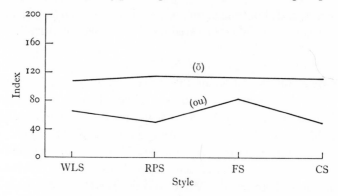

Fig. 29   (ou) and (ō) by style: MMC

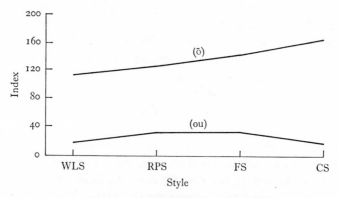

Fig. 30   (ou) and (ō) by style: LMC

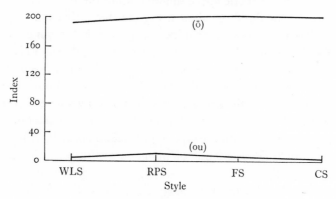

Fig. 31   (ou) and (ō) by style: UWC

of what is usually termed 'phonemic overlapping' of (ou) and (ō), much larger than the amount mentioned by Labov, for instance, in his discussion of variance analysis (1966*a*, pp. 520–4; and see Wetmore, 1959). In traditional phonemic studies this type of phenomenon is usually described as being the result of a linguistic change in progress: an imminent phoneme merger. In fact, in 'taxonomic phonemic' terms there is no other way of handling this 'almost-but-not-quite' type of merger. There is in this case, however, no sign whatsoever of any linguistic change. The situation portrayed in fig. 29 is the normal state of affairs in MMC Norwich English. The most satisfactory explanation of this phenomenon is that there are, in all varieties of Norwich English, two distinct underlying phonological elements which are realised at the phonetic level, in the speech of the MMC, in two areas of the phonetic continuum that almost entirely overlap. Alternatively, it is possible that the two areas overlap entirely, and that each phonemic unit is simply realised more frequently in one portion of the area than another (see Postal, 1968, ch. 9). The evidence in any case provides a strong argument in favour of a theory of phonology which permits the recognition of two different levels of the systematic phonemic and systematic phonetic type.

Fig. 30 shows that the LMC realisations of the two underlying phonemes are phonetically much more distinct than those of the MMC, and, interestingly, that the amount of differentiating phonetic space increases as the formality of style decreases. The downward dip of the (ou) line between RPS and WLS can perhaps be regarded as the result of pressures operating in phonetic space, with the opening of the first element of (ō) vowels in formal styles leading to a less RP-like pronunciation of (ou) items in order to preserve the distinction. This process, which is presumably unconscious, explains the unusual shape of the LMC line in fig. 28. It also helps to confirm the hypothesis developed in connection with (yu) above (7.5.4) that stylistic variation can be the result of systemic pressures. Further, it provides a small amount of empirical evidence to show that pressures in phonetic space *do* exert some influence on the realisation of vowels. Fig. 31 shows that the UWC makes a large distinction in phonetic space between the two sets, with an (ou) norm of around [ɒu] and an (ō) norm approaching [uː].

Now, some linguists might wish to argue that the contrast between the UWC and MMC graphs is due to a mixture of two systems. They might wish to say that the situation illustrated here is simply the result of the interference of one system which has lost the (ou):(ō) distinction (RP) on another which has maintained it. What we have here could, in other words, be described as an example of dialect mixture. (This is presumably the position that would be adopted by Bickerton (1971).) Such an explanation may in fact be an adequate historical account of how the situation arose in the first place. It is not, however, a satisfactory analysis of the current position. There are, it is true, some (RP) speakers in Norwich who never have the distinction, and a few speakers who always have the maximum [ɒu]:[u:] differentiation. For the vast majority, however, there is considerable variation along a continuum of differentiation, with no clear cut-off point between one group of speakers and another. For this reason there can be no question of establishing two separate systems, with two sets of rules, for a description of Norwich English. The variation demonstrated above is a characteristic of most Norwich speakers and a characteristic of Norwich English as a single system. It is not possible, that is, to divide speakers into those who consistently have a particular phonetic distinction, and those who consistently have either some other distinction or none at all. We therefore prefer to describe this situation as the result of *inherent variability* of the system (to be handled by variable rules – see chapter 8).

7.8.2   The variables (er) and (ɛr). We have already discussed (ɛr) above (7.5.3). The other variable, (er), is the vowel in *here, fear, idea.* Fig. 32 shows that there is a considerable amount of stylistic variation of this variable, but that, especially in CS, there is little differentiation between the four lowest classes. The fact that in CS the UWC and LMC have scores higher than the MWC and LWC suggests that a linguistic change may be in progress (see 6.2; 7.5.3), although the score differences are very small. The scores also indicate that in CS even the MMC uses a vowel more open than [eə ~ e:], while the norm for the other classes is around [ɛ: ~ ɛ̣:].

Because the same index is used for both variables we can now use (er) and (ɛr) scores to investigate the nature and extent of the phonetic distinction between items of the *fear* and *fair* sets, as it is made by different groups of Norwich speakers. This is exemplified in fig. 33, which shows the scores for MMC speakers for both (er) and (ɛr), by contextual style. The index scores shown along the ordinate have been reversed so that 000 is at the top of the graph and 200 at the bottom. This symbolises 'phonetic space', with scores for more open vowels at

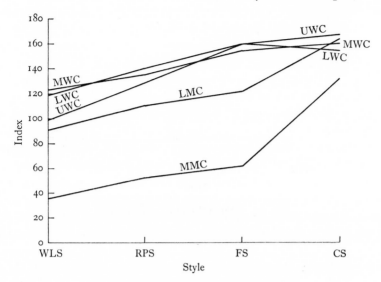

Fig. 32 Variable (er) by class and style

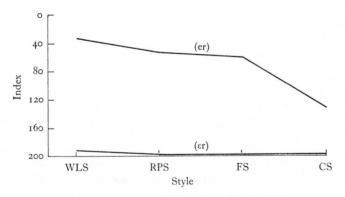

Fig. 33 (er) and (εr) by style: MMC

the bottom of the graph, as in conventional vowel diagrams. The graph shows quite clearly that, in spite of our discussion of the homophony of *fear* and *fair* in chapter 6, the MMC makes a definite distinction between the two lexical sets. It also shows, though, that the amount of phonetic space employed to effect this distinction decreases in the more informal styles. Thus even the MMC is involved in the Norwich tendency to merge (er) and (εr), the distinction in CS being on average only that between [ε] and [ẹ]-type vowels.

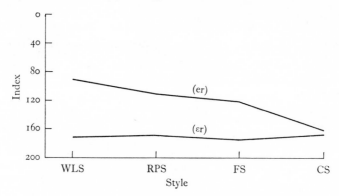

Fig. 34   (er) and (ɛr) by style: LMC

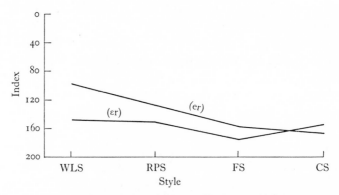

Fig. 35   (er) and (ɛr) by style: UWC

Fig. 34 shows that the LMC makes a certain amount of distinction, but much smaller than one would normally associate with a 'phonemic' distinction, between (er) and (ɛr) in formal styles. In CS, however, the merger is more or less complete. That is to say that in normal, everyday speech LMC speakers do not distinguish between (er) and (ɛr) items, but are able to do so in more formal styles, including even FS. This of course again argues very persuasively for a theory of phonology which distinguishes between a surface phonetic level and a deep phonological level, and in which it is possible for two distinct underlying phonological units to have one identical surface realisation.[1]

[1] (er) and (ɛr) provide a true example of 'complete overlapping', in contradistinction to (ō) and (ou) where there is a tendency for the realisation of one unit to predominate in one particular section of the phonetic area, and vice versa.

Fig. 35 shows a similar picture for the UWC, but with an even smaller amount of distinction of (er) and (εr), and a complete merger in CS. The more open vowel for (εr) items in FS can be interpreted as the result of pressures operating in phonetic space, of the same type that we saw illustrated in the case of (ou) and (ō). More open (er) vowels result in more open vowels for (εr) as well, in order to preserve the distinction. Where the distinction is not made, in CS, (εr) vowels can revert to their 'natural' level again. Fig. 36 shows the same sort of picture for the MWC, but with the distinction only minimally preserved. Once again, (εr) vowels are more open in FS, because of systemic pressure, but are closer again in CS. Fig. 37 shows that LWC speakers distinguish the two sets only in WLS and RPS, and then minimally.

An interesting point emerges from figs. 35, 36 and 37. For the UWC and MWC in CS, and, particularly, for the LWC in FS and CS, (er) vowels are more open than (εr) vowels. This indicates pronunciations something like: *fear* [fɛ̞ː] : *fair* [fɛ̞ː]. The implications of this may seem somewhat surprising: both historically, in linguistic change, and synchronically, in stylistic variation, two originally distinct vowels have, as it were, gone past each other in phonetic space. At first sight, this would appear to contradict everything we know about linguistic change: once two vowels have become phonetically the same, then they must subsequently be treated, it has always been thought, as the same vowel – a phonemic merger has taken place. It is certainly the case, moreover, that the vowels of *fear* and *fair* are perceived as the same by Norwich speakers. (We discussed in chapter 6 the fact that no distinction is made in many Norwich varieties, and in the pairs test a very large number of speakers pronounced pairs of this type identically.)

Our observation, however, ties in in an interesting way with a discovery made by Labov. He writes (1970a) 'chain shifts show that word classes move through phonological space in a manner that preserves their relative distances. Yet contrastive function is not necessarily the only factor which determines phonological output, since we now find that some word classes are preserved as distinct, although they appear to be "the same" to native speakers in a minimal pair test' (p. 304). The example of (er) and (εr) is clearly a case in point. Native speakers think of them as 'the same', yet in natural speech a small amount of phonetic distinction is made. (This distinction increases in formal speech – proof that the two are phonologically distinct. It seems likely that the distinction may be effected in CS through the presence or

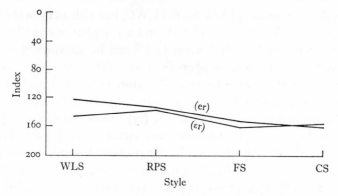

Fig. 36   (er) and (ɛr) by style: MWC

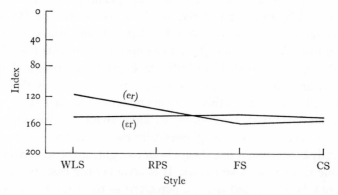

Fig. 37   (er) and (ɛr) by style: LWC

absence of a slight schwa off-glide, or by a secondary articulation of palatalisation on (er) vowels.) The phonetic distinction, although not consciously perceived, is sufficient to maintain the phonological distinctiveness of two phonetically very similar vowels, so that 'cross-overs' of the type illustrated above can take place. This has two implications. First, the minimal pairs test must now be regarded as very unreliable for revealing contrasts in language of this type, as must also, in these cases, native speakers' evaluations. (My own feeling as a native Norwich speaker is that *fear* and *fair* are the same – but not in the same unambiguous way that *meet* and *meat* are, for instance.) Secondly, the fact that this can happen may lead to a reinterpretation by linguists of certain reconstructed sound changes which are otherwise quite difficult to explain. A possible example is the well-known merger and subsequent

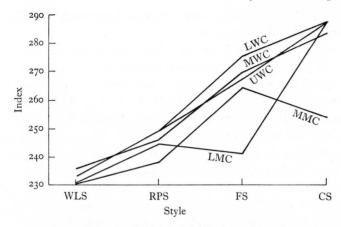

Fig. 38   Variable (ū) by class and style

split of *made, mate* with *mead, meat* in the the history of English (see Halle, 1962; Samuels, 1972; Labov, forthcoming).

7.8.3   The variables (ū) and (ō). The variable (ū) is the vowel in *boot, spoon, roof,* and deals with variation in this lexical set over /uː/, /ʉː/ and /ʊ/. Class and style differentiation of (ū) is shown in fig. 38. While this shows that there is significant style variation, there appears to be little or no class differentiation, except that the MMC is quite clearly distinct from the other classes in CS. One explanation for the apparently irregular behaviour of the MMC in this style is that RP-type speakers do not have the Norwich distinction /uː/ – /ʉː/, but instead have a whole range of vowels either as free variants or as contextually determined allophones.

The extent of the stylistic shifting of /uː/ to /ʉː/ in Norwich, and vice versa, can be gauged from the following list, which cites all the (ū) items recorded in the interviews in CS and FS.

Item with /uː/, /ʉː/ and /ʊ/: *room*
Items with /uː/ and /ʉː/: *school, move, to, fool, boot, improve, after-noon, mood, smooth*
Items with /uː/ only: *pool, wound, group, approve, troop, food*
Items with /ʉː/ only: *too, two, do, lose, you, through, who, shoe, soon, Waterloo, root*
Items with /ʊ/ only: *proof, Tombland*

In addition, the following items were recorded in the interviews only with /ʉː/, but can frequently be heard in Norwich with /uː/: *saloon, scooter, hoop, Doonican, goose, scoop, croupier, honeymoon. Tombland* is also pronounced with /u:/ and /ʉ:/.

WLS and RPS material. Of the above items, the following also occur in the word list and the reading passage: *room, proof, boot* (WL only) and *food, too, do, you, who, soon, school, move, fool* (WL and RP). The much larger amount of material obtained in these two styles shows that *proof* also occurs with /ʉ:/ and /u:/, that *food* also has /ʉ:/, and that *too, who* and *soon* can also occur with /u:/. The full list of items occurring in either the word list, or the word list and the reading passage, is as follows: *fool, cool, school, food, move, spoon, roof, soup, soon, too* (in the WL and the RP), and *hoof, proof, room, broom, boot* (WL only). (*You, who* and *do* also occur, but are overwhelmingly although not entirely pronounced with /ʉ:/, and will not be discussed further.)

The very large amount of variation that occurs in this variable in Norwich can be gauged from the fact that, although only ten of these items occur in both the word list and the reading passage, as many as 48 informants had at least one case of stylistic shift: there was at least one item that had a pronunciation in RPS different from that in WLS. This differentiation cannot in most cases properly be termed stylistic variation, since there is no clear tendency to shift in a particular direction. In the case of *cool*, for example, twelve ($= 20\%$) of the informants had a pronunciation in RPS different from that in WLS. In six of these cases, the informant switched from WLS /u:/ to RPS /ʉ:/, and in the other six cases the opposite switch occurred. Furthermore, although altogether only twenty-five instances of (ū)-items occur in the reading passage and word list combined, only two groups of informants, one consisting of three, the other of two, were identical to each other in their usage of /u:/, /ʉ:/ and /ʊ/ with respect to (ū) items in these two styles.

This switching of (ū) items from /ʉ:/ to /u:/ has implications, of course, for the merger of (ō) and (ū) items under /u:/. It will be remembered that the index scale for these two variables is as follows:

$$(\bar{o})\text{--}1, (\bar{u})\text{--}1 = /\text{ɒu}/ = 000$$
$$(\bar{o})\text{--}2, (\bar{u})\text{--}2 = /\text{əʊ}/ = 100$$
$$(\bar{o})\text{--}3, (\bar{u})\text{--}3 = /\text{u:}/ = 200$$
$$(\bar{u})\text{--}4 = /\text{ʉ:}/ = 300$$
$$(\bar{o})\text{--}4 \qquad = /\text{ʊ}/ = 300$$

The nature and extent of the merger of *boat* and *boot*-type items is illustrated in table 7.12. This shows the amount of distinction, in index

TABLE 7.12. *Difference in index points between (ō) and (ū) scores*

	Style			
Class	WLS	RPS	FS	CS
MMC	127	124	151	142
LMC	115	119	098	126
UWC	039	049	070	089
MWC	049	063	101	109
LWC	048	069	117	120

points, made between the two lexical sets by members of the different social classes in different contextual styles. The amount of distinction is calculated by subtracting (ō) index scores from (ū) index scores. This procedure, however, cannot be followed when both scores are over 200, since this implies the usage of some (ō)–4 and some (ū)–4, which are distinct, and therefore signify a differentiation. In these cases, therefore, we must subtract 200 from each score, and sum the results. Thus for example:

$$(ū) \ 185 : (ō) \ 145 = 040$$

but

$$(ū) \ 285 : (ō) \ 245 = 130$$

The figures shown in table 7.12 can, of course, represent only a rough guide as to the extent of the merger of (ō) and (ū), since some lexical items, such as *do, who, you,* only very rarely have /u:/ as opposed to /ʉ:/, so that (ō) and (ū) scores are never likely to be identical. The table shows, however, that in FS and CS, where the figures are most reliable since the proportions of (ō) and (ū) items most closely reflect those of normal speech, the biggest differentiation occurs in the two most extreme class groups, the MMC and the LWC (and also, in CS, the LMC). In the case of the MC, the large differentiation is due to an RP-type /əʊ/ : /u:/ distinction, while in the case of the LWC it is due to a maintenance of the distinction by usage of more (ū)–4 /ʉ:/ and (ō)–4 /ʊ/ forms. The LMC and MWC also have a fairly high differentiation rate. It is the UWC which has the greatest amount of merged forms, more particularly in WLS, and which can be said to be in the vanguard of this merger[1] as a linguistic change, because of its reluctance to use (ū)–4 and (ō)–4 forms and its inability or unwillingness to use (ō)–1 or (ō)–2 forms. The

---

[1] Note that this is a merger of the lexical sets of (ō) and (ū), and not a phonetic merger of /ʉ:/ and /u:/.

TABLE 7.13. *Percentage of monophthongal (ō)–3 and (ū)–3 in RPS*

	(ō)	(ū)
MMC	10	78
LMC	35	83
UWC	63	70
MWC	66	76
LWC	63	69
	(*boat*, etc.)	(*boot*, etc.)

general increase of differentiation as the formality of style decreases is attributable to an increase in the number of (ū)–4 forms.

This merger of *boot* and *boat* items, through the reallocation of the *boot* class to /u:/, also has implications for our discussion of the nature of sound changes in phonetic space in 7.8.2, under (er) and (ɛr). Some Norwich speakers distinguished pairs of this type, in the pairs test, as /buːt/ : /beʊt/; or /bʉːt/ : /buːt/. (Others distinguish them in CS as /bʉːt/ : /bʊt/.) A majority, however, had /buːt/ in both cases, and claimed, when asked, that *boot* and *boat* sounded 'the same'. In normal speech, though, most of these speakers, while having a high back rounded vowel of the /u:/ type for both sets, often made some kind of distinction between the two. The data indicates that this distinction is not consistently made in the manner of similar distinctions discussed by Labov (1970*a*). Rather, the two underlying phonological elements are 'kept apart' in the subconscious linguistic knowledge of speakers because a small phonetic distinction is sometimes made between sets of items which they perceive as phonetically 'the same', and because the elements are involved in two distinct sorts of stylistic alternation: *boat* /u:/ > /ʊ/; *boot* /u:/ > /ʉ:/. This lends further strength to the hypothesis developed in 7.8.2 (and, incidentally, provides additional support for a two-level type of phonological theory). As far as the nature of the small phonetic distinction is concerned, we noted in chapter 6 that rural Norfolk speakers had an [ǫu] type of vowel in (ō) items, whereas Norwich speakers tended to have [u: ~ ʉ:]. The diphthongised form is, however, also used in Norwich, and appears to be available to most speakers. This is also true of (ū) items such as *boot* but, apparently, to a lesser extent. Table 7.13 shows the percentage of /u:/ forms that were monophthongal [u:] in RPS, where all informants read the same items, for each of the five social classes, both for (ū) items and (ō) items. In each case, there are more (ō) diphthongs than there are (ū) diphthongs. A small phonetic distinction is therefore made, on average, between (ō) and (ū) items when they are realised as /u:/, although this is not done consistently. This demonstrates that the two phonological elements, in spite of the fact that they can be realised in a phonetically identical or similar manner (to the extent that native speakers cannot hear a difference), do remain phonologically distinct. At some future date they could develop in different directions under linguistic change.

It should be noted at this point that this phenomenon is distinct from that discussed by Labov (forthcoming). We have noted above that when (ū) items such as *boot* are transferred from the /ʉ:/ class to the /u:/ class, they still remain phonologically distinct because of different stylistic alternations and a tendency to a slightly different phonetic realisation. Labov, on the other hand, in a small-scale study of his own of Norwich English, has noted the inability of at least one Norwich informant to discriminate between /ʉ:/ and /u:/: this informant could not tell the difference between *too* (pronounced with /ʉ:/) and *toe* (pronounced with /u:/) when these were read aloud to him by his best friend. Part of his confusion was probably due to the complex series of alternations we have noted between /ʉ:/ and /u:/ of items such as *to*, *too*, and *two*, but it also demonstrates that, as a phenomenon quite distinct from the transference of (ū) words to /u:/, /ʉ:/ and /u:/ are becoming phonetically less distinct, owing to the fronting of /u:/ which is illustrated by spectrographic data in Labov's paper.

7.9 Geographical factors

7.9.1 It was observed during the course of the survey that there seemed to be more signs of some internal geographical variation of the diphthongisation of /u:/ that we have just been discussing (7.8.2) than of any other variable. In order to investigate this point we must of course compare the index scores of informants from different parts of the city. To avoid the possibility of introducing social class bias into these investigations we will base the comparison on the scores of one class only, and we shall select the largest class, the MWC, for this purpose. Unfortunately, we shall have to leave two of the five Norwich areas studied in the survey out of consideration because of the small numbers of members of the MWC living in these areas. We can, however, make a valid comparison of the scores from the other three areas, the electoral wards

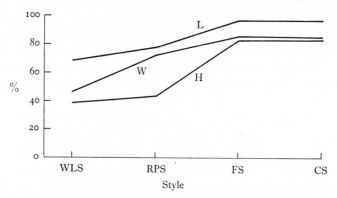

Fig. 39   Hellesdon, Lakenham and Westwick:
MWC (ō)–3, percentage of monophthongs by style

Hellesdon, Lakenham and Westwick (see chapter 1). Fig. 39 gives the average scores obtained by MWC informants in the four contextual styles in these three areas. It shows quite clearly that the in part newer and more peripheral area of Lakenham has fewer diphthongised forms than the older or more central areas of Westwick and Hellesdon. Parts of Lakenham, however, are in fact considerably older than Hellesdon, and so the differentiation cannot be ascribed solely, if at all, to the area-age factor. It is not clear, in fact, how we should explain this difference. The answer may lie in factors involved with dialect mixture and immigration. It is possible that migrants from different areas of Norfolk may have brought different pronunciations with them, or that some areas of the city have (or have had) a higher proportion of in-migrants than others.

7.9.2   The variable (h). The fact that in-migration can have an effect on the pronunciation of the city can be illustrated by means of the variable (h). Fig. 40 shows that (h) has a fairly normal type of class and style differentiation, except that the LWC and MWC are indistinguishable in their use of this variable. We saw in chapter 6 that rural East Anglia is an 'h-pronouncing' region, and commented that Norwich appeared to be an island of 'h-lessness' within the region. It is therefore interesting to see that (h) in Norwich exhibits all the characteristics of a normal phonological variable, since this indicates that 'h-lessness' is well established in Norwich and has been for many years. At the same time, however, it should be noted that the LWC and MWC use about

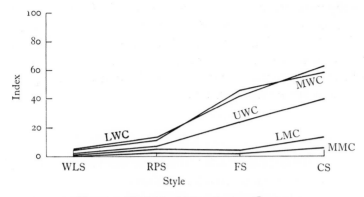

Fig. 40   Variable (h) by class and style

TABLE 7.14. (*h*) *indices: rural-born v. total informants*

		Style			
Class		WLS	RPS	FS	CS
LMC	Total	000	005	004	014
	Rural-born	000	000	002	012
UWC	Total	001	007	024	040
	Rural-born	000	000	007	012
MWC	Total	004	012	043	059
	Rural-born	000	004	023	050
LWC	Total	005	013	041	061
	Rural-born	000	008	000	000

40% 'h-ful' forms even in CS. This is probably a higher percentage than would be found in other English areas.

Since we have noted that there is a difference between rural and urban speech as far as (h) is concerned it is informative at this point to compare the scores for this variable of informants born and brought up in rural districts with those of the informants who were born and have remained in the city. Table 7.14 shows the average (h) scores for rural-born informants compared to the average (h) scores for their social class as a whole, by contextual style. (No MMC scores are included, since none of this group was rural-born.) Table 7.14 shows that informants born and brought up in rural areas have consistently lower (h) scores than city-born informants. This is particularly true of the UWC and the LWC. This means that the rural–urban dichotomy is still a linguistically valid one in the area around Norwich. As far as (h) is concerned, it is not a distinction which is valid only at the level of the conservative dialects of the elderly. The figures suggest that patterns of in-migration have had an effect on Norwich speech, and that they may therefore have played some part in the growth of the pattern of geographical differentiation of /u:/.

7.10   Summary

We can summarise the main points of interest that have arisen out of our study of the phonological variables as follows:

1. Not all variables subject to class variation participate in stylistic variation. Stylistic variation takes place only if one of four factors (7.5.4) is present.

2. Unusual patterns of class or sex differentiation are generally the result of a linguistic change in progress. Changes 'from below' tend to be led by younger male MWC and UWC speakers.

3. The amount of distinction in phonetic space between some pairs of variables varies with class and style. Cross-over patterns provide empirical evidence in support of the view that pairs of vowels perceived as the same by native speakers can in fact remain distinct. This has very important implications for the value of the minimal pairs test, and for an explanation of certain types of sound change. It also lends support to a theory of phonology which recognises an underlying and a surface level, and which permits complete overlapping of the realisations of phonological units.

4. The facts of variation in the Norwich speech community are more satisfactorily handled in terms of inherent variability than by attempted explanations in terms of dialect mixture.

8 The Norwich diasystem

8.1 The Norwich speech community

The heterogeneity of the Norwich speech community has been illustrated in some detail in chapter 7. We have described and discussed some of the ways in which different groups of Norwich speakers are distinguished from each other linguistically. We have shown that different social class, sex and age groups have pronunciations of the phonological variables that differentiate them from other groups, and that most speakers have variant realisations of many of the variables in different social contexts. The fact remains, however, that in spite of these significant differences, all the informants investigated in the course of this study were distinctively speakers of the same variety of English: Norwich English. This chapter will be taken up with a discussion of Norwich English that will be as concerned with the similarities to be found within the Norwich speech community as with the differences. As in chapters 6 and 7, the discussion will be mainly limited to segmental phonetic and phonological features of Norwich English. (Non-segmental features will certainly prove to be of very great importance, but analysis of this aspect of the data has still to be carried out.)

It must of course be recognised that Norwich English is not an isolated, distinct or discrete linguistic variety. Geographically, it merges into the other varieties of Norfolk, East Anglian and southern British English. Socially, it merges with the non-localised varieties of RP and standard English. It is not, however, unreasonable to regard Norwich as if it were a distinct variety. We have already shown, for example, that there is some evidence of the existence of a linguistic rural–urban dichotomy in the areas surrounding Norwich. There are, moreover, many linguistic characteristics which are peculiar to the urban area of Norwich. Speakers of Norwich English, that is to say, belong to a particular speech community which has very many common linguistic features. Many of these features are not shared by any other speech community. In this chapter we shall be attempting to establish a common framework that will, in some sense, incorporate all types of Norwich English. We hope to show that these different types are derived from a single underlying framework that is the same for the whole community. We shall call this underlying framework (together with the rules which produce the different types and relate them to each other) the Norwich *diasystem*. We believe that this diasystem, since it is concerned solely with phonological and phonetic aspects of Norwich English, can most usefully be constructed within the theoretical framework of generative phonology. Many writers have demonstrated the usefulness of generative phonology in dialectology (Keyser, 1963; King, 1969; O'Neil, 1963; Saporta, 1965; Thomas, 1967; Troike, 1969; Vasiliu, 1966; 1967), and others have pointed out the drawbacks and deficiencies of the so-called taxonomic phonemic diasystem of the type initially proposed by Weinreich (1954) (see Cochrane, 1959; King, 1969; Moulton, 1960; Pulgram, 1964; Trudgill, 1971). I shall not therefore attempt to justify this decision here.

8.2   The reality of the diasystem

There are two main justifications for attempting to establish this kind of diasystem. The first is that a model of this nature provides a common basis for the description and comparison of closely related varieties. The second is that there is some sense in which members of, in this case, the Norwich speech community, can be said to have internalised this diasystem, in that they are able to draw upon it in their variable speech production, and to use it in the comprehension and social interpretation of utterances produced by other speakers. We therefore believe that there is a need to establish some kind of model of this internalised diasystem. The diasystem can be said in some sense to 'exist', and must therefore be described in order correctly and fully to describe the native speaker's linguistic competence. The diasystem, that is, should provide a model of the linguistic competence of the individual as a native speaker of Norwich English *and* as a member of the Norwich speech community. (The term *diasystem* will be used ambiguously to apply to the knowledge of the native Norwich speaker, and to the partial model of this knowledge developed below.) The 'competence' we are dealing with here, then, has perhaps more in common with some aspects of the (communicative) competence of Hymes (1971) than with the more familiar competence of Chomsky (e.g. 1964, p. 9).

Now, it might be thought that it would be reasonable to attempt to set up a diasystem for any pair or group of mutually intelligible varieties (cf. Cochrane, 1959, who compares Yorkshire and Australian accents), or to establish a polylectal or panlectal grammar for all varieties of English in the manner advocated by Bailey (1972). There are two reasons why I do not believe this to be justifiable. First, it would be extremely difficult to set up in any meaningful way a common underlying system for many pairs of English accents. It is true, of course, that the phonological systems of most types of American, Canadian, Australian, New Zealand and South African English are closely related to each other and to the accents of the south of England. This will also be true of many accents associated with standard English in other parts of the United Kingdom and Ireland. In all these cases, rules could be established which would relate these varieties to each other in a coherent way. Consider, however, the difficulties of incorporating the following data (from Gregg, 1964) into any such system:

	RP	G
have	/hæv/	/he:/
home	/heʊm/	/he:m/
move	/mu:v/	/me:v/
none	/nʌn/	/ne:n/
straw	/strɔ:/	/stre:/

G is in fact the Scotch–Irish rural dialect of Glenoe, near Larne, Northern Ireland, but the same sort of problem would arise with very many phonological systems from Northern Ireland, lowland Scotland or parts of the north or Midlands of England. The correspondences are not regular enough to permit incorporation into a single system.

Secondly, there can be no justification (for combining varieties of this kind) of the type advanced for treating Norwich English as a single system. Most varieties of English, it is true, are mutually intelligible to a fair degree, but there can be no real sense in which speakers can be said to have internalised a diasystem of this kind. Australian speakers cannot switch, for stylistic reasons, into a Yorkshire accent; neither can they faultlessly imitate it for humorous or other reasons; nor can they assign fine sociological meanings to different types of pronunciation. Norwich speakers can do all these things with different varieties of Norwich English. There are, moreover, no discrete varieties of Norwich English. The incorporation of different Norwich speech forms into a single system is not simply, therefore, an intellectual exercise. (For further arguments on this topic, see Trudgill, 1973.)

8.3   The generative phonological diasystem

The diasystem outlined below will involve the systematic phonemic and systematic phonetic levels of generative phonology. The phonological features used, however, will not be of the acoustic or articulatory type more commonly found in works on generative phonology. Rather, we shall employ, at the systematic phonemic level, abstract features of the type proposed by Fudge (1967) and illustrated there and in Fudge (1969a; 1969b), Garman (1973) and Tay (1970). Fudge has argued the advantages of this type of approach (1967; 1972) and I do not propose to repeat his arguments here. It is perhaps useful to add, however, that these arguments are particularly strong when one is comparing a number of accents that are phonetically or phonologically distinct.

Fudge develops a phonological grammar of English the first component of which is a syllable generator which produces the type of syllable structure illustrated in fig. 41. A different underlying phonemic system can be shown to operate at each place in syllable structure. The systems operating at places 1, 2, 4, 5 and 6 in syllable structure are shown in tables 8.1 to 8.5. (Place 6 is used only in word-final syllables. A full justification for these arrangements including, for example, the counter-phonetic positions of /s/, /z/ and /r/ has been given in Fudge (1969a). /k/ : /s/ alternations of the type *opaque* : *opacity* are partly responsible for the position of /s/, for instance.) The place of the syllable in generative phonology, it is true, is not uncontroversial. Since, however, this part of Fudge's theory is not crucial for the approach adopted here, I shall not discuss this point further.

Fudge's abstract underlying phonological system for English, although it by no means claims to be all-embracing, is intended to be diasystemic. Fudge states, for example, that 'the inclusion of post-vocalic *r* must not be taken as implying that the scheme does not apply to "*r*-less" dialects': *r* is an 'abstract element which in some dialects (notably RP) may often have no realisation of its own, but which will, so to speak, contribute to the realisation of the preceding vowel' (1969a). It is quite clear, however, that the systematic phonemic system proposed by Fudge for English vowels (place 3 in syllable structure) is not adequate for Norwich English. The system is illustrated in table 8.6. The abstract distinctive features are X, β, 1 and so on, and the systematic phonemes (enclosed in double slants in the text) are of the form //Xα1//. For simplicity, however, these will often be represented mnemonically, as in

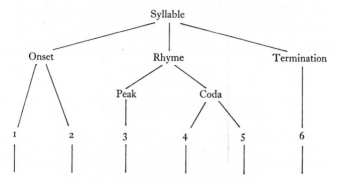

Fig. 41   English syllable structure

TABLE 8.1. *Systematic phonemic system at place 1*

	A	B	C	D
1 a	p	t	č	k
b	b	d	j	g
c	sp	st		sk
2 a	f	θ	š	s
b	v	ð		z
3	w	l	y	r
4	m	n		
	←——— h ———→

TABLE 8.2. *Systematic phonemic system at place 2*

	A	B	C	D
3	w	l		r
4	m	n		

TABLE 8.3. *Systematic phonemic system at place 4*

	A	B	C	D
3		l		r
4	←——— N ———→

TABLE 8.4. *Systematic phonemic system at place 5*

	A	B	C	D
1 a	p	t	č	k
b	b	d	j	g
c	sp	st		sk
2 a	f	θ	š	s
b	v	ð		z
3		l		r
4	m	n		

TABLE 8.5. *Systematic phonemic system at place 6*

	A	B	C	D
1 a/b		T		
c		st		
2		θ		S

TABLE 8.6. *Systematic phonemic system at place 3*

	X α	X β	Y α	Y β	Z α	Z β
I	i	ʌ	ī	ʌ̄	au	oi
II	e	u	ē	ū		
III	a	o	ā	ō	a:	ɔ:

table 8.6, in the form //i//. (The vowels under X will be realised as the short vowels of *pit, pet, pat, putt, put, pot*; the vowels under Y as the vowels of *bite, beat, bait, Bute, boot, boat*.)

If this system is compared with the facts of Norwich phonology outlined in chapter 6, it will be seen that it does not permit us to generate the distinction made in many types of Norwich English between the lexical sets of *nail* and *name* (6.2), which are often /næil/ and /nɛ:m/. For this purpose we need an extra systematic phoneme in addition to //ā//. It is also clearly not possible to produce the Norwich distinction of the lexical sets of *nose* and *knows* (variables (ō) and (ou), distinguished as /u:/ and /ɒu/) from the above system. We therefore need a further systematic phoneme in addition to //ō//. It is also impossible to generate

TABLE 8.7. *The Norwich diasystemic phonological vowel system: A*

	X		Y		Z
	α	β	α	β	
I	i	u	ī	ū	↑
II a			ē	ᴧ̄	│
b	e	ᴧ	ɛ̄	au	oi
III a			ā	ō	│
b	a	o	ai	ou	↓

the *weak* : *week* distinction made by older East Anglian speakers (and minimally in Norwich). Although it is not too important to do this for present-day Norwich English, it is useful for purposes of exemplification.

The solution to this problem is to amend Fudge's vowel system to that shown in table 8.7. The vowels portrayed here are the abstract elements that underlie phonetic vowels in all types of Norwich English. The differences between the two systems (tables 8.6 and 8.7) are as follows:

1. The addition of the element mnemonically represented as $//\bar{\varepsilon}//$, which will be realised as /e:/ in *weak*, allows the *weak*:*week* distinction to be made.

2. The additional element $//ai//$ will be realised as /æi/ in *nail* while $//\bar{a}//$ will produce /ɛ:/ in *name*.

3. The additional element $//ou//$ will be realised as /ɒu/ in *knows*, while $//\bar{o}//$ will give /u:/ in *nose*.

4. The switching of $//u//$ and $//\bar{u}//$ with $//\Lambda//$ and $//\bar{\Lambda}//$, and the inclusion of $//au//$ under Y instead of Z vowels, makes the system more symmetrical. More importantly, it means that morphological alternations of the type *profound/profundity* can be handled as well as those of the type *produce/production*.

5. a: and ɔ: have been omitted altogether. This, together with 4, has the effect of underlining the peripheral nature of $//oi//$ in the English vowel system. One justification for this omission lies in the fact that a: and ɔ: do not occur in many types of English, and can usually be produced at the phonetic level from various combinations of phonemic elements, for example, $//o// + //r// = /ɔ:/$. Perhaps more important though is the small number of instances of post-vocalic *r* recorded in the

Norwich survey. (It may be, however, that the omission of a: and ɔ: is unrealistic in present-day Norwich English, and that by omitting them we are guilty of trying to extend the diasystem to cover varieties other than those of Norwich. The implication, that is, of omitting them – which is that they are elements of a rather different order from the other vowel elements – may not be justifiable any longer.) The vowel system shown in table 8.7 will be called the Norwich diasystemic phonological vowel system.

8.3.1 Diasystemic inventory rules. The Norwich phonological vowel system shown in table 8.7 can be characterised as diasystemic because, as it underlies all forms of Norwich English, some of its units are redundant for many Norwich speakers as far as speech production is concerned: they are not necessary for the phonological feature part of lexical entries for these speakers.

We shall now, therefore, develop a set of rules which will relate this overall diasystemic vowel system (table 8.7) to the particular phonological vowel systems used by speakers of various Norwich accent types in their speech production. For example, as we have already seen, many Norwich speakers do not distinguish the vowels in the lexical sets of *name* and *nail*. We therefore require, for these speakers, the diasystemic rule, rule 1:

(1) $//Y\alpha III\begin{Bmatrix} a \\ b \end{Bmatrix}// \longrightarrow //Y\alpha III//$

That is $\begin{rcases} //\bar{a}// \\ //ai// \end{rcases} \longrightarrow //ai//$

(Note that the choice of symbol to the right of the arrow in the second formulation is totally arbitrary, since all the units involved are abstract.) Rule 1 is a *diasystemic inventory rule*. It is a statement to the effect that some Norwich speakers have no systematic phonemic contrast of $//ai//$ and $//\bar{a}//$: lexical entries for items such as *name* and *nail* will have the same underlying vowel. One justification for the development of this type of rule is that it permits all types of Norwich English to be derived from the same underlying system without any redundancy for individual speakers. A further justification is that one must assume that this type of rule is used by speakers who do not themselves make a particular distinction in the interpretation of utterances in which the distinction is made (see also Troike, 1970). Fig. 42 illustrates this point.

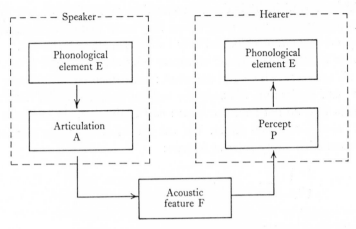

Fig. 42   The act of communication

Fudge (1967) has proposed the model of the act of linguistic communication illustrated in fig. 42, which 'shows the steps involved in inducing the hearer to select the same phonological element E as the speaker has selected'. In the case of Tone 1 in Mandarin Chinese, for example, the following takes place:

E   Mandarin Tone 1
A   Vocal cords tense, vibrating at frequency which is high, and remains constant throughout the syllable
F   Fundamental frequency of sound wave constant and high
P   High level pitch
E   Mandarin Tone 1

In the case of this particular Norwich distinction, however, it would seem that selection of //ā// on the part of the speaker can induce selection of //ai// on the part of a hearer who does not have the //ā// : //ai// distinction. This is made possible because the hearer has internalised the diasystemic inventory rule, rule 1. This assumption is partially justified by the fact that many speakers appear to be able, in some way, to reverse the direction of application of the rule. In other words, speakers who normally never make this distinction are able to do so, *without error*, if they wish to for humorous or other similar purposes. Empirical evidence for this is that a small number of younger informants who did not have the distinction were able to produce it, consistently and correctly, when asked to read out the reading passage as they thought older speakers

would have read it. This demonstrates that, while they do not themselves have distinct underlying forms, they know that other members of
the speech community do, and they know what these forms are.

As far as other diasystemic inventory rules are concerned, it is a fact
that all speakers who have the *weak* : *week* distinction also have the
name : *nail* distinction, although the reverse does not apply. Similarly,
speakers who do not have the *name* : *nail* distinction, do not have the
weak : *week* distinction either. We can therefore postulate additional
diasystemic inventory rules as follows:

(2) $//Y\alpha_{11}\begin{Bmatrix}a\\b\end{Bmatrix}// \longrightarrow //Y\alpha_{11}//$

That is $\begin{rcases}//\bar{e}//\\//\varepsilon//\end{rcases} \longrightarrow //\bar{e}//$

This rule applies to older speakers, except for the very oldest who
preserve this distinction. For younger speakers, who do not have either
of the two above distinctions, the more general rule, rule 3, applies.

(3) $//Y\alpha\begin{bmatrix}11\\111\end{bmatrix}\begin{Bmatrix}a\\b\end{Bmatrix}// \longrightarrow //Y\alpha\begin{bmatrix}11\\111\end{bmatrix}//$

That is $\begin{rcases}//\bar{e}//\\//\varepsilon//\end{rcases} \longrightarrow //\bar{e}//$

and $\begin{rcases}//\bar{a}//\\//ai//\end{rcases} \longrightarrow //ai//$

(Rule 1, that is, is now unnecessary.)

As, however, a and b occur only under 11 and 111, rule 3 is better
expressed in the more general, simpler form of rule 3 *a*.

(3*a*) $//Y\alpha\begin{Bmatrix}a\\b\end{Bmatrix}// \longrightarrow //Y\alpha//$

(This rule then applies vacuously to $//Y\alpha_{1}//=//\bar{\imath}//$ as well.)

It has been suggested that rule simplification plays an important part
in the process of linguistic change (see King, 1969, ch. 4). The increase
in generality of application of this diasystemic inventory rule, as expressed above in the switch from rule 2, which older speakers have, to
rule 3 *a* for younger speakers, would appear to provide a very good

TABLE 8.8. *Norwich phonological vowel system: B*

	X		Y		Z
	α	β	α	β	
I	i	u	ī	ū	↑
II a				Ā	↓
b	e	ʌ	ē	au	oi
III a			ā	ō	
b	a	o	ai	ou	↓

TABLE 8.9. *Norwich phonological vowel system: C*

	X		Y		Z
	α	β	α	β	
I	i	u	ī	ū	↑
II a				Ā	↓
b	e	ʌ	ē	au	oi
III a				ō	
b	a	o	ai	ou	↓

example of precisely this phenomenon. This point can be more clearly illustrated if we restructure the above rules to read as follows:

$$(2) \quad \begin{Bmatrix} a \\ b \end{Bmatrix} \longrightarrow \emptyset \; / \overline{\mathrm{Y}\alpha\mathrm{II}}$$

$$(3a) \quad \begin{Bmatrix} a \\ b \end{Bmatrix} \longrightarrow \emptyset \; / \overline{\mathrm{Y}\alpha}$$

(This also shows that at least one theoretical advance made in the field of generative phonology is not surrendered because we have rejected phonetically based features in favour of abstract features.) Rules 2 and 3 a are the only two diasystemic inventory rules in the Norwich diasystem. This means that, in addition to a phonological vowel system which is identical to the diasystemic phonological vowel system illustrated in table 8.7, there are the two additional phonological vowel systems produced by application of the diasystemic inventory rules, shown in tables 8.8 and 8.9. All Norwich speakers have one of these three systems.

It should be noted at this point that the failure to distinguish the lexical sets of *name* and *nail* is not of the same order as the failure of some speakers to distinguish the lexical sets of *nose* and *knows*. Some MC Norwich speakers, it is true, might appear to have merged the two latter sets, since they make little phonetic distinction between the two types (see 7.8.1). The merger, however, is *not* total: it is a phonetic rather than phonological merger. This can be demonstrated most clearly by results obtained in the pairs test. All those speakers who, during the course of the interviews, made little or no distinction between items of the type *nose : knows* could always be induced to make this distinction by presenting them with a pair of this type to be read side by side. The same did *not* apply to pairs of the type *days : daze*, even in those cases where the distinction could be made for humorous purposes. (An exception to this was provided by a few older speakers who clearly had both //ai// and //ā// but tended to merge them phonetically. In these cases, and in the cases of apparent *nose/knows* merger, we are dealing with a lower level rule handling the realisation of two distinct systematic phonemes, and not with a diasystemic inventory rule.) There are therefore three types of speaker, as far as the *name/nail* distinction is concerned: those who do not have rule 3 *a*, and always maintain the distinction; those who do not have rule 3 *a*, but who merge the two sets in certain styles in the manner of those who merge //ō// and //ou//, by means of a lower level rule; and those who do have rule 3 *a* – these speakers have identical vowels in their lexical entries for *name* and *nail*, since they never distinguish pairs of this sort (except as a joke – and this they do by some kind of operation in reversal of rule 3 *a*).

8.3.2   Lexical entries. It is at this point in the phonological grammar that the link-up with the lexicon must occur, so that items can be listed in the lexicon in terms of one of the phonological systems shown in tables 8.7, 8.8 and 8.9. For speakers who have the *nail/name* distinction, *name* will be listed as:

$$//B_4 \cdot Y\alpha_{111}b \cdot A_4 \cdot //$$

or

$$//n \cdot \bar{a} \cdot m \cdot //$$

where //B₄// at place 1 in syllable structure is realised as /n/ and //A₄// at place 5 as /m/. (Dots indicate places in syllable structure which remain empty.) For speakers who do not make the distinction, the lexical entry, along with the semantic and syntactic information, will be:

$$//B_4 \cdot Y\alpha_{111} \cdot A_4 \cdot //$$

or

$$//n \cdot ai \cdot m //$$

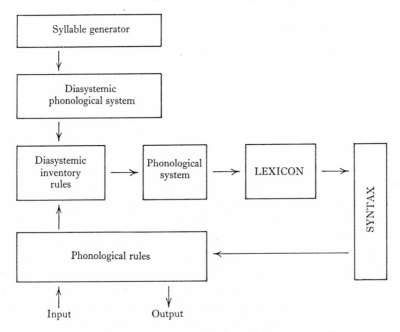

Fig. 43   The place of the diasystemic inventory rules

The fact that lexical entries are made in terms of one of the three phonological systems A, B or C rather than the diasystemic phonological system means that the diasystemic inventory rules must be allowed to operate before the lexicon stage is reached for recognition purposes as well as for production. We must therefore postulate a model of the type illustrated in fig. 43. The diasystemic phonological system will include the vowel system shown in table 8.7 (p. 139); the diasystemic inventory rules are rules 2 and 3 a; and the phonological system will include one of the vowel systems A, B and C – and it is in terms of these that entries in the lexicon will be made. The second stage of the phonological grammar (the phonological rules of fig. 43) will then come into operation after lexical items have been introduced and all the syntactic rules have been run through. These phonological rules will include rules of the type normally found in the phonological components of generative grammars, but there will be additional rules of a diasystemic nature.

8.4   Phonological rules

8.4.1   Morphological alternations. Rules of morphological alternation can be handled most satisfactorily within the sort of framework outlined here, by rules of the form:

$$Y \longrightarrow X \quad / \text{ in certain contexts.}$$

By converting Y vowels to X vowels (see table 8.7, p. 139), this rule will
produce alternations of the type: *divine/divinity*; *serene/serenity*; *opaque/*
opacity. The arrangement of the systematic phonemic vowel system
means that the vowels which alternate most frequently differ by only
one (abstract) feature: X as opposed to Y. Comparable rules that have
been developed within the distinctive feature framework are relatively
complex and cumbersome (see Chomsky & Halle, 1968, ch. 4). Note
that the two Y phonemes //au// and //ʌ̄// correspond to the single
X vowel //ʌ//. This means that the distinction of //au// and //ʌ̄// is
neutralised under this kind of alternation. In the same way, //ō// and
//ou// correspond to the single X vowel //o//, so that the distinct vowels
of *know* and *provoke* are merged under alternation to *knowledge* and
provocative:

$$//ou// \longrightarrow //o//$$

and
$$//ō// \longrightarrow //o//$$

similarly
$$//ai// \longrightarrow //a//$$

and
$$//ā// \longrightarrow //a//$$

(*explain/explanatory*; *profane/profanity*)

8.4.2   Diasystemic incidence rules. The rules of this second section
of the phonological grammar that are of diasystemic interest are those
which we shall call *diasystemic incidence rules*. As we have seen in
previous chapters, there is a large amount of variation in Norwich
English of the type that is usually described as resulting from differences
in phoneme incidence. The two main sources of this variation are the
following:

(*a*) Vowels which are reflexes of ME ǭ are subject to shortening in
   Norwich English from [uː] to [ʊ] in closed syllables – the East
   Anglian short *o*. The item *road*, for example, can be pronounced
   either [ruːd] or [rʊd].

(*b*) Items such as *boot, soon, hoof,* in which the vowels result from ME ǭ, can be pronounced in Norwich English either with an [ʉː]-type vowel, with the [uː] vowel also found in *road,* or with the short [ʊ] of *road, hood.*

Now it could be claimed that these alternations in pronunciation are simply the result of a series of alternative forms in the lexicon. The item *road* might be listed both as //r·ō·d·// and as //r·u·d·//. But this would suggest the various alternative pronunciations were entirely unmotivated, and would fail to reveal the underlying regularity, demonstrated in chapter 7, that these alternations affect whole lexical sets in exactly the same way. It would suggest that the fact that alternations like [ruːd]/[rʊd], [stuːn]/[stʊn] etc. are identical is entirely accidental. We propose, on the other hand, that there is a significant generalisation to be made here. The relationships that obtain between the systematic phonemic elements //ō//, //ū// and //u//, as exemplified in the above alternative pronunciations and in chapter 7, are not simply accidental relationships of alternation among phonemes. They are, rather, subject to rule, and ought to be accounted for in a phonological grammar. There is a definite and constant relationship between the pronunciations of these sets of lexical items, and the amount of variation is so large (and, as we saw in chapter 7, stylistically determined) that it cannot be handled satisfactorily simply by listing alternative forms in the lexicon.

The type of rule proposed by Thomas (1967) to handle features of this type in Welsh is relatively complex compared to the form of the rules required in Norwich English. For example, to handle the alternations associated with the lexical set of *road,* we must assume the following. The item *road* is listed in the lexicon as //r·ō·d·//. We take the //ō// form rather than the alternative //u// form as basic, since rules of morphological alternation must have Y ('long') vowels to operate on if they are to produce the correct output. (If, for example, we listed *provoke* with //u// rather than //ō//, the item *provocative* would not have the correct phonetic form.) It is also true that the variant [ruːd] is the more common, particularly in more formal styles. Historically, too, the long vowel is the original one.

We then require the (optional) diasystemic incidence rule, rule 4.

(4) //Yβɪɪɪa// ⟶ //Xβɪ//

That is, //ō// ⟶ //u//. This eventually produces the output [rʊd]. If the rule does not apply, the output is [ruːd].

To handle the alternation of items such as *boot*, we assume that we have lexical entries of the type //b·ū·t·//. This is partly because [bʉːt] appears to be the older East Anglian form, and partly because we have already allotted //ō// to *road*-type items. (The element //u//, too, must be allotted to items of the type *wood, put.*)

We then require the diasystemic incidence rule, rule 5.

(5) //Yβɪ// ⟶ //Yβɪɪɪa//

That is, //ū// ⟶ //ō//. This eventually produces the output [buːt]. If these two rules are re-ordered, so that rule 5 precedes rule 4, then these two rules between them will also produce the output [bʊt]. Thus:

$$//r·ō·d·//   //b·ū·t·//$$

(4) //ō// ⟶ //u//://r·u·d·//   //b·ū·t·//
(5) //ū// ⟶ //ō//://r·u·d·//   //b·ō·t·//

Output: [rʊd], [buːt]

(5) //ū// ⟶ //ō//://r·ō·d·//   //b·ō·t·//
(4) //ō// ⟶ //u//://r·u·d·//   //b·u·t·//

Output: [rʊd], [bʊt]

If rule 5 only is applied to both entries, the output will be [ruːd], [buːt]; and if no incidence rules are applied, [ruːd], [bʉːt].

It should now be noted that there are alternative ways of handling this type of alternation which do not require diasystemic incidence rules. One method would be to allow for the possibility of //ō// having a continuous range of realisation, at the phonetic level, from [uː] through to [ʊ]. This scheme, however, fails to reveal the fact that a genuine switch in pronunciation occurs. Many of the Norwich informants, for instance, recognised that there are two distinct pronunciations of items like *road*, and not a graded series. Comments such as 'sometimes I say [hʊm] and sometimes I say [huːm]' were common in the interviews. But it is also true that some intermediate pronunciations do occur. This is because the phonetic realisation ranges of //ō// and //u// overlap. (It should also be noted that it is much less plausible to permit //ū// to have a phonetic realisation range stretching from [ʉː] through [uː] to [ʊ].) Another alternative would be to regard the switch from [uː] to [ʊ] not as the result of a systematic phonemic level rule but as a consequence of a lower level phonetic rule shortening the vowel in rapid speech. The counter-argument to this is that [ʊ] frequently occurs in citation forms, such as in the responses to the word list test of the Norwich questionnaire.

The diasystemic incidence rules that we have developed for the Norwich diasystem will therefore handle the distribution of systematic phonemes over lexical items, and reflect the structured nature of the relationships that hold between them. The rules must be optional, since speakers fluctuate considerably in their usage, particularly according to social context. If diasystemic incidence rules *do* become obligatory in certain environments or in the case of particular lexical items, this results in the rewriting of entries in the lexicon. And if (importantly), for some speakers, they become obligatory throughout the vocabulary, they will then be re-interpreted as diasystemic inventory rules. If they then become generalised to the whole speech community, this can lead to the complete loss of systematic phonemes from the diasystem (and therefore to the loss of the appropriate diasystemic inventory rules themselves).

We can, for example, imagine that at an earlier stage of Norwich English there was introduced, as an innovation, a diasystemic incidence rule:

$$//\bar{\varepsilon}// \longrightarrow //\bar{e}//$$

which permitted items of the type *wheat* to be realised optionally as /wɪit/ or as /weːt/ in the speech of younger members of the community (older speakers would have had only /weːt/). As this rule became obligatory for certain speakers it became a diasystemic inventory rule, because the $//\bar{\varepsilon}//:\!//\bar{e}//$ distinction was redundant in the phonological systems of these speakers. This is the situation in Norwich today, as presented above – but only just. The number of speakers remaining who use this distinction is so small that the rule will soon apply obligatorily to all Norwich accents, with the result that the phoneme $//\bar{\varepsilon}//$ (and the rule itself) will drop out of the diasystem altogether.

The diasystemic inventory rule, rule 3, described above (8.3.1), provides a similar example. That section of the rule presented as:

$$\left.\begin{array}{c} //\bar{a}// \\ //ai// \end{array}\right\} \longrightarrow //ai//$$

was discussed as an inventory rule. It is clear, however, that in the speech of some older informants, this rule is a diasystemic incidence rule:

$$//\bar{a}// \longrightarrow //ai//.$$

These speakers, in other words, can and do choose, in normal everyday speech, to pronounce words like *name* either with [ɛ:] or with [æi]. (These speakers will include among their ranks those who produced the //ā// : //ai// distinction only, or mainly, in the pairs test in the interviews.)

8.4.3   Further problems. There are some complications that arise in connection with diasystemic incidence rules 4 and 5. Some items such as *do* and *lose* must be marked −rule 5 in the lexicon, as they are pronounced only with /u:/. The major problem, however, is probably that, as was amply illustrated in chapter 7 in the discussion of (ō) and (ū), the application of rules 4 and 5, although optional, is dependent on the social class of the speaker and stylistic context. We therefore need to build this information into the model in some way, if we are correctly to characterise the competence of the native Norwich speaker. The most successful way of doing this would appear to be by means of variable rules, in the manner of Labov (1964; 1969; 1970) and Weinreich *et al.* (1968). We shall therefore indicate that the Norwich diasystemic rules are not only optional but also dependent on sociological factors by the following type of notation:

(4) x//ō// $\longrightarrow$ //u//
      x (rule 4) = f (style, class, age, sex)

The operation of rule 4, this states, is a function of style, class, age level and sex of the speaker. Rule 5 can be rewritten in a similar way:

(5) x//ū// $\longrightarrow$ //ō//
      x (rule 5) = f (style, class, age)

The value of x can in each case be deduced from the material presented in chapter 7. This kind of rule, Labov states (1964) is 'one means of showing the structure which relates competence to performance'. The competence of a speaker is given in terms of rules like 4 and 5. But this may mean that in actual performance a given speaker may never actually use, say, rule 5, so that for him:

      $x = $ f (style, class, age) $= $ o[1]

For a much more sophisticated formulation of variable rules, one should now consult Cedergren & Sankoff (forthcoming).

Another problem associated with diasystemic incidence rules is that, as we saw in chapter 7, they are applied to some lexical items more frequently than others (this was particularly true of the 'short *o*' pronunciation). It is not at all clear how we should handle this. One possibility would be to mark some items [+rule 5] and others [+ +rule 5]. Another possibility would be to allow the value of *x* in these rules to depend on semantic features – items connected with, for example, family life, appear to be more likely to run through these rules than other items. In any case, it would seem to be true to say that what we are dealing with here is an example of 'lexical diffusion' (see Wang, 1969; Chen & Hsieh, 1971). Chen & Hsieh suggest that this problem should be handled in a synchronic description by the introduction of 'rule features in the lexical entries'. It is probable, therefore, that we may need a rather more refined approach. For the moment, though, it is perhaps sufficient to suggest the following kinds of lexical entry:

home:	//h·ō·m·//	[+ +rule 4]
bloke:	//blō·k·//	[+rule 4]
float:	//flō·t·//	
remote:	//r·e···-m·ō·t·//	[−rule 4].

8.4.4 Mutation and realisation rules. Diasystemic incidence rules and rules of morphological alternation deal with elements at only one level – the systematic phonemic level. (Note, incidentally, that the incidence rules must be ordered after the alternation rules. If this were not done, forms like //pro···-v·ō·k·// would be liable to 'shortening' of //ō// to //u//, and produce *provocative* */pʰɹəvʊ́k'ət'ɪv/.) Other rules which operate solely at this level include many of the type discussed by Chomsky & Halle (1968), including those relating to stress. (These rules are of little interest to us here, since they are the same for all types of Norwich English, and indeed many other varieties.) Rules like diasystemic incidence rules which apply at or within a particular level are mutation rules, with the product of the rule or process being 'an element of the same stratum as the input to the process' (Fudge, 1969*b*). Rules which relate one level to a lower level are realisation rules. (This division of rules into two clearly distinct types is a concomitant of Fudge's strict separation of the phonemic and phonetic levels. This avoids the ambiguities that result from an approach like that described in Chomsky (1964) where there are intermediate levels of no systematic status at all.)

8.4.5   Phonological realisation rules. Having discussed those rules which operate within the systematic phonemic level in the Norwich diasystem, we can now move on to a discussion of the rules that relate this level to the systematic phonetic level. These rules convert the abstract underlying phonemes into potentially concrete systematic phonetic elements. We shall call them *phonological realisation rules.*

The problem we now have to face is two-fold: what form are these phonological realisation rules to take; and what exact status is the systematic phonetic level to have? According to Fudge's early formulation (1967), phonological realisation rules are of the following form:

$$//A// \longrightarrow \text{Front of tongue highest}$$
$$//2// \longrightarrow \text{Tongue low}$$

for the realisation of vowel phonemes (in terms of features), and

$$//B// \longrightarrow \text{Velar place of articulation}$$

for the realisation of consonant phonemes. A later formulation (1969*b*) has realisation rules of the form:

$$//A// \longrightarrow \text{Labiality 2} / \underline{\quad\quad} //2//$$

for the realisation of consonant phonemes. (Fudge gives no examples of realisation rules as they apply to vowels according to this later type of approach.) In these rules, the symbols $//A//$, $//B//$, $//2//$, etc., refer to the abstract features of the systematic phonemic level. Features of the type: Labiality 2, are derived from Ladefoged's attempt to establish a set of universal phonetic categories (1967*b*, 1971).

One disadvantage associated with rules of this type is that they often appear to attempt to produce generalisations where there are none to be made. For example, Fudge (1969*b*) sets up the 'Latin' phonological subsystem for English consonants as portrayed in table 8.10. For very good reasons associated with patterning and morphological alternation, the elements mnemonically represented as k, g, s, j and r are presented in the same column in this table – they all share the abstract features $//D\alpha//$. This arrangement has many advantages at the systematic phonemic level, and enables us to handle rules at this level in a very simple and convenient way. Fudge, however, attempts to extend the advantages gained at this level to the realisation rules themselves. It is,

TABLE 8.10. *The 'Latin' subsystem*

	A	B	D	
			α	β
1 a	p	t	k	qu
b	b	d	g	gu
2 a	f	s	s	
b	v	z	j	
3		l	r	
4	m	n		

of course, a desirable objective to discover generalisations and establish natural classes of the type illustrated in rules such as:

$||B||$ ——→ Alveolar place of articulation

but rules of the following type show that, once we have abandoned phonetically based features in favour of abstract features, the fact that natural classes are phonetic natural classes means that the objective cannot be attained.

$$||D|| \longrightarrow \begin{cases} \text{Postalveolar p.a. } / \begin{cases} [\_\_2a]\ [i]\ [Vowel] \\ \_\_2b \\ \_\_3 \end{cases} \\ \text{Alveolar p.a. } /\_\_2a \\ \text{Velar p.a.} \end{cases}$$

or:

$$||a|| \longrightarrow \begin{cases} [\text{Glottal constriction } 9]/2\_\_ \\ \begin{bmatrix} \text{Glottal constriction } 9 \\ \text{Glottal timing} \quad 5 \end{bmatrix} / \begin{array}{l} \text{initial in} \\ \text{stressed syllable} \end{array} \\ \begin{bmatrix} \text{Glottal constriction } 9 \\ \text{Glottal timing} \quad 3 \end{bmatrix} / \#[\text{B2a}]\ [\_\_] \\ \begin{bmatrix} \text{Glottal constriction } 9 \\ \text{Glottal timing} \quad 4 \end{bmatrix} \end{cases}$$

Since we do not have a natural phonetic class under D, there is little point in setting up a realisation rule which pretends that we do. Natural classes at the phonemic level can only be indicated by means of phonetically based features such as those used by linguists working within the distinctive feature approach.

Similar disadvantages occur, with this approach, in the realisation of vowel phonemes. For the realisation of Hungarian vowels, for instance, Fudge (1967) has rules like the following:

$$
B \longrightarrow \begin{cases} \text{Front of tongue highest} & /\underline{\hspace{1.5em}}\text{1a} \\ \text{Middle of tongue highest} & /\underline{\hspace{1.5em}}\text{2a(ii)} \\ \text{Back of tongue highest} \end{cases}
$$

We can obtain no generalisations because there are none to be made at precisely those points where the phonemic system is counter-phonetic and where the abstract nature of the system is most clearly emphasised. It would therefore seem better to allow phonological realisation rules to apply individually to systematic phonemes. This is the approach we shall adopt here. It might be argued that, if we allow rules to apply to systematic phonemes individually, there is little point in 'subdividing' phonemes into features at all. This argument would be false since there are two very good reasons why it is crucial to maintain features. First, phonological mutation rules such as diasystemic incidence rules and rules of morphological alternation are couched in terms of features and capture thereby the generalisations that are to be made. Secondly, the use of features illustrates the relationships which hold between the different systematic phonemes. These relationships, moreover, can still be read out from the form of the realisation rules. (In those cases where Fudge's realisation rules illustrate 'the generalization that...features... manifest a "natural" situation (since the realization rules show that they correlate one-to-one with phonetic features)' (1972), this information, in the approach outlined here, will have to be read out from the form of the phonological realisation rules together with lower level rules of the type discussed below.)

8.4.6   The status of the systematic phonetic level. The function of the systematic phonetic level has been defined as to 'indicate the way the physical system of articulation is to perform' (Postal, 1968, p. 273). Typically, the systematic phonetic level forms the output stage of the phonological component of a generative grammar. But any examination of a large amount of (particularly casual urban) speech material makes it clear that there is a very big disparity between the outputs of phonological components as they are usually presented, and what speakers actually say. That is to say, the output fails by a very long way to indicate the way in which the physical system of articulation is to perform. This disparity, when it is not ignored, is often dismissed with the argu-

ment that it must be assumed to be the result of 'performance phenomena'. There are reasons, however, for arguing that a phonological
grammar should be able to produce as its output something which
closely approaches what people actually say, or should at least allow
for various different possibilities of performance. There are obviously
many things which affect performance that cannot be handled by a
grammar of this type – like a mouthful of food or a cold in the head.
But on the other hand many of the so-called performance phenomena
can be shown to be structured, determined, and subject to rule, albeit
perhaps of a statistical probability type, in just the same way as higher-
level linguistic features. It is also the case that these so-called performance phenomena vary geographically and socially. They are not the
same, for instance, in London speech as they are in Norwich, and even
within Norwich itself they vary to a certain extent from social class to
social class. For this reason alone, a Norwich phonological grammar
ought to incorporate them. As an example, consider the following
perfectly normal Norwich utterances transcribed from the tape-recorded
interviews.

[ʔʌ̈s ʒəs ɐʔ °gwæ̃n]
That's just how it go on

[wɛ ë fm °gõw æ̈ʔ ɜ sæ̈ʔ ë̤ næ̈ʔ]
Well, if I'm going out on a Saturday night

[nʌ̈ ə ë̤ʔ ˌb dæ̃ lɛ̰ læ̈iʔlëi]
No, I haven't been down there lately

These utterances are quite typical of casual speech. They are also
quite distinctively Norwich utterances, even as they stand on paper with
no indication of prosodic features, and for that reason the Norwich
diasystem should be able to produce them as output. They do not,
of course, much resemble the outputs that are usually associated with
phonological grammars. It is therefore clear that if the systematic
phonetic level is to indicate how the articulatory system is to perform,
it can only do so very imprecisely. There is therefore little virtue in
having narrowly articulatory outputs of the type developed by Ladefoged
and Fudge at this stage, since the outputs do not correspond to actual
articulations.

   The systematic phonetic level in the Norwich diasystem, therefore,
will not deal with actual articulations or pronunciations, but with

potential or ideal pronunciations. Units at this level will represent un-
ambiguously idealised pronunciation types. The level will therefore be
an extrinsic allophonic level, since intrinsic allophones result from actual
overlapping articulations. Phonological realisation rules in the Norwich
diasystem will be of the form:

$$||Y\beta 111a|| \longrightarrow /u:/,$$

where /u:/ is an extrinsic allophone indicating the approximate region
of the phonetic continuum where this idealised but phonetically determined unit is to be realised. It represents, in other words, the phonetic
'area' to be 'aimed at'. (Note that systematic phonetic elements are
enclosed by single slants, phonemic elements by double slants.)

(Ladefoged's articulatory features will be reserved for the realisation
of the extrinsic allophones at the lowest phonetic level, which we shall
call the phonetic realisation level. It will be at this lowest level that
intrinsic allophones will be produced and other 'performance phenomena' will be handled. At this level we will be able to indicate much
more precisely how the articulatory system is to perform – see p. 171
below.)

8.4.7   Phonological realisation rules for consonants. We can begin
our discussion of the phonological realisation rules in the Norwich
diasystem by examining those which convert the consonantal systematic
phonemes (members of systems at places 1, 2, 4, 5 and 6 in syllable
structure) into systematic phonetic elements. We are first of all faced
with the following problem: should the phonological realisation rules
take form 6*a* or form 6*b*?

$$(6a) \quad ||B1a|| \longrightarrow \begin{cases} /t^h/ \, / \, (\#) \, \underline{\quad} \, (\acute{V}) \\ /t/ \, / \, \underline{\quad} \, \# \\ /t'/ \end{cases}$$

$$(6b) \quad ||B1a|| \longrightarrow \begin{cases} /t^h/ \, / \, (\#) \, \underline{\quad} \, (\acute{V}) \\ x\langle /t/ \sim /t?/ \sim /?/\rangle \, / \, \underline{\quad} \, \# \\ x\langle /t'/ \sim /\underset{\smile}{t}?/ \sim /?/\rangle \end{cases}$$

$$x = f \, (\text{style, class})^{1}$$

It seems fairly clear that features such as the lateral release of [t] before
laterals must be handled at the lower phonetic realisation level, since

---

[1] For the angle-bracket notation, see Labov (1969).

they are due to overlapping articulations. It is also clear that $/t^h/$, $/t^h/$ and $/t/$ are extrinsic allophones which belong at the systematic phonetic level. But what is the status of t̰ʔ and ʔ? The solution we prefer to adopt here is that these are not extrinsic allophones, but variant realisations, depending on sociological variables, of the extrinsic allophones $/t^h/$ and $/t/$, at the phonetic realisation level. (This means that we are able to confine our study of the 'phonological' variables discussed in chapter 7 to the phonetic realisation level. Since it is actual articulations we were comparing in the index scores presented in chapter 7, this would appear to be where they belong.) It is also the case that [t̰ʔ] and [ʔ] resulting from $/t^h/$ and $/t/$ occur mainly in casual or rapid speech, and it is the phonetic realisation level which is designed to handle features of this type. The glottal stop also occurs automatically before heavily stressed initial vowels, in which case it can hardly be said to be an extrinsic allophone. The low-level nature of this feature is therefore best emphasised by confining the glottal stop to the realisation level. Perhaps the most important reason, however, is that this arrangement permits us to handle mutation rules at the systematic phonetic level in a much simpler way. We can, for example, have an assimilation rule of the type:

$$/t/ \longrightarrow /p/ \ / \text{———} \ /p^h/$$

instead of:

$$\begin{bmatrix} /t/ \\ /t̰ʔ/ \\ /ʔ/ \end{bmatrix} \longrightarrow \begin{bmatrix} /p/ \\ /p̰ʔ/ \\ /ʔ/ \end{bmatrix} \ / \text{———} \ /p^h/$$

We will therefore have phonological realisation rules of type 6*a*, and produce [t̰ʔ], [ʔ] etc., by means of phonetic realisation rules or realisation level mutation rules.

The other consonant phonological realisation rules include the following:

(7) $\quad //\text{A1b}// \longrightarrow \begin{cases} /_{\circ}\text{b}/ \ /\# \text{———} \\ /\text{b̥}/ \ / \text{———} \ \# \\ /\text{b}/ \end{cases}$

(8) $\quad //\text{A1c}// \longrightarrow \begin{cases} /\text{s}/ + /\text{p}/ \ /\# \text{———} \\ /\text{s}/ + /\text{p}^h/ \end{cases}$

(9) $\quad //\text{A2a}// \longrightarrow /\text{f}/$

(10) $\quad //\text{A2b}// \longrightarrow \begin{cases} /_{\circ}\text{v}/ \ /\# \text{———} \\ /\text{v̥}/ \ / \text{———} \ \# \\ /\text{v}/ \end{cases}$

(Note that it would also be possible to specify the contexts for realisations of this kind in terms of the places in syllable structure at which the systematic phoneme occurs.)

(11) $//A3// \longrightarrow /w/$

(12) $//A4// \longrightarrow /m/$

Systematic phonetic elements resulting from other phonological realisation rules are the following:

/tʰ/, /tʻ/, /t/, /ₒd/, /d̥/, /d/, /θ/, /ₒð/, /ð̥/, /ð/, /l/, /ł/, /n/, /tʃ/, /ₒdʒ/, /dʒ̊/, /dʒ/, /ʃ/, /pʰ/, /ₒz/, /z̧/, /z/, /j/, /kʰ/, /kʻ/, /k/, /°g/, /g̊/, /g/, /r/, /ə/, /h/.

There is at least one other element that results from a phonetic mutation rule, which we shall discuss below. Special rules are also needed to realise the archiphonemes at places 4 and 6. In the case of $//N//$, these rules result in a new systematic phonetic element /ŋ/:

(13) $//N// + //g// \longrightarrow /ŋ/$, for example.

8.4.8   Phonological realisation rules for vowels. Phonological realisation rules for the vowels are as follows:

(14) $//Xαι// \longrightarrow /ɪ/$ as in *bid*
(15) $//Xαιι// \longrightarrow /ɛ/$ as in *bed*
(16) $//Xαιιι// \longrightarrow /æ/$ as in *bad*
(17) $//Xβι// \longrightarrow /ʊ/$ as in *put*
(18) $//Xβιι// \longrightarrow /ɔ/$ as in *bud*
(19) $//Xβιιι// \longrightarrow /ɒ/$ as in *pod*
(20) $//Yαι// \longrightarrow /ɒi/$ as in *buy*
(21) $//Yαιιa// \longrightarrow /ɪi/$ as in *bee*
(22) $//Yαιιb// \longrightarrow /e:/$ as in *wheat*
(23) $//Yαιιιa// \longrightarrow /ɛ:/ \sim /e:/$ as in *name*
(24) $//Yαιιιb// \longrightarrow /æi/$ as in *nail*
(25) $//Yβι// \longrightarrow /ʊu/$ as in *soon*
(26) $//Yβιιa// \longrightarrow /ʊu/$ as in *tune*
(27) $//Yβιιb// \longrightarrow /æu/$ as in *now*
(28) $//Yβιιιa// \longrightarrow /ʊu/$ as in *go*
(29) $//Yβιιιb// \longrightarrow /ɒu/$ as in *know*
(30) $//Z// \longrightarrow /ʊi/$ as in *boy*.

Rule 26 should in fact read:

$$//\text{Y}\beta\text{11a}// \longrightarrow x\langle/\text{ɵu}/ \sim /\text{jɵu}/\rangle$$
$x = \text{f (style, class)}$

since although $//\bar{\text{ʌ}}//$ and $//\bar{\text{u}}//$ can have identical realisations at the systematic phonetic level, variations such as *tune* /tjɵun/ ~ /tɵun/ occur in the speech of many people. (Rules 14–30 apply only to vowels in stressed syllables.) Note that the elements previously written as /ʌ/ and /u:/ now appear as /ɔ/ and /ʊu/.

8.5 A problem of Norwich phonology

In addition to those already illustrated, there are other systematic phonetic vowels that we must take into consideration. Consider, for example, the following three sets of Norwich pronunciations:

A		
	third	/θɜːd̥/
	fern	/fɜːn/
	far	/faː/
	fur	/fɜː/
	for	/fɔː/

These vowels are historically products of short vowels plus *r*.

B			C		
	fire	/faː/		*trying*	/tʰrɑːn/
	fear	/fɛː/		*seeing*	/sɛːn/
	fair	/fɛː/			
				saying	/sæːn/
	tour	/tʰɔː/		*booing*	/ˌbɔːn/
	pure	/pʰɜː/		*knew it*	/nɜːt/
	store	/stɔː/		*going*	/°gɔːn/
				knowing	/nɒːn/
	tower	/tʰɑː/		*allowing*	/əlɑ́ːn/
	employer	/ɛmplɔ́ː/		*employing*	/ɛmplɔ́ːn/

The vowels under C are, with two exceptions, identical with those listed under B, although the B vowels are historically products of long vowels plus *r*, and the C vowels are not. C vowels are produced from the same underlying vowels, but in conjunction with the reduced vowel [ə]. (We can be quite sure of this because older speakers quite often have /°gɔ:ən/, for example, rather than /°gɔ:n/.)

Clearly, if we solve this problem by having two types of rule, one to produce these vowels from forms with *r* and another for forms with schwa, an important generalisation will be lost. We know, both from synchronic and historical evidence, that post-vocalic *r* developed to schwa before disappearing, in those cases where it has disappeared. These vowels therefore result, in both cases, from the same kind of process. We have here, that is to say, an opportunity of illustrating that a historical sound change is reflected in a synchronic phonological rule. For example, just as the vowel /ɪi/ in *here*, presumably /hɪir/, has developed to /ɛ:/ in conjunction with the schwa descended from *r*, to produce /hɛ:/, so the vowel /ɪi/ in *see* develops, in modern Norwich English, to /ɛ:/ in conjunction with the schwa resulting from unstressed //i//, to produce alternations of the type: /sɪi/ – /sɛ:n/: *see – seeing*.

If we were to have two sets of rules, moreover, they would have to be of two different types. Post-vocalic //r// occurs only at the systematic phonemic level in most types of Norwich English, so the rule handling forms with *r* would have to be a phonological realisation rule. Schwa, on the other hand, occurs only at the systematic phonetic level, as a realisation of unstressed phonemic vowels.

8.6   Phonetic mutation rules

The solution to this problem is as follows. First of all we require phonological realisation rule 31:

$$(31) \quad //r// \longrightarrow /ə/ \; / \underline{\hspace{1em}} \begin{cases} \# \\ C \end{cases}$$

(Rule 31 will have /r/ rather than /ə/ as output for those very few members of the speech community who have post-vocalic *r*.) The /ə/ which forms the output to this rule is identical with the /ə/ produced by other phonological realisation rules acting on unstressed vowels. Subsequent rules to generate the vowels portrayed above (8.5, A, B, and C) must therefore operate at the systematic phonetic level. They will act on systematic phonetic elements to produce other systematic phonetic elements. They will therefore be termed *phonetic mutation rules*.

In order to produce the systematic phonetic vowels listed under A (8.5) we need the following obligatory *phonetic mutation rules*:

(32) /ɪ/ ⎫
(33) /ɛ/ ⎬ $\longrightarrow$ $x\langle$/ɜ:/ ~ /ɑ:/$\rangle$ / ___ /ə/
(34) /ɔ/ ⎭

$$x = f \text{ (age, class)}$$

These rules will produce the variable outputs discussed under (ir) in chapter 7 (7.7.1).

(35) /æ/ $\longrightarrow$ /ɑ:/ / ___ /ə/
(36) /ɒ/ $\longrightarrow$ /ɔ:/ / ___ /ə/.

These rules produce the required vowels in *third, fern, fur, far*, and *for*. They are the only rules required for the oldest Norwich speakers, who retain /ə/ and have no vowel mutation in items like *fire* = /fɒɪə/. For other speakers, we need the following set of phonetic mutation rules, which are optional, and operate in the context / ___ /ə/.

(37) /ɵʉ/ $\longrightarrow$ /ɜ:/   *pure, brewer, knew it*
(38) /ʊu/ $\longrightarrow$ /ɔ:/   *store, going, go it, Noah*
(39) /ʊi/ $\longrightarrow$ /ɔ:/   *royal, enjoying, enjoy it*
(40) /ɒi/ $\longrightarrow$ $x\langle$/ɑ:/ ~ /ɑ:/$\rangle$ *fire, higher, try it, quiet*
(41) /æʉ/ $\longrightarrow$ $x\langle$/a:/ ~ /ɑ:/$\rangle$ *tower, allowance, allow it*
           $x = f$ (class)
(42) /ɪi/ $\longrightarrow$ /e:/ ~ /ɛ:/   *pier, seeing, see it*
(43) /æ:/ $\longrightarrow$ /æ:/ /‡ ___ /ə/   where ‡ is a morpheme boundary:
                                              player, say it
(44) /ɒu/ /ɔ:/ ~ /ɒ:/   *knowing, mow it*

There is also the obligatory rule, rule 45:

(45) /æi/ $\longrightarrow$ /ɛ:/ / ___ /ə/   *there*

Finally, we require the (optional) rule to delete /ə/:

(46) x/ə/ $\longrightarrow$ ø (after vowels except diphthongs)
           $x = f$ (age)

Note that in the case of *tour, poor*, pronounced with /ɔ:/, it is necessary for the diasystemic incidence rule //ū// $\longrightarrow$ //ō// (rule 5) to have applied in order to produce the required /ɔ:/ from /ʊu/ + /ə/. (Failure to do this produces /ɜ:/, which can in fact be heard in *tour*. It is much more common, however, in items like *booing*, which can be /₀bɜ:n/ as well as /₀bɔ:n/). These optional rules are applied more frequently morph-internally (as in *fire*) than word-internally (as in *higher*), and more frequently here than across word boundaries (as in *try it*).

For example: *tour*   //t·ū·r·//   rule 5 ⟶ //t·ō·r//
phonological realisation rules
/tʉuə/   /tʊuə/
phonetic mutation rules
/tɜ:ə/ – rule 37   rule 38 – /tɔ:ə/
/tɜ:/   – rule 46 –   /tɔ:/

We thus have a number of systematic phonetic vowels, /ɜ:/, /ɔ:/, /ɑ:/, /æ:/, /ɒ:/, /a:/, to add to those produced by the phonological realisation rules 14–30. /ɔ:/, /æ:/, and /a:/ can result from other sources also, as we shall see below.

8.6.1   The problem of 'intrusive r'. Now that we have written out post-vocalic *r* at the systematic phonetic level, by realising //r// in this position as /ə/, we are faced with the problem of how to generate intrusive and linking *r* in forms like *law and order* and *lore and language*. By 'intrusive *r*' is meant a pronunciation with /r/ where this is not histori-cally 'justified', i.e. where the *r* is not descended from Early Modern English *r*, and does not occur in the spelling. Intrusive and linking *r*'s occur only where /ɑ:, ɔ:, ɜ:, ɪə, ɛə, ʊə, ə/ (as in *pa, paw, her, idea, there, sure, banana*) or their Norwich equivalents occur immediately before another vowel. (There is a restriction in Norwich English that intrusive *r* does not occur in contexts like *extra eggs*, where an /r/ precedes an un-stressed /ə/ in the same syllable.) Examples from the Norwich inter-views include:

idea of   [ʁidˈɛ:ɹəv]
lot of old   [lˈɑ·ʔəɹˈɳuɬ]
out to eat   [æʉʔtʰəɹẹiʔ]
quarter to eight   [kʰwˈɔ:ʔtəɹˈæiʔ]

Intrusive *r* was originally set up as a phonological variable but this proved to be of no interest since all the Norwich informants used 100% intrusive *r*. There was some class differentiation in the number of intrusive *r*'s used by speakers, but this was due to the fact that working-class speakers established more contexts for the insertion of *r* by reducing more unstressed vowels to [ə], as in *quarter to eight*, above.

One way of handling this problem would be to amend rule 46 as follows:

$$/\text{ə}/ \longrightarrow \begin{cases} \text{ø} & / \underline{} \begin{cases} \# \\ C \end{cases} \\ /\text{r}/ & / \underline{} V \end{cases}$$

This might seem to be to some extent an unfortunate arrangement, in that the systematic phonemic $//\text{r}//$ is written out by phonological realisation rules, only to have $/\text{r}/$ written in again by this mutation rule. This is necessary, however, since the above rule writes in $/\text{r}/$ even where $/\text{ə}/$ is not derived from $//\text{r}//$ (which is the whole point of calling it 'intrusive *r*', of course). It is also possible to deduce the relationship between the two phenomena simply from the *form* of the two rules:

$$//\text{r}// \longrightarrow /\text{ə}/$$
$$/\text{ə}/ \longrightarrow /\text{r}/$$

There is, in other words, an indication, if rather an obscure one, that only accents without post-vocalic $/\text{r}/$ have intrusive $/\text{r}/$.

There is a good reason, however, why a modified rule 46 is not adequate here. So far we have been considering how to produce intrusive and linking *r* only with respect to forms produced from vowel $+ [\text{ə}]$, whatever its origin, for example:

far off $/\text{faːr ɒf}/$ from $/\text{æ}/ + /\text{ə}/$
    where $/\text{ə}/ < //\text{r}//$
he have often said $/\text{heːr ɒfən sɛd̥}/$ from $/\text{ɪi}/ + /\text{ə}/$
    where $/\text{ə}/ < //\tilde{\text{æ}}//$

We also have to consider, though, how to handle items such as *law* and *pa*, which also produce intrusive *r*, and where no [ə] appears to be involved. We cannot list *law* and *pa* as $//\text{l·o·r·}//$ and $//\text{p·a·r·}//$ since this would produce the wrong output both for post-vocalic *r* retainers and for those who have only linking and not intrusive *r*. Rules 35 and 36 suggest another possibility. It might be possible to list *law* and *pa* as $//\text{l·o···}//$ and $//\text{p·a···}//$ and then have the following phonological realisation rules:

$$//\text{o}// \longrightarrow /\text{ɔːə}/ / \underline{}' \#$$
$$//\text{a}// \longrightarrow /\text{aːə}/ / \underline{}' \#$$

Rules 35, 36 and (modified) 46 would then produce the correct output. This solution, however, is particularly counter-intuitive and indeed unnecessary. It writes in $/\text{ə}/$ where there is no motivation for doing so either in the lexical entry, or, particularly, in actual speech – simply in order to produce intrusive /r/ at the right place. It is also complicated by the need to make schwa-deletion obligatory in these two cases, since */paːə/ and */lɔːə/ never occur. A much more acceptable solution is to write *pa* and *law* as //p·a···// and //l·o···//, as suggested above, but to have phonological realisation rules as follows:

(47) //a// ⟶ /aː/ / ___'___ #

(48) //o// ⟶ /ɔː/ / ___'___ #

If we accept this interpretation, it forces on us the most satisfactory (and simplest) solution to the linking and intrusive /r/ problem. It is, however, a solution which makes it impossible to show that only '*r*-less' accents have intrusive /r/ – or at least this information will have to be read from the form of three rules.

The solution is as follows. We allow the phonetic mutation rules 32–45, together with the phonological realisation rules 47 and 48, to produce the systematic phonetic vowels: /ɜː/, /aː/, /ɔː/, /ɑː/, /eː/, /ɛː/, /æː/ and /ɒː/. Some of these also result from other sources. For example:

(49) //a// ⟶ $x\langle$/aː/ ~ /æː/$\rangle$/ ___ $\begin{cases} //f// \\ //\theta// \\ //s// \\ //nt// \\ //nš// \\ //ns// \end{cases}$

$x = f$ (age) (see 6.2)

(e.g. *laugh* /laːf/; *path* /pʰaːθ/).

We then, finally, apply the optional phonetic mutation rule, rule 50, which produces linking and intrusive *r*:

(50) ø ⟶ /r/ / $\begin{cases} /ɜː/ \\ /eː/ \\ /ɛː/ \\ /æː/ \\ /aː/ \\ /ɔː/ \\ /ɒː/ \\ /ɑː/ \\ /ə/ \end{cases}$ ___V

Rule 50 stresses the automatic and low-level nature of the /r/-insertion process. Speakers who do not have linking and intrusive /r/ do not have rule 50. Speakers, on the other hand, who have linking but not intrusive /r/ (a very small group) cannot be handled in terms of these rules. The only way to treat this problem is to mark items like *law*, *idea*, *drawing* [– rule 50] in the lexical entries for these speakers. This has the favourable result of stressing the somewhat artificial nature of this type of speech. Speakers of this type, it seems, rely heavily on spelling in order to achieve the correct /r/-less result in items of this type.

8.6.2 Of the above systematic phonetic elements, /ɜ:/, /ɒ:/ and /ɑ:/ result only from phonetic mutation rules. This is in many cases also true of the elements /æ:/ and /e:/. /e:/ can be a realisation of //ɛ̃// and of //ã//, but in most cases it is an alternative form to /ɛ:/ in items of the set *fear*. For example, the lexical entries for *fear* and *fair* are:

$$//f\cdot\bar{e}\cdot r\cdot//\qquad//f\cdot ai\cdot r\cdot//$$

At the systematic phonetic level this results in:

$$/f\text{\scriptsize I}iə/\qquad/fæiə/$$

The relevant phonetic mutation rule for *fear* (42) is optional, that for *fair* (45) obligatory. This means that we can have the following contrasts:

$$/f\text{\scriptsize I}iə/\qquad/fɛ:ə/$$

or $\qquad/f\text{\scriptsize I}iə/\qquad/fɛ:/$

If rule 42 selects /e:/, we have the contrasts:

$$/fe:ə/\qquad/fɛ:ə/$$

or $\qquad/fe:/\qquad/fɛ:/$

If, however, rule 42 selects /ɛ:/, the result is:

$$/fɛ:ə/\qquad/fɛ:ə/$$

or $\qquad/fɛ:/\qquad/fɛ:/$

The consequence of this is the variation portrayed in the discussion of (er) and (ɛr) in chapter 7.

At least one other phonetic mutation rule has the effect of resulting in a new consonantal systematic phonetic element.

$$(51)\quad /z/\longrightarrow/ʒ/\;\Big/\;\begin{Bmatrix}/\text{\scriptsize I}/\\/j/\end{Bmatrix}\;\underline{\quad}\;V$$

For example, *pleasure* will be derived from the lexical entry:

//plē·z·// plus the suffix //y·ᴧ·r·//.

This will give //ple·z-y·ᴧ·r·// by the rule of morphological alternation. This will result in the systematic phonetic representation: /pʰlɛzjəə/. Phonetic mutation rules will delete one of the final schwas, and rule 51 will give us:

$$/pʰlɛʒə/$$

Rule 51 is obligatory.

There are also other phonetic mutation rules which are of no particular diasystemic interest – for example, the rules of /w/ and /j/ insertion (see 8.7, 8.9.1), and of resyllabification (8.9.1).

8.7   The systematic phonetic vowel system

As a result of the phonological realisation and phonetic mutation rules, we now have a phonetic system of vowels and consonants consisting of extrinsic allophones. The vowel system consists of a series of subsystems, as portrayed in table 8.11. A majority of speakers have subsystems A, B and D exactly as shown in table 8.11. There are, however, several alternatives to subsystem C. Two of these are illustrated in tables 8.12 and 8.13.

The symbolisation used for these systematic phonetic elements shows approximately how the articulatory system is to perform, and stresses the phonetic symmetry of the system. This symmetry is by no means entirely a linguist's artificial construct. Indices for the variables of the type discussed in chapter 7, for example, show that there is a close correlation in scores between (ī) (7.6.2) and (au) (not illustrated). There is therefore justification for tabulating /ɒi/ and /æʉ/ as parallel elements. There is also considerable symmetry in the development of A and B vowels in conjunction with the D vowel to produce C vowels. Thus the four highest A vowels: /ɪ/, /ɛ/, /ʊ/ and /ɔ/ all become /ɜ:/ in combination with /ə/ (see rules 31–4). The two parallel vowels /ɒi/ and /æʉ/ both become /ɑ:/ (rules 40–1); while /ɪi/ and /æi/ can both become /ɛ:/ (rules 42 and 45), and /ʊu/ and /ɒu/ can both become /ɔ:/ (rules 38 and 44). (Note, too, that Ba vowels trigger off a /j/-insertion rule, and Bb vowels a /w/-insertion rule which parallel the C and D vowels' /r/-insertion rule (rule 50).)

TABLE 8.11. *The Norwich systematic phonetic vowel system*

A		B				C		
		a		b				
ɪ	ʊ	ïi	ʊ̈i	ʉ̈ʉ̈	ʊu			
ɛ	ɔ					ɛː	ɜː	ɔː
æ	ɒ	æi	ɒi	æʉ̈	ɒu	æː		ɒː
						aː		ɑː

$$\dfrac{\text{D}}{/ə/}$$

TABLE 8.12. *Sub-system C (i)*

C		
ɛː	ɜː	ɔː
aː		

TABLE 8.13. *Subsystem C (ii)*

C			
ɛː	ɔː	*face*	*paw*
ɛːə	ɔːə	*fierce*	*pore*
aː		⎰ *farce* ⎱ *first*	

8.7.1   Phonetic space.

One of the drawbacks of Fudge's scheme (of which he is aware) is that his phonological system does not allow for the possibility of indicating or explaining how innovating structural pressures can lead to sound change. There is no system in which forces of this kind can be played out. Fudge sets up, as an alternative to the vowel system shown in table 8.6, the system given here in table 8.14. Fudge states (1969a): 'although table [8.6] is the one we adopt, it must be admitted that the relationships of table [8.14] do exert an influence on the phonological system – sound changes set up phonetic structural pressure in an innovating direction, while morphological relationships which persist through a sound change tend to pull in the direction of conserving the old phonemic system. There is therefore a struggle, and the implication of our approach is that this struggle is one between

TABLE 8.14. *Alternative phonemic vowel system*

X		Y		W	
α	β	α	β	α	β
i	u	i:		yu:	u:
e	o	ei	oi		ɔ:
a	ʌ	ai		au	ou

present-day phonetics and present-day morphology: we do not need to bring in diachronic considerations at the basic theoretical level. On the other hand, dissimilarities between phonemic patterning and phonetic patterning will normally reflect sound change in some way: the position of [ʌ] as the realisation of /Xıβ/ [Table 8.6] is a case in point – it reflects the sound change [u] ⟶ [ʌ], but without implying that Modern English [ʌ] is a high back rounded vowel, even at an underlying level. Chomsky & Halle's approach implies exactly this, with the further implication that the "struggle" mentioned above is between present-day phonetics and the phonetics of a past stage of the language; it thus lacks descriptive adequacy – can we expect the (untrained) native speaker to know anything at all about the past history of his language?'

While Fudge's criticisms of Chomsky & Halle are clearly well-founded, it is plain that by rejecting table 8.14, Fudge loses the possibility of explaining past sound changes of the type he describes and of predicting and allowing for future sound changes. All one is able to do with his scheme is to deduce what past sound changes have occurred. Sound changes of this type, however, must have some kind of system within which to operate – we must have some means of indicating how structural pressures can cause sound change.

Fudge's problem would appear to be his attempt, in the scheme presented in table 8.14, to handle this type of phenomenon at the systematic phonemic level. It is certain – Fudge admits as much by implication himself – that structural pressures of this type take place at the phonetic level; because the phonemic level is abstract, sound change has only a very indirect effect on the phonemic system. This is why we have throughout preferred the term 'phonetic space' to the more usual 'phonological space'. This view is also shared by Kiparsky (1968): 'real enough tendencies towards phonological symmetry exist, but...they have nothing to do with the autonomous phonemic level for which they are often claimed. Rather they are probably brought about by simplificatory phonological changes such as rule simplification and rule re-ordering, and the symmetry they result in is phonetic rather than phonemic symmetry.'

What Kiparsky does not say is that these tendencies towards phonetic symmetry, and structural pressures at this level generally, may well be found to be one *cause* of phonological changes such as rule simplification and rule re-ordering. What is even more likely is that purely phonetic changes and dialect differences which are of little phonological interest but of considerable diasystemic importance may be the result of this type of pressure.

Justification for this belief is provided by the work of Martinet (1952, 1955) and of other linguists such as Moulton (1962). Martinet has shown that the concept of 'phonological' space is a very useful one in the study of linguistic change, and that terms such as 'holes in the system' and 'drag chain' are certainly not without value in this field. Martinet himself does not overemphasise the importance of this particular cause of sound change: 'On ne se lassera pas de répéter que personne n'a jamais prétendu que les facteurs phonologiques internes soient le seuls, ni même nécessairement les plus décisifs' (1955, p. 54), but some of his claims can be substantiated by reference to the Norwich material.

(1) 'Une opposition phonologique qui sert à maintenir distincts des centaines de mots parmi les plus fréquents et les plus utiles n'opposera-t-elle pas une résistance plus efficace à l'élimination que celle qui ne rend service que dans un très petit nombre de cas?' (p. 54).

One of the Norwich mergers we have dealt with in this work is that between items of the sets *fear* and *fair*. As we saw above, Fry (1947) has shown that /ɛə/ and /ɪə/ are respectively seventeenth and eighteenth out of a total of twenty RP vowels in their degree of frequency, and that they between them account for only 0.55 % of all RP segments. By way of comparison, /ɪ/ and /ə/ between them account for 19.07 %.

(2) 'Nous avons...indiqué...comment les nécessités physiologiques peuvent contrecarrer l'intégration phonologique...Il y aura, entre [o] et [u] une plus petite différence d'ouverture qu'entre [e] et [i], bien que l'angle maxillaire soit le même dans les deux cas' (p. 98). In other words, 'the physiological asymmetry of the vocal tract interferes with the achievement of permanent symmetry (for example, in the matter of distinctive degrees of height in vowel phonemes, there is more latitude for keeping the front vowels apart than for the back vowels)' (Robins,

TABLE 8.15. *Subsystem A (i)*

A	
ɪ	ʊ
ɛ	ɔ
æ	

TABLE 8.16. *Subsystem A (ii)*

A	
ɪ	ʊ
ɛ	ɔ

1967, p. 224). Martinet himself gives as an example the fronting of /u/ in Azores Portuguese, which releases more space for the maintenance of the contrast between the remaining back vowels, /o/, /ɔ/ and /a/.

As far as the Norwich material is concerned, in the case of the short (A) vowels the fact that there is less space for the realisation of the back vowels /ʊ/, /ɔ/ and /ɒ/ has led to the fronting and lengthening of /ɒ/ in the speech of many individuals to the extent that there is no contrast between /aː/ and /ɒ/ – in the pairs test items such as *barks* and *box* are not distinguished in spite of the fact that they are placed side by side. This results in the less symmetrical but (physiologically) more comfortable system of table 8.15. Other tendencies are at work, however, which are moving in the direction of reconstituting the phonetic symmetry of the system: many younger speakers lengthen the vowel /æ/ so that there is no contrast between /æ/ and /æː/. Forms such as *sat* and *say it* are not distinguished. This of course results in the once more symmetrical system of table 8.16. Other manifestations of pressures operating in phonetic space were illustrated in the figures given in chapter 7, notably in the case of the variables (er) and (ɛr), and (ō) and (ou).

The deficiencies of Fudge's scheme with respect to phonetic space are made good in the Norwich diasystem by the phonetic vowel system or inventory shown in table 8.11. It is this systematic phonetic vowel system which demonstrates how and why structural pressures of this kind can occur. This system is, of course, in conflict with the systematic phonemic vowel system shown in table 8.7. But events at the phonetic level are important from the point of view of phonemic change, since, through time, they can affect lexical entries and the systematic phonemic system itself. It is possible, for example, that the loss of the diasystemic element //ɛ̄// in Norwich is the result of pressures at the phonetic level (a consequence of the proliferation of long front vowels, /ɪi/, /eː/, /ɛː/, /æː/, /aː/), leading to a merger of /eː/ and /ɪi/, together with the fact that there are no important morphological alternations which require //ɛ̄// to be distinguished from //ē//. This proliferation of front vowels may also have led to the merging of *fear* and *fair* items, of course, particularly since all C vowels have been squashed, as it were, towards the bottom end of the vowel trapezium, as can be seen from table 8.11. Note that whereas previous Norwich generations may not have had /eː/ and /æː/ in *here* and *player* respectively, they probably did have these vowels in items of the type *wheat* or *face* and *half* respectively.

8.8   Phonetic realisation rules

We now need a series of rules to realise the extrinsic allophones of the systematic phonemic level at the lowest phonetic level, the phonetic realisation level, where we shall produce intrinsic allophones and handle other 'performance phenomena'. The function of this level is to indicate as precisely as possible how the articulatory system is to perform. We have already stated that Ladefoged's articulatory features, also employed by Fudge, will be reserved in this approach for use at this level. There will, however, be two major alterations in the way in which these features are treated by Ladefoged and Fudge.

(1) The Ladefoged features will be totally specified for each segment. If a parameter is relevant for Norwich English, its value must always be given, where possible, if the physical system of articulation is to receive exact instructions. Much of the information would of course be redundant at higher levels.

(2) Only consonants will be specified in terms of Ladefoged's features. These are by no means sufficiently specific for vowels, and Ladefoged's approach is in any case phonological-contrastive rather than strictly phonetic. In other words, if there are three distinctive vowel heights in a particular language, Ladefoged's parameter *auditory height*: 1, 2, 3, will be perfectly adequate if we wish simply to indicate which vowel it is. If, however, we wish to indicate how the articulatory system is to perform in order to obtain precisely the right pronunciation, then it is

certainly not adequate. This is particularly evident in the construction of a diasystem where it is necessary to indicate slight differences in pronunciation. The outputs of realisation rules applying to vowels at the phonetic realisation level will therefore be given in terms of IPA alphabet symbols which will indicate as exactly as possible the vowel quality to be produced. This level will form the output of the diasystemic phonological grammar, and will be a linguist's attempt to produce and reproduce as closely as possible what speakers actually say. As an example, we can give the following four rules which will convert an abstract systematic phonemic element into one of its possible realisations:

Phonological

   realisation rule: $||D2b|| \longrightarrow |z|$

Phonetic

   mutation rule (51): $|z| \longrightarrow |ʒ| \,/\, |j| \underline{\quad\quad} V$

Phonetic

   realisation rule: $|ʒ| \longrightarrow$

$$
\begin{bmatrix}
\text{Articulatory place} & 3 \\
\text{Glottal constriction} & 5 \\
\text{Nasality} & 0 \\
\text{Stricture} & 2 \\
\text{Affrication} & 0 \\
\text{Glottal timing} & 1 \\
\text{Laterality} & 0 \\
\text{Lip rounding} & 0 \\
\text{Secondary articulation} & 0
\end{bmatrix}
$$

   i.e. $|ʒ| \longrightarrow [ʒ]$

Realisation level

   mutation rule:
$$
\begin{bmatrix}
\text{Articulatory place} & 3 \\
\text{Glottal constriction} & 5 \\
\text{Nasality} & 0 \\
\text{Stricture} & 2 \\
\text{Affrication} & 0 \\
\text{Glottal timing} & 1 \\
\text{Laterality} & 0 \\
\text{Lip rounding} & 0 \\
\text{Secondary articulation} & 0
\end{bmatrix}
\longrightarrow
\begin{bmatrix}
3 \\
6 \\
0 \\
2 \\
0 \\
1 \\
0 \\
0.5 \\
0
\end{bmatrix}
\Big/
\begin{array}{l}\text{in certain}\\ \text{contexts}\end{array}
$$

   i.e. $[ʒ] \longrightarrow [ʒ̞]$, e.g. *closure* [kl̥ᵊɥːʒ̞ᵊ]

Realisation level mutation rules produce intrinsic allophones, and alter pronunciations in rapid casual speech to permit the production of the types of utterances shown above (8.4.6). They will be discussed further below.

Obvious phonetic realisation rules for converting ideal into actual pronunciations would be the following:

$$/k^h/ \longrightarrow [\underset{+}{k}^h] / \underline{\quad} /\text{ɪi}/$$
$$/æ/ \longrightarrow /æ^{\cdot \breve{e}}/ / \underline{\quad} /\mathring{g}/$$
$$/ɔ/ \longrightarrow [ʌ^{\text{'}\dashv}]$$
$$/ɜ:/ \longrightarrow [ɐ̞:]$$

We have already stated above that rules of this type should be formulated in terms of the framework developed by Ladefoged, as far as consonants are concerned, except that all relevant parameters for a particular language should be totally specified for each segment. The phonetic realisation rule for /k^h/ above should therefore read:

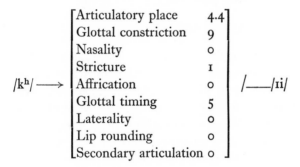

$$/k^h/ \longrightarrow \begin{bmatrix} \text{Articulatory place} & 4.4 \\ \text{Glottal constriction} & 9 \\ \text{Nasality} & 0 \\ \text{Stricture} & 1 \\ \text{Affrication} & 0 \\ \text{Glottal timing} & 5 \\ \text{Laterality} & 0 \\ \text{Lip rounding} & 0 \\ \text{Secondary articulation} & 0 \end{bmatrix} / \underline{\quad} /\text{ɪi}/$$

Other realisations of /k^h/ will depend on the following vowel and other items constituting the phonetic environment. For example, the full phonetic realisation rule for /k^h/ would also have to include:

$$/k^h/ \longrightarrow \begin{bmatrix} \text{Articulatory place} & 5.7 \\ \text{Glottal constriction} & 9 \\ \text{Nasality} & 0 \\ \text{Stricture} & 1 \\ \text{Affrication} & 0 \\ \text{Glottal timing} & 5 \\ \text{Laterality} & 0 \\ \text{Lip rounding} & 0.5 \\ \text{Secondary articulation} & 0 \end{bmatrix} / \underline{\quad} /ɔ:/$$

Rules of this type can also be made more general so as to, in this case, apply to /°g/ as well, for example.

It is also at this point that we are able to produce the different variants of the phonological variables that we discussed above (8.4.7). For example, we have the diasystemic phonetic realisation rule, rule 52:

(52)

$$
/t/ \longrightarrow x \left\langle
\begin{bmatrix}
\text{A.p.} & 2 \\
\text{G.c.} & 9 \\
\text{Nas.} & 0 \\
\text{Strict.} & 1 \\
\text{Affric.} & 0 \\
\text{G.t.} & 3 \\
\text{Lat.} & 0 \\
\text{L.r.} & 0 \\
\text{S.a.} & 0
\end{bmatrix} \sim
\begin{bmatrix}
\text{A.p.} & 2 \\
\text{G.c.} & 1 \\
\text{Nas.} & 0 \\
\text{Strict.} & 1 \\
\text{Affric.} & 0 \\
\text{G.t.} & 3 \\
\text{Lat.} & 0 \\
\text{L.r.} & 0 \\
\text{S.a.} & 0
\end{bmatrix} \sim
\begin{bmatrix}
\text{A.p.} & 0 \\
\text{G.c.} & 1 \\
\text{Nas.} & 0 \\
\text{Strict.} & 1 \\
\text{Affric.} & 0 \\
\text{G.t.} & 3 \\
\text{Lat.} & 0 \\
\text{L.r.} & 0 \\
\text{S.a.} & 0
\end{bmatrix}
\right\rangle
$$

That is, /t/ ⟶ x ⟨[t] ~ [t̞ʔ] ~ [ʔ]⟩

x = f (style, class, age)

This rule specifies that the variable (t) is the realisation of, in this case, the systematic phonetic element /t/ at the phonetic realisation level, and that the realisation of /t/ will be [t], [t̞ʔ] or [ʔ] according to the factors specified. This rule is a diasystemic rule which applies to the whole speech community. We can assume that all speakers have this rule as part of their linguistic competence. Performance, however, will vary widely from speaker to speaker. Rules of this type are presumably also applied in a reverse direction in the social interpretation of utterances made by other speakers. The rules will in fact be somewhat more complex than presented above because intrinsic allophonic features such as lip rounding must also be indicated. We must also build in a restriction on the selection of the variant [ʔ]. The following Norwich pronunciations, for example, must be taken into consideration:

get it [°gɛ́t̞ʔɪʔ] but not *[°gɛʔɪʔ]
not at all [nɑ̈:ʔət‘ɔ̣:ɫ] but not *[nɑ̈:ʔəʔɔ̣:ɫ]
isn't it [ínt‘əʔ] but not *[ínʔəʔ]
put it [pʰɵ̣t‘əʔ] but not *[pʰɵ̣ʔəʔ]
about it [bəu̯t‘əʔ] but not *[bəu̯ʔəʔ]
get her to come [gɛʔət‘əkʰɛ̣m] but not *[gɛʔəʔəkʰɛ̣m]

The following, however, do occur:

won't have to go to [wŏʔɛ̨·ʔəgǫ̆ʔə]
don't ought to [dŏʔɔ̨̌:ʔə]
went into [wɛʔíʔ]

The restriction is, therefore, that a glottal stop cannot occur both before and after /ə/ or unstressed /ɪ/. (The *went into* example shows that this is possible in the case of stressed /ɪ/.) Note too that in the phrase *get her to come*, with /ǯ:/ rather than /ǯ/ in *her*, two glottal stops are possible. The restriction also appears to force the *first* of the /t/ or /tʻ/ consonants to be realised as [t], [tʻ] or [tʔ], rather than [ʔ], except where the second /tʻ/ is in initial position, as in *get her to come* and *not at all*. (The form *at all* is pronounced /ə-tʻɔ:ɫ/ rather than /ət-ɔ:ɫ/.) We must therefore modify rule 52 to read:

$$
/t/ \longrightarrow x \begin{cases} \langle [t] \sim [t\underset{\cdot}{ʔ}] \rangle & \Bigg/ \begin{cases} \underline{\quad} \begin{Bmatrix} /ə/ \\ /ɪ̆/ \end{Bmatrix} /t/ \\[2ex] /t/ \begin{Bmatrix} /ə/ \\ /ɪ̆/ \end{Bmatrix} /-/ \underline{\quad} \end{cases} \\[6ex] \langle [t] \sim [t\underset{\cdot}{ʔ}] \sim [ʔ] \rangle \end{cases}
$$

Symbols like [tʔ] are of course shorthand devices representing complexes of Ladefoged-type features as shown above.

This, then, is the form that phonetic realisation rules will take for consonants. We have already indicated above that the realisation rules for vowels will have to be of a different form. This is not without justification in the literature. It has been shown, for example, that kinaesthetic and tactile feedback are much more important for the production of consonants than the production of vowels. Auditory feedback, on the other hand, is more important for vowel production. Ladefoged (1967a) writes, for example: 'When auditory feedback was absent many vowel sounds were considerably affected both in length and in quality.' This is a further argument against the use of distinctive features, since the same features are used both for vowels and consonants at the phonetic as well as the phonemic level. Chomsky &

Halle (1968) point out, as a justification for this (as does Ladefoged (1967*b*) himself in his development of phonetic parameters), that there are many parallels between consonant production and vowel production. Öhman (1966), on the other hand, has shown that vowels and consonants appear to be produced by two different types of mechanism, with consonants being in some sense superimposed on a continuous stream of vowels. If there are two different types of production mechanism, then we have every justification for postulating that phonetic realisation rules for vowels are of a somewhat different type from those for consonants.

We are now, therefore, faced with the problem of the exact form these rules are to take. We will, as we have already indicated above, allow the output of these rules to take the form of phonetic symbols indicating as precisely as possible the area of the vowel trapezium where the vowel is to be realised – the vowel quality the speaker aims at, as it is affected by overlapping articulations, and which he controls for auditorily. One alternative is, therefore, to have rules of the form:

$$/\varepsilon/ \longrightarrow [\underset{\cdot}{e}] \sim [\varepsilon]$$

This, however, suggests that there are certain discrete pronunciation types open to speakers, which, as we have seen in chapter 6 and elsewhere, is not the case. We shall therefore adopt a set of realisation rules of the following type:

$$/\varepsilon/ \longrightarrow [\underset{\cdot}{e}\text{-}\varepsilon\text{-}\underset{\cdot}{\ddot{e}}\text{-}\ddot{e}]$$

where the forms within the square brackets signify not different possible pronunciation types but the complete phonetic area over which the realisation can range. (Note that we have to do this for vowels, but that it would also be possible for consonants, since, although it is easier to discriminate auditorily between different consonantal variants, these are in many cases also simply areas of different phonetic continua.)

The full set of vowel phonetic realisation rules for the Norwich diasystem is as follows.

(53) $/\text{I}/ \longrightarrow x \begin{cases} \langle[\ddot{\text{e}}\text{-}\ddot{\text{e}}\text{-}\text{ə}]\rangle/ \underline{\quad} /\text{ɬ}/ \\ \langle[\text{i}\text{ɩ-}\ddot{\text{e}}\text{-}\ddot{\text{e}}]\rangle \end{cases}$

      $x = \text{f (style, class, age)}$

(54) $/\varepsilon/ \longrightarrow \begin{cases} x\langle[\underset{\cdot}{e}\text{ɩ-}\varepsilon\text{ɩ-}\underset{\cdot}{\ddot{e}}\text{-}\ddot{\ae}\text{-}\text{ɐ}]\rangle/ \underline{\quad} /\text{ɬ}/ \\ [\text{e-}\varepsilon\text{-}\underset{\cdot}{\ddot{e}}\text{-}\ddot{e}] \end{cases}$

      $x = \text{f (style, class, age, sex)}$

(55) $/æ/ \longrightarrow x$ $\begin{cases} \langle[\varepsilon\text{-}\varepsilon\text{:-}æ\text{-}æ\text{:-}ææ\text{-}æi\text{-}\varepsilon i]\rangle / \underline{} \begin{cases} /\mathring{g}/ \\ /k/ \end{cases} \\ \langle[\varepsilon\text{-}\varepsilon\text{:-}æ\text{-}æ\text{:-}\ddot{æ}\text{-}\text{ɐ}]\rangle \underline{} /ł/ \\ \langle[\varepsilon\text{-}\varepsilon\text{:-}æ\text{-}æ\text{:-}ææ\text{-}æ\ddot{e}\text{-}\varepsilon\ddot{e}]\rangle \end{cases}$

$x = f \text{ (style, class, age)}$

(56) $/ʊ/ \longrightarrow \begin{cases} [\ddot{o}\text{-}\text{ǫ}] /\!/ \begin{matrix} /p^h/ \\ /_\circ b/ \end{matrix}\!/ \\ [\ddot{ÿ}\text{-}\ddot{ö}] \end{cases} \underline{}$

(57) $/ɔ/ \longrightarrow x \langle[\text{ɔ}^\dashv\text{-}\text{ʌ}^\dashv\text{-}\text{ɐ}]\rangle$
$x = f \text{ (age)}$

(58) $/ɒ/ \longrightarrow x \langle[\text{ɒ-ɒ:-ɑ-ɑ:-a:}]\rangle$
$\text{x} = f \text{ (style, class, age, sex)}$

(59) $/ɪi/ \longrightarrow x \langle[\ddot{ï}\text{ɨ-}\ddot{ë}\text{ɪ-}\text{əɨ-}\text{əi}]\rangle$
$x = f \text{ (class)}$

(60) $/æi/ \longrightarrow x \langle[\text{ęë-}æ\ddot{e}\text{-}æ\text{ɪ-}æ̨i]\rangle$
$x = f \text{ (style, class)}$

(61) $/ʊi/ \longrightarrow x \langle[\ddot{ö}\text{i-}\text{ɔ}̟\ddot{ë}]\rangle$
$x = f \text{ (class, age)}$

(62) $/ɒi/ \longrightarrow x\langle[\text{ɑę-a}ę\text{-}ɐ\ddot{e}\text{-}ɐ\text{i-}\text{ɔ}ˤi]\rangle$
$x = f \text{ (style, class, age, sex, } /æʉ/)$

(63) $/ɵʉ/ \longrightarrow x \langle[\text{ʉ:-ɵʉ-ɵʉ-}3\text{ʉ}]\rangle$
$x = f \text{ (class)}$

(64) $/æʉ/ \longrightarrow x \langle[\text{ɑö-aö-}\varepsilon\text{ʉ-}3\text{ᵼʉ}]\rangle$
$x = f \text{ (class, age, } /ɒi/)$

(65) $/ʊu/ \longrightarrow x \langle[\text{u:-ʉ}\dashv\text{:-}\ddot{ö}\text{u-}\text{ɵö}]\rangle$
$x = f \text{ (style, class)}$

(66) $/ɒu/ \longrightarrow x\langle[\text{aʉ-ɑʉ-ɒʉ-ɔʉ-ɵö}]\rangle$
$x = f \text{ (class, age) (see 7.8.1)}$

(67) $/e:/ \longrightarrow [\text{ę:-}\varepsilon\text{:-}\ddot{\varepsilon}\text{:-}\ddot{e}\text{:}]$

(68) $/\varepsilon:/ \longrightarrow [\text{ę:-}\varepsilon\text{:-}\ddot{\varepsilon}\text{:-}\ddot{\varepsilon}\text{:}]$

(69) $/æ:/ \longrightarrow [\text{ɛ̨:-}æ\text{:-}æ^\vdash\text{:-}\varepsilon^\vdash\text{:}]$

(70) $/a:/ \longrightarrow x \langle[\text{a:-ɑ}\dashv\text{:}]\rangle$
$x = f \text{ (class)}$

(71) $/ɔ:/ \longrightarrow [\text{ǫ}\dashv\text{:-ɔ}^+_\top\text{:}]$

(72) $/ɒ:/ \longrightarrow [\text{ɔ}\dashv\text{:-ɒ}\dashv\text{:-ɒˤ:}]$

(73) /ɑː/ ——→ [ɑː-ɑ˔ː]

(74) /ɜː/ ——→ [ɜː-aː]

These rules are in some cases relatively simplified (although they give a good idea of the form phonetic realisation rules in the Norwich diasystem must take): we will also need, for example, rules to lengthen vowels before voiced consonants.

Note that these rules allow for the possibility of the following pairs of systematic phonetic vowels not being distinguished at the phonetic realisation level:

/æ/ : /æː/

/ɒ/ : /ɒː/

/aː/ : /ɑː/

/æ/ : /æi/

/ɒ/ : /aː/

/ɜː/ : /aː/

Other cases of possible overlapping realisations include /eː/ and /ɛː/, /ɔː/ and /ɒː/, /æ/ and /ɛː/, and /ɪ/ and /ɛ/. Note, finally, that all realisations of A, C and D vowels have voiceless counterparts which are realisations of /h/.

8.9 Realisation level mutation rules

We have now reached a stage in our Norwich diasystemic phonological grammar which is probably much more detailed than that normally achieved by the phonological components of generative grammars. We have the stated aim, however, of generating an output which approaches much more closely what different Norwich speakers actually say. The level we have so far reached is adequate for fairly slow, careful Norwich speech. It is not adequate for rapid, casual speech. To produce forms of the type illustrated in the three Norwich utterances quoted earlier on (8.4.6), and to handle casual rapid speech in general, we will now develop a set of rules which will be relevant only for this type of speech. These rules, which will incidentally demonstrate that at least some 'performance' phenomena are subject to rule, will of course be optional. Since they will apply to and produce elements at the phonetic realisation level, we shall call these rules *realisation level mutation rules*.

It is preferable to have this type of phenomenon handled at the lowest level, because it is then a relatively simple matter to derive casual speech from careful speech. It is not desirable to handle 'performance' phenomena of this type by phonetic realisation rules such as:

$$/\text{ɛnt}/ \longrightarrow [\ddot{\text{e}}ʔ], \quad \text{e.g. } plenty, twenty$$

because this complicates the realisation rules and means that, in addition to the rules producing intrinsic allophones, there will have to be several alternative rules, with the one we have just postulated as only one of the alternatives. In this particular case, for example, the omission of [n] in items like *plenty* occurs only where /t/ is [ʔ], so the above rule would have to be presented in just that form, if a complication of levels is not to arise. We will therefore have instead rules of this type:

$$[n] \longrightarrow \text{ø} / [\ddot{\text{e}}] \underline{\quad} [ʔ]$$

The true form of this realisation level mutation rule is the following:

(75)

A.p.	2		A.p.	0
G.c.	5		G.c.	1
Nas.	1		Nas.	0
Strict.	1		Strict.	1
Affric.	0	$\longrightarrow$ ø /[ę-ɛ̨-ɛ̈-ë̈] __	Affric.	0
G.t.	1		G.t.	3
Lat.	0		Lat.	0
L.r.	0		L.r.	0
S.a.	0		S.a.	0

Such a statement stresses the very low level nature of this type of phenomenon. It might be thought that the rather cumbersome formula representing the realisation of the systematic phonetic vowel /ɛ/ within the square brackets could be more simply expressed at the higher level. However, the virtue of this formulation can be judged from the fact that in the speech of many Norwich people, the rule applies in the more general environment:

$$[e-\varepsilon-\ddot{\varepsilon}-\ddot{e}] \underline{\quad} [ʔ]$$

That is, the rule applies to items such as *didn't* [dę̈ʔ] and *isn't* [ë̈ʔ] as well as to *plenty* etc. In this way, we can indicate that a rule of this kind applies, not to a systematic phonetic element, but to a phonetic area. The justification for such an arrangement is provided by the fact that speakers who use the higher variant [ɨ] of /ɪ/ do not have this rule in the case of *didn't* and *isn't* items. The rule, therefore, quite clearly does not apply to /ɪ/, but to the particular phonetic area indicated in the rule. The development /ɪnt/ ——→ /ɪt/ can only take place: (*a*) where /t/ = [ʔ], and (*b*) where /ɪ/ has a quality more open than [ɪ̈]. (It must be conceded that this case is not conclusive, since the [ɪ̈] realisation of /ɪ/ is found mostly in the speech of older informants. It could therefore be assumed that the above facts are simply the result of older speakers having rule 75 in a form slightly different from that of younger speakers.)

Realisation level mutation rules are a very complex problem, and a great deal of work remains to be done on this subject. Some of the more important of these rules in the Norwich diasystem, however, have been developed, in a rather tentative way. These are presented below. Note that shorthand forms such as [n] are used where this does not obscure the true nature of the rule.

(76)

$$
\begin{bmatrix}
\text{A.p.} & 2 \\
\text{G.c.} & 5 \\
\text{Nas.} & 1 \\
\text{Strict.} & 1 \\
\text{Affric.} & 0 \\
\text{G.t.} & 1 \\
\text{Lat.} & 0 \\
\text{L.r.} & 0 \\
\text{S.a.} & 0
\end{bmatrix}
+
\begin{bmatrix}
\text{A.p.} & 1 \\
\text{G.c.} & 5 \\
\text{Nas.} & 0 \\
\text{Strict.} & 2 \\
\text{Affric.} & 0 \\
\text{G.t.} & 1 \\
\text{Lat.} & 0 \\
\text{L.r.} & 0 \\
\text{S.a.} & 0
\end{bmatrix}
\longrightarrow
\begin{bmatrix}
\text{A.p.} & 2 \\
\text{G.c.} & 5 \\
\text{Nas.} & 0 \\
\text{Strict.} & 3 \\
\text{Affric.} & 0 \\
\text{G.t.} & 1 \\
\text{Lat.} & 1 \\
\text{L.r.} & 0 \\
\text{S.a.} & 3
\end{bmatrix}
$$

That is, [nð] ——→ [ɫ]. It is possible that this rule should be of wider application, since, although no examples of this were recorded during the survey, forms like [waˈdəɫæˈi̯sæˈi] *what do they say* have been heard. This increase in generality could be achieved by leaving the value for nasality unspecified.

(77)   [ˌð̥] ——→ ø /# ——

Rule 77 handles pronunciations like *that* [æ·ʔ], *this* [ë̥s]. Note that in cases like this it is possible to generalise the rule to all intrinsic allophones of /ˌð̥/ by omitting, not fully specifying, or allowing for variable specification of features such as lip rounding, so that the rule applies to [ˌð] as well as to [ˌð̥].

(78)   [æ-a-ɑ˞] ——→ [≃],   e.g. *that* [æ̃·ʔ]

Rule 78 nasalises all open vowels within the phonetic area indicated by the symbols, even in non-nasal environments. This therefore provides another example of a rule which applies to a phonetic area rather than to particular systematic phonetic elements. A vowel will only be nasalised if it falls into this area, regardless of its origin. The element /ɒ/ is not nasalised, for instance, only certain of its realisations.

(79) [ɪ̈-ɛ̈] ⟶ [ə]
(80) [ɛ̈-ɛ-ɛ̈] ⟶ [ɛ̈]
(81) [æ] ⟶ [æ̈-ɐ-ʌ̈]
(82) [ö-ɤ̈] ⟶ [ö-ɤ̈]
(83) [ɔ̈˧-ʌ˧] ⟶ [ʌ˧]
(84) [ɑ-a] ⟶ [ä]

These rules centralise and open short vowels in rapid speech. Note, too, that rule 81 applies not to /æ/ but only to [æ].

(85) [ɜ:-a:] ⟶ [æ-ɐ-a]

This rule shortens the vowel in *bird*, *first*, etc., and produces the typical East Anglian short forms with the wide range of phonetic distribution discussed and described by Kökeritz and Lowman, and in chapter 6 above (the variable (ir)). Note, however, that as it applies to a phonetic area rather than to a systematic phonetic element it has the effect of optionally shortening all [a:]-type forms, not only those derived from //i//, //e// and //ʌ//+//r//. This is a desirable effect, since pronunciations such as *partner* [pʰɐʔnə] were recorded during the survey. We have, moreover, seen that /ɒ/, too, can have a realisation in the region of [a:]. It is therefore satisfying for our thesis concerning the input to these rules to note that forms such as *bob* [ˌbʌ̈b̥], *job* [dʒɐb̥] (rhyming with *hub*) were frequently recorded during the survey. The input is therefore, once again, a phonetic area rather than a systematic phonetic element: [a:] ⟶ [ɐ] whatever its origin.

(86) [ɵu-au-ɒu-ʊu] ⟶ [ɵ-a-ɒ-ʊ]

This rule deletes the glide from all diphthongs that result from systematic phonetic Bb vowels.

(87) [Stricture 1] ⟶ [Stricture 2]
(88) [Stricture 2] ⟶ [Stricture 3]

These rules convert stops into fricatives, and stops and fricatives into approximants. They account for occasional Norwich pronunciations such as:

he paid [ëiɸ̊ǣëd̥]

(89) [Glottal timing 3] ⟶ [Glottal timing 2 ∼ 1]

TCS

This converts voiceless segments into segments that are partially or completely voiced. It accounts for Norwich pronunciations such as:

$$he\ called\quad [\ddot{e}\underset{\circ}{i}\gamma\ddot{\jmath}\cdot\underset{\circ}{l}\d{d}]$$

(90) [ə-ə̰] ⟶ ø

(91) [ɫ] ⟶ ø/ ___ #

(92) [n] ⟶ ø/ ___ #

(93) [ʔ] ⟶ ø/ ___ [s]

(94) [voiceless vowel] ⟶ ø

These rules all delete sounds as indicated. Note that rule 94 must also have a corresponding phonetic realisation rule:

$$/h/ \longrightarrow ø$$

to account for speakers who 'drop their *h*'s' even in careful speech.

(95) [Vowel] ⟶ [~]/ ___ [Nasalisation l]

This rule nasalises vowels which precede nasal consonants.

(96) ø ⟶ [ʔ]/ ___ #V́

This rule introduces a glottal stop before initial vowels in stressed syllables, as in:

$$awful\quad [\d{P}\acute{\underset{\circ}{\jmath}}{\cdot}{:}f\underset{\circ}{l}]$$

Many other realisation level mutation rules are of course required, in particular to delete vowels and consonants in certain contexts and to shorten long vowels.

We are now in a position to demonstrate how our three Norwich utterances (8.4.6) can be generated by the Norwich diasystem.

8.9.1   Exemplification

A *That's just how it go on*

We can assume that the systematic phonemic underlying form for this would be something approaching the following:

Systematic phonemic level

$$//ð{\cdot}a{\cdot}ts+j{\cdot}ʌ{\cdot}st{\cdot}+h{\cdot}au{\cdots}+{\cdots}i{\cdot}t{\cdot}+g{\cdot}\bar{o}{\cdots}+{\cdots}o{\cdot}n{\cdot}//$$

There are no diasystemic incidence rules that apply in this case and, subsequent to the phonological rules of stress, boundary deletion, etc., the phonological realisation rules convert this into the systematic phonetic representation:

Systematic phonetic level

$$/_{\circ}\text{ðæts } _{\circ}\text{ʤəst hæʉ ət } {}^{\circ}\text{gʊu ɒn}/$$

Phonetic mutation rules now apply, in this case rules of glide insertion and resyllabification, to produce the following:

$$/_{\circ}\text{ðæts } _{\circ}\text{ʤəst hæʉ ət } {}^{\circ}\text{gʊu wɒn}/$$

The next set of rules to be run through are the phonetic realisation rules, which convert this to the level of actual articulations. The result is something like the following:

Phonetic realisation level

$$[_{\circ}\text{ðæ˞ʔs } _{\circ}\text{ʤəs æ̈ë̈ʉ əʔ } {}^{\circ}\text{gəu wän}]$$

This represents a possible slow, careful type of Norwich pronunciation. Now the final set of realisation level mutation rules comes into play:

(1) Rule 77 deletes the initial [ₒð] in *that's*.
(2) Rule 93 deletes the glottal stop before [s] in *that's*.
(3) Rule 87 converts [ₒʤ] into [ʒ].
(4) Rule 86 converts [æ̈ʉ] and [əu] into [æ̈] and [ə] respectively.
(5) Rule 81 centralises and lowers the vowels of *that's* and *how* to [ɐ̈] and [ɐ] respectively.
(6) Rule 90 deletes [ə] in *it* and in *go*.
(7) Rule 95 nasalises the vowel of *on*.
(8) Rule 94 deletes the [æ̈] < /h/.
(9) Finally, rule 96 inserts the initial glottal stop.

The result is the required output:

$$[\text{ʔɐ̈s ʒəs ɐʔ } {}^{\circ}\text{gwän}]$$

B *Well, if I'm going out on a Saturday night*

Systematic phonemic level

$$//\text{w·e·l· + ··i·f· + ··ï·m· + g·ō··-··iNg· + ··au·t·}$$
$$+ ··o·n· + ··a··· + s·a··-t·e·r-d·ē··· + n·ï·t·//$$

Systematic phonetic level

/wɛɫ ɪf əm °gʊuən æʉt ənə sæt'ədɹi nɒit/

The phonetic mutation rules convert this to:

/wɛɫ ɪ fəm °gʊuwən æʉt ənə sæt'ədɹi nɒit/

Phonetic realisation level

[wɛ̧ɫ ë fəm °gǫ̈uwən æ̈ʉʔ ənə sæ̈ʔədëi̧ nʌ̈i̧ʔ]

(1) Rule 91 deletes the [ɫ] in *well*.
(2) Rule 90 deletes [ə] in *I'm, going, a* and *Saturday*.
(3) Rule 86 deletes the [u] in *going* and the [ʉ] in *out*.
(4) Rule 95 nasalises the vowels in *on* and *going*.
(5) Rule 92 deletes the [n]'s in *on* and *going*.
(6) Rule 78 nasalises the [æ̈] in *Saturday*.

This produces the required output:

[wɛ̧ ë fm °gǫ̃w æ̈ʔ ɔ̃ sæ̧̈ʔëi̧ nʌ̈i̧ʔ]

except that we need an additional rule to delete the [d] in *Saturday*. The exact environment for the operation of this rule is not yet clear.

C   *No I haven't been down there lately*

Systematic phonemic level

//n·ou··· + ··ī··· + ··iNt· + b·ē·n· + d·au·n· + ð·ā·r· + l·ā·t-l·ē···//

Systematic phonetic level

/nɒu ə ɪnt ˳bən ˳dæʉn ˳ðæiə læitlɹi/

The phonetic mutation rule (rule 45) produces:

/nɒu ə ɪnt ˳bən ˳dæʉn ˳ðɛ: læitlɹi/

Phonetic realisation level

[nʌ̃ų̈ ə ɛ̧nʔ ˳bən ˳dæ̈ʉn ˳ðɛ̧˞: læ̧i̧ʔlëi̧]

(1) Rule 86 deletes the [u] in *no* and the [ʉ] in *down*.
(2) Rule 75 deletes the [n] in *haven't*.
(3) Rule 76 produces [ɫ] from [n] + [˳ð].
(4) Rule 95 nasalises the vowel in *down*.
(5) Rule 90 deletes [ə] in *been*.
(6) Rule 92 deletes the [n]'s in *been* and *down*.

We also require a rule to shorten the vowel in *there*. We now have the correct output: [nɐ̃ ə ë̞ʔ ₒb ₒdæ̃ ɨ̞ɹ læ̞iʔlë̞i]

We have finally, therefore, reached the stage where we are, in theory at least, able to generate all types of Norwich English, including casual, rapid speech, from the same underlying system. One of the obstacles in the way of achieving this in practice is the complexity of the phonetic realisation rules and the realisation level mutation rules. In the next section we shall be making a few suggestions on how to attempt to simplify this problem. The large amount of variety to be found in Norwich English is the result of the numbers of optional rules, at all levels, and the socially determined rules with variable outputs which constitute the Norwich diasystem. We have been able to present only a part of this diasystem above. Note that all Norwich speakers have, in principle, access to the entire diasystem. In their actual speech production, however, optional rules are either employed or rejected, with the result that any given speaker only reflects part of the diasystem in his performance.

8.10 Articulatory settings

Finally in this chapter we shall briefly discuss a topic which should be of some assistance in formulating and simplifying the phonetic realisation rules and realisation level mutation rules. It is a striking fact that the speech of many Norwich informants whose individual segments are otherwise quite or perhaps very similar actually sounds very different. This difference is due to the use by very many (particularly younger) WC speakers of what several informants referred to during the course of the interviews as 'a Norwich voice'. In those cases where there are slight differences in the pronunciation of individual segments, moreover, these often seem to be due to the same overall difference in the mode of articulation. Both these types of difference can be described as differences of *setting* (see Honikman, 1964).

Setting has been described by Laver[1] as one of the components of voice quality. (The other main component is the 'anatomical and physiological foundation of a speaker's vocal equipment'.) Settings are 'long-term muscular adjustments...once acquired idiosyncratically, or by

---

[1] Laver (1968). Note that Laver's model of voice quality is based on Abercrombie (1967, ch. 6). I am extremely grateful to John Laver for his help with this section.

social imitation, and now unconscious, of the speaker's larynx and supralaryngeal vocal tract'. Settings can therefore be divided into two types:

1. Settings of the larynx.
2. Settings of the supralaryngeal vocal tract.

Type 1 settings can be divided into three groups:
1. (*a*) phonation types
   (*b*) pitch ranges
   (*c*) loudness ranges

There are also four subgroups of type 2 settings:
2. (*a*) longitudinal modifications
   (*b*) latitudinal modifications
   (*c*) tension modifications
   (*d*) nasalisation

This classification of setting components enables us to analyse and
describe reasonably accurately the distinctive setting employed by
Norwich WC speakers. This type of setting distinguishes Norwich WC
speakers not only from MC speakers but also from East Anglian rural
speakers and, of course, from speakers of many other types of English.
It also characterises some otherwise MC speakers as having come from
a WC background. The setting typical of Norwich WC speech can be
described in the following way.

8.10.1   Settings of the larynx

Phonation types. There is a tendency for Norwich WC speakers to
employ the phonation type which has been characterised as 'creaky
voice' (Catford, 1964). There is no corresponding tendency in the
speech of MC informants.

Pitch ranges. The pitch range used by both male and female Norwich
WC speakers tends to be high rather than medium or deep.

Loudness ranges. The loudness range selected by Norwich WC
speakers tends to be loud rather than medium or soft.

8.10.2   Settings of the supralaryngeal vocal tract

Longitudinal modifications. One of the more obvious components
of the Norwich working-class setting is what has been termed 'raised
larynx voice' (Laver, 1968). This results from the vertical displacement
of the larynx in an upward direction from the neutral position.

Latitudinal modifications. Latitudinal modifications of the supra-laryngeal vocal tract include 'settings of the tongue that result in a constrictive or expansive tendency somewhere in the oral cavity'. The Norwich working-class 'raised larynx voice' is often accompanied by a modification of this type, in that the centre of gravity of the tongue is fronted and probably also lowered from the neutral position. The effects of this modification are most noticeable in the case of vowels in the mid and open front vowel region. These tend to be more front and more open in WC speech than in MC speech – see, for example, the index scores for (a:) and (ā) in chapter 7.

Tension modifications. Norwich WC speech is generally produced with a large amount of muscular tension throughout the vocal tract.

Nasality. An auditory quality which can be loosely labelled as nasality is a frequent component of the Norwich working-class setting, and is particularly noticeable in association with the pronunciation of low front vowels (see performance mutation rule, rule 78). We shall see below that nasality may well be an inadequate term for this feature.

8.10.3   The combined effect of these components of the setting is to produce a type of speech that is somewhat harsh and metallic. Many of the MC informants in the survey considered this type of voice quality to be particularly unpleasant. Most of the various components of this setting would appear to have little or no effect on the articulation of individual segments. This is evident from the fact that 'MC segments' can be superimposed on the WC raised larynx voice (and WC segments on the MC neutral larynx voice). The features of nasalisation and vowel fronting and lowering, on the other hand, could be considered to have a more significant effect on individual segments. This is entirely due to the fact that they *appear* to affect only certain vowel segments: front and low vowels. It is not in fact possible to divorce consideration of any of the components from a consideration of the setting as a whole, since there are good reasons for believing that all the components are anatomi-cally and physiologically linked in some way. The nasalisation and vowel fronting and lowering, in other words, cannot be considered to be properties of those particular segments where their effects are auditorily the most marked. They must be considered as integral features of the overall setting.

The general connectedness of the different components of the setting can be described, somewhat tentatively, in the following way. It would seem to be the case that the component of tension modification is the most important and fundamental component in the production of this particular type of setting. It is not simply tension modifications of the supralaryngeal vocal tract that we must consider, however, but modifications of the vocal tract as a whole. We must also take into consideration muscular tension and effort at the subglottal level. The facts suggest, for instance, that the Norwich working-class setting is characterised by a relatively high degree of effort and muscular tension throughout the speech production apparatus. Thus, the three laryngeal components of the Norwich working-class setting – with the possible exception of phonation type – appear to be controlled by this single overall tendency to high muscular tension. The high degree of tension, for example, produces the high pitch range typical of this kind of setting, since increased vocal cord tension leads to a higher frequency of vibration. The amplitude of vibration of the vocal cords, and thus the high loudness range typical of Norwich WC speech, can also be ascribed to relatively high subglottal pressure resulting from increased muscular effort. The physiological causes of creaky voice, however, are open to question, although there is a possibility that it is at least partly due to muscular tension.

The same overall tendency also controls the four supralaryngeal components. For example, high muscular tension in certain supralaryngeal muscles leads to the longitudinal modification of the raised larynx, and thus to 'raised-larynx voice'. The raising of the larynx, in turn, may well have the effect of facilitating the fronting and possibly also the lowering of the centre of gravity of the tongue, which leads to the fronting (and lowering) of vowels described above. This fronting of the tongue can, in its turn, lead to a tendency to lower the velum, because 'some of the depressor-relaxer muscles of the velum...have their point of origin in the tongue' (Laver, 1968). This is most marked in the case of low front vowels, and results in the nasalisation already described (see also Pike, 1947, p. 22, on 'faucalization'). The high muscular tension is, of course, also present as a tension modification of the muscular walls of the supralaryngeal vocal tract – which is one factor contributing to the metallic nature of this type of speech. It is also possible that the feature we have called nasality is due, at least in part, to resonance features associated with the high muscular tension of the walls of the pharynx. The term 'nasalisation' employed above is for this reason probably not adequate.

8.10.4   In view of the fact that all the components of the setting appear
to be so closely interconnected, it would seem legitimate to reinterpret
rule 78 as a setting rule, of a rather different type from the realisation
level rules which delete segments and handle certain assimilations.
The nasalisation associated with low front vowels will then be seen not
simply as an unmotivated phenomenon to be found in casual WC
speech, but as part of an overall articulatory process. Note, too, that not
only rule 78 is involved here. For example, rules 79–84, which centralise
and open short vowels, can also be accounted for, at least in part, by
a setting where the centre of gravity of the tongue is optionally lowered in
casual speech as a correlation of the raising of the larynx. It would clearly
be an advantage if we could replace these six performance mutation
rules by one setting rule. There is therefore some justification for
proposing a set of setting rules of the following type:

(97)   Vocal organs $\longrightarrow$ x $\langle$ Setting 1 $\sim$ Setting 2 $\rangle$
      $x = $ f (class)

(98)   Setting 2 $\longrightarrow$ High muscular tension

(99)   High muscular tension $\longrightarrow$ $\begin{cases} \text{High pitch range} \\ \text{High loudness range} \\ \text{Tense vocal tract} \\ \text{Raised larynx} \end{cases}$

(100)   Tongue $\longrightarrow$ Fronted and lowered/Raised larynx

(101)   Velum $\longrightarrow$ Lowered/Tongue fronted

(Rules 100 and 101, at least, are optional since, for example, the fronting
of the tongue that is facilitated by the raising of the larynx is not physiologically inevitable: it is possible for muscular adjustments to be made so
that the centre of gravity of the tongue is not fronted.) The rules produce:

(*a*)   The high pitch, loudness, metallic quality and raised larynx typical
      of Norwich WC speakers;

(*b*)   The fronting and lowering of vowels in phonetic space;

(*c*)   Blade rather than tongue-tip articulation of alveolar consonants;

(*d*)   The nasalisation of low front vowels.

These rules indicate that the components of the Norwich working-class
setting are initially dependent on the relatively high muscular tension
in the vocal tract. They also suggest (it is only a suggestion) that some
interconnected sound changes occurring ostensibly as the result of
pressures in phonetic space may in fact be due to changes in the setting.

Note, for instance, that the above rules account not only for the fronting, lowering and nasalisation of certain vowels – which do not occur to a very marked extent in the speech of older informants – but also for the fronting of /ɒ/ from [ɑ̠˖] to [a̠˖], which we have discussed above as a sound change. We can hypothesise that the fact that many young and middle-aged speakers have a front vowel in the lexical set of *box* is due in part to the fronting of the centre of gravity of the tongue. It is also possible that other Norwich sound changes, such as the [ɛː] vowel in items of the lexical set of *fear*, are due to the lowering of the centre of gravity of the tongue, although this is more doubtful. It is instructive, on this point, to compare the pronunciation of older Norwich speakers with that of younger speakers. (The categories 'older' and 'younger' represent only certain statistical tendencies associated with different age-groups, of course.) Consider the following:

	Older	Younger
hymn	[hɪ̝m]	[əm]
better	[bɛ̝tʔə]	[bä̠ʔə]
hammer	[hæ̝·mə]	[ɛ̃mə]

Changes of this type can be dealt with much more easily if they are regarded as the result of a single change in setting than if each change is regarded as an individual event.

If we incorporate synchronic rules of this type into the Norwich diasystem, moreover, the statement of both the phonetic realisation and realisation level mutation rules can be much simplified. We can, for example, replace a phonetic realisation rule of the type:

$$/ɪ/ \longrightarrow x\langle[\mathfrak{i}\text{˖-ë}]\rangle$$
$$x = \text{f (class, age)}$$

by the rule: $/ɪ/ \longrightarrow [\mathfrak{i}\text{˖}]$

and allow the setting rules to produce the more open vowel where appropriate. Another advantage of setting rules is that they can relate different types of Norwich English to each other in the diasystem in a much more generalised and significant way than a series of individual rules. Different social types of Norwich English may be characterised by the presence or absence of, say, rule 100, rather than by a whole series of rules. This is an important point, since it is clear that perhaps the single socially most significant feature of linguistic differentiation in

Norwich is the type of voice quality produced by the particular type of setting employed by a speaker. It is in any case this feature which most clearly distinguishes WC from MC speakers. This point, of course, did not emerge at all from our atomistic analysis of the co-variation of linguistic and sociological phenomena in chapter 7.

Setting rules can be regarded as ancillary to the phonetic realisation rules, and must come into play either before or simultaneously with these rules. If we place the setting rules before the phonetic realisation rules, this will permit us to realise systematic phonetic elements according to an already established type of setting. The outputs of the phonetic realisation rules will then have been filtered through the setting rules to produce the particular output required in each case. Exactly how this is to be done in our model is not clear (see Kim, 1970), but we might propose a mechanism such as the following:

if Tongue ⟶ Fronted and lowered

then /ɒ/ ⟶ [ɑ·]

⇓

/ɒ/ ⟶ [a·]

Note, however, that if we are to allow setting rules to play any part in sound changes of the 'phoneme merger' type, we must allow for the filtering effect of the setting to be skewed in some way, so that, say, back vowels can be more affected by fronting of the centre of gravity of the tongue than front vowels.

8.10.5   Summary   In this chapter we have partially developed a diasystem the aim of which is to produce all forms of Norwich English from a common underlying base. The diasystem comprises a single underlying systematic phonemic system, and the following types of rule:

Diasystemic inventory rules

$$//\text{Y}\alpha\text{III} \left\{ \begin{matrix} a \\ b \end{matrix} \right\} // \longrightarrow //\text{Y}\alpha\text{III}//$$

$$\text{i.e.} \quad \left. \begin{matrix} //\bar{a}// \\ //ai// \end{matrix} \right\} \longrightarrow //ai//$$

Rules of this type relate the overall diasystemic systematic phonemic system to the particular phonological systems used by Norwich speakers.

Phonological mutation rules: diasystemic incidence rules

$$//Y\beta_{111}a// \longrightarrow //X\beta_{1}//$$
$$\text{i.e. } //\bar{o}// \longrightarrow //u//$$

Rules of this type handle diasystemic alternations of the type: *road* /ru:d/ : /rʊd/.

Phonological realisation rules

$$//A_{2}b// \longrightarrow /v/$$
$$\text{i.e. } //v// \longrightarrow /v/$$

These rules convert systematic phonemic elements into the extrinsic allophones of the systematic phonetic level.

Phonetic mutation rules

$$/ʊu/ \longrightarrow /ɜ:/ / \underline{\quad} /ə/ \qquad \text{e.g. } brewer$$

These rules convert systematic phonemes into other systematic phonemes. Some systematic phonemes result only from rules of this type.

Phonetic realisation rules

$$/ɛ/ \longrightarrow [ȩ\text{-}ɛ̧\text{-}ȩ̈\text{-}ë] \qquad \text{e.g. } [_{o}bȩd_{o}] \; bed$$

Rules of this type convert systematic phonemes into the actual articulations of the phonetic realisation level. Rules for consonantal systematic phonemes have outputs in terms of the features developed by Ladefoged (8.8).

Realisation level mutation rules

$$[_{o}ð̊] \longrightarrow ø / \# \underline{\quad} \qquad \text{e.g. } [æʔ] \; that$$

Realisation mutation rules handle phenomena found in casual speech and ensure that the output to the grammar resembles as closely as possible what speakers actually say. It is of some considerable theoretical interest that, at least in the case of vowels, inputs to these rules have the form of phonetic areas rather than of reflexes of particular systematic phonemes.

Articulatory setting rules

Velum ——→ Lowered / ——————————
$\qquad\qquad\qquad$ Tongue fronted

Although as yet only very crudely developed, rules of this type may prove to be of considerable significance, particularly in the simplification of phonetic realisation and realisation level mutation rules.

Appendix

THE QUESTIONNAIRE

I 'First of all, we'd like to ask you a few questions about your local background.'

1. (i) Where in your time have you lived apart from Norwich, and for how long.
    (ii) What different parts of Norwich have you lived in, and for how long?
    (iii) Where did your father, mother, grandparents, husband/wife come from?
2. (i) What job do you (and/or your husband) do now? (*Ascertain exactly*.)
    (ii) What other jobs have you done previously?
    (iii) What is/was your father's (last) job?
3. (i) Which schools did you go to?
    (ii) How old were you when you left school?
    (iii) Do you have any O- or A-level passes? (or equivalent: e.g. 'Cambridge'.)
    (iv) Do you have any further night-school, college or university education?

II *Word List* (Cards 1–12)

'Now we'd like you to read out the words on these cards as naturally as you can.'

III *Lexical*

'A few questions about some Norwich or Norfolk words.'

1. (i) Do you know what a *dwile* is?
    (ii) Have you ever heard anybody say this word?
    (iii) Do you ever use it yourself?
        (Similarly: *mardle, mawther, squit, swad.*)
2. What do you call that stuff you can buy on the fish stalls on the market and fry up for your tea – it's fish eggs really, some of it hard, some soft? (*Milts* and *roes*.)
3. Do you know any other local words?

IV *Reading Passage*

'We'd like you now to read this short story. Please don't read it as if you were in the classroom at school, but as naturally as you possibly can. We'd like to see just how naturally you can read it.'

V *Norwich*

'Some questions about Norwich itself.'
1. (i) What do you think of Norwich as a place to live?
   (ii) What do/don't you like about it?
   (iii) Would you rather live somewhere else/in some other part of the city?
   (iv) Since you can remember, has Norwich changed very much? For the better/worse?
2. (i) Do you take much interest in what the city council do?
   (ii) What do you think of the council?
   (iii) If you were a councillor, what would you have done in the city?
3. (i) Do you take an interest in football at all?
   (ii) Do you ever watch Norwich City? (If so, introduce some topic of interest, e.g. promotion.)
4. (i) Do you find there's very much to do in Norwich?
   (ii) Would you say to someone who was thinking of moving here that you could enjoy yourself here O.K. if you wanted to?
   (iii) Have you been in a situation, recently or some time ago, where you had a good laugh, or something funny or humorous happened to you, or you saw it happen to someone else?

VI *Rapid Word List* (Cards A–C)

1. 'Would you now read out the words on these cards as rapidly as you can but without being incomprehensible.'
2. (i) 'And would you now please say for me the days of the week.'
   (ii) '...count from 1 to 20.'

VII *Pairs* (Cards i–iv)

'There's one last set of words we'd like you to read out, at a normal speed. Would you please read these out in pairs.'

VIII *Subjective Attitudes*

'Some questions on the way people speak in Norwich.'

1. (i) Do you like the way people in Norwich speak?
    (ii) What in particular do/don't you like?
    (iii) Is there anything you don't like about the way you speak your-self/your children speak?
    (iv) Have you ever tried to do anything about it?
    (v) Would you like to hear local radio or TV announcers with Norwich accents? Why (not)?
2. (i) Has anybody outside Norwich or Norfolk ever laughed at you for the way you speak?
    (ii) Has anybody ever recognised/made a mistake about where you come from by the way you speak?
    (iii) Do you think people outside Norwich or Norfolk like the way we talk here?
3. Do you think people in Norwich speak differently from the country people in Norfolk? If so, how?

IX *Self Evaluation* (Chart One)

'You're now going to hear some different pronunciations of a number of different words. All these pronunciations are used in Norwich. We would like you to mark which pronunciation of each word is nearest to the one you generally use yourself. If you use more than one, mark more than one. If you can hear no difference, leave a blank.'

X *Linguistic Insecurity*

'This is the last thing we're going to ask you to do. You're going to hear two different ways of saying ten different words. We'd like you to tick which way you think is correct, and then to underline the way you say it yourself, either if it's the same or different.'

XI 1. Age Group.
2. Income Group.

WORD LIST

Paper	Soon	Underneath	Cart
Baker	Music	Roof	Alone
Silly	Lost	Huge	Coal
You	Year	Off	Queue
Avoid	Pepper	Pear	Bared
Girl	Buckle	See	Pip
Undone	Better	Time	Back
Soup	Like	Tell	Me
Hoof	Bottom	Dreadful	Days
First	Late	Shore	Daze
Bear	Know	Threshold	Loud
Doing	Head	More	Hate
Bit	Stone	Jealous	Fool
Very	Spoon	Poor	Few
Please	View	Matter	Curse
Made	Near	Face	Beer
Own	Walking	There	Tomorrow
Hill	Water	Under	Joint
Old	Manner	Whole	Law
Boot	Cat	Broom	Thread
Due	Coat	Dog	Paw
Turkey	Now	Yellow	Sawing
Beard	After	What	Cool
Wanted	Comb	Stop	Gear
Evening	Proof	Knew	Yet
Pipe	Worst	Certain	Healthy
Man	Dear	Boy	Froth
City	Laughing	Path	Early
Go	Bottle	Only	Bloke
My	Really	Nuisance	Daze
Asked	Arm	Coming	Hair
Aerodrome	Round	Here	Yarmouth
Food	Out	Going	Susan
Duty	Clerk	Thought	Alan
Cough	Won't	Floor	Castle Meadow
Pier	Room	Drawing	Decided
People	Suit	Get	Work
Blacken	Idea	Met	Suppose
Lip	Morning	Both	Road
Beauty	Button	Hundred	Pure
Night	Leave	Twelve	Fool
Her	Make	Boil	Take
Home	Pail	Shriek	Mind
Stout	Playing	Ride	Wait

Moor	Helping	Henry	Yelled
Aunt	Stupid	Tuesday	Great
Derby	Cheer	Elmo's	It
Bertie	Quite	School	Ate
Elsie	Arrive	Move	Gull
Hugh	Too	Never	They
Ernie	Last	British Home	Three
David	Ninety	Stores	
Wandering	Wanted	Nearly	
Hellesdon	Metal	Together	

PAIRS TEST

Boot – Boat	Soup – Soap
Hair – Here	Bear – Beer
Bust – Burst	Paw – Poor
Daze – Days	Cool – Coal
Moon – Moan	More – Moor
Do – Dew	Bird – But
No – Know	Heart – Hurt
Girl – Gull	Hoarse – Horse
Face – Fierce	Fear – Fair
Poor – Pore	Cure – Sewer
Pore – Paw	Hurt – Hut
Bard – Bird	Rude – Road
First – Fast	Man – Manner
Father – Farther	Met – Metal
No – New	Road – Rowed
Are – Our	News – Nose
Herd – Heard	Sole – Soul
Nose – Knows	Falling – Fallen
Wonder – Wander	Soaring – Sawing
Boat – Boot	Helen – Ellen
Far – Our	On – Arm
Pure – Purr	Hold – Old
Pear – Peer	Under – Wander
Boy – Buoy	Firs – Furze
Rays – Raise	Home – Put
Gate – Gear	Own – Old
Bird – Bad	Meet – Meat
Two – Too	Tale – Tail
Buy – Boy	Week – Weak
Box – Barks	Tern – Turn
Fire – Far	Rode – Road

READING PASSAGE
MY BROTHER

My brother David and me live here together. It's quite a laugh, I can tell you. He's a funny bloke, I suppose. (And he's got a beard!)

He's a bit of a nuisance at times. Take the other day. He was late for work in the morning. But I thought that *that* would be the last I saw of him the whole day.

I saw him splash some water on his face, put on his coat, and run down the stairs, three at a time.

'You won't make it!' I yelled. He pulled the paper out of the door, and ran down the path. He just made it to the 93 bus stop down the bottom of the road as the bus was drawing up.

That's another great day started, I thought.

After all that, I wasn't very pleased when I met him that evening. He was wandering in a daze down St Stephens – by the British Home Stores, or Elmo's, or somewhere near there.

I was going out to eat with Aunt Angela and Uncle Hugh, and our cousins Susan and Alan. They live out at Hellesdon, close to the aerodrome. But I didn't want my fool of a brother to come along as well.

I'd got a bottle of beer under my arm. Of course, he saw it. And he wanted to know all about it.

'What are you doing with that?' he asked.

I knew he would like the idea of helping me have a night out. He likes his food, too. And Sue's a bit of a beauty. He likes her, and so do I. But she's always rather cool to both of us, poor girl! Anyway, I had to tell him. Then I said: 'Cheerio! See you tomorrow.' Then I got a move on.

I decided I'd better get the 86. There wasn't much of a queue, just a few people, so I waited on Castle Meadow. It was years before the bus arrived. They're supposed to come every 12 minutes.

I was still early, though. They were all at home when I got there. Sue was dressed in what she called 'the latest gear' – a yellow dress with a metal zip down the front. She was playing pop music on the wireless. (I'm certain her mother hates it!)

She never had very good manners, and now they've got worse. All she said to me was: 'Hello dear! Leave me alone, I'm busy!' (Pure nonsense, of course.) And she only said *that* after she'd combed her hair for about 5 minutes.

She was the first one up the table. And then she ate her turkey soup with a fruit spoon!

But I soon got my own back, by telling everybody how I saw her admiring the view on Yarmouth pier on Tuesday! She was with a boy who's still at school. Aunt Angela nearly hit the roof! (Mind you, she was due for a shock.)

I didn't think I ought to have said it really. It looked as if there was a row coming. But it didn't matter. Just then there was a knock on the door, and in walked my stupid brother David!

Bibliography

Abercrombie, D. (1967). *Elements of general phonetics* (Edinburgh: University Press)

Abercrombie, D., Fry, D. B., MacCarthy, P. A. D., Scott, N. C. & Trim, J. L. M. (eds.) (1964). *In honour of Daniel Jones* (London: Longmans)

Anderson, C. A. & Bowman, M. J. (eds.) (1965). *Education and economic development* (Chicago: Aldine)

Avis, W. S. (1971). 'The "New England short *o*": a recessive phoneme'. *Language* XXXVII, 544–58

Bach, A. (1950). *Deutsche Mundartforschung* (Heidelberg: Winter)

Bach, E. & Harms, R. T. (1968). *Universals in linguistic theory* (New York: Holt, Rinehart and Winston)

Bailey, C-J. N. (1972). 'The integration of linguistic theory: internal reconstruction and the comparative method in descriptive analysis', in R. Stockwell & R. Macaulay (eds.), *Linguistic change and generative theory* (Bloomington: Indiana University Press)

Baratz, J. C. & Shuy, R. W. (eds.) (1969). *Teaching black children to read*, Urban Language Series, 4 (Washington, D.C.: Center for Applied Linguistics)

Barber, B. (1957). *Social stratification* (New York: Harcourt, Brace and World)

Bendix, R. & Lipset, S. M. (eds.) (1953). *Class, status and power: a reader in social stratification* (Glencoe: Free Press)

Berry, D. J. L. & Pred, A. (1961). *Central place studies* (Philadelphia: Regional Science Research Institute)

Bickerton, D. (1971). 'Inherent variability and variable rules', *Foundations of Language* VII, 457–92

Bottomore, T. B. (1965). *Classes in modern society* (London: Allen & Unwin)

Briers, F. (ed.) (1961). *Norwich and its region* (Norwich: British Association for the Advancement of Science)

Bright, W. (ed.) (1966). *Sociolinguistics* (The Hague: Mouton)

Bunge, W. (1966). *Theoretical geography* (Lund: Royal University of Lund)

Catford, J. C. (1964). 'Phonation types: the classification of some laryngeal components of speech production', in Abercrombie *et al.* (eds.)

Cedergren, H. & Sankoff, D. (forthcoming). 'Variable rules: performance as a statistical reflection of competence'. To appear in *Language*

Chen, M. & Hsieh, H-I. (1971). 'The time variable in phonological change', *Journal of Linguistics* VII, 1–13

Chomsky, N. (1964). *Current issues in linguistic theory* (The Hague: Mouton)

Chomsky, N. & Halle, M. (1968). *The sound pattern of English* (New York: Harper & Row)

Cochrane, G. R. (1959). 'The Australian English vowels as a diasystem', *Word* xv, 69–88

Crystal, D. & Davy, D. (1969). *Investigating English style* (London: Longmans)

Davies, A. F. (1952). 'Prestige of occupations', *British Journal of Sociology* III, 134–47.

DeCamp, D. (1958). 'The pronunciation of English in San Francisco. Part I', *Orbis* VII, 372–91

(1959). 'The pronunciation of English in San Francisco. Part II', *Orbis* VIII, 54–77

Dickinson, R. B. (1967). *The city region in western Europe* (London: Routledge & Kegan Paul)

Duncan, O. D. (1961). 'Properties and characteristics of the socioeconomic index', in Reiss

(1961). 'A socio-economic index for all occupations', in Reiss

Duncan O. D. & Duncan, B. (1955). 'Residential distribution and occupational stratification', *American Journal of Sociology* LX, 493–503

East Anglia Economic Planning Council (1968). *East Anglia: a study* (London: H.M.S.O.)

Eastern Evening News (1968). 'Norwich – the way ahead', Supplement, 22 October

Enderlin, F. (1911). *Die Mundart von Kesswil im Oberthurgau* (Frauenfeld: Bachmann)

Fasold, R. W. & Shuy, R. W. (eds.) (1970). *Teaching standard English in the inner city* (Washington, D.C.: Center for Applied Linguistics)

Finch, F. A. & Hoehn, A. J. (1951). 'Measuring socio-economic or cultural status: a comparison of methods', *Journal of Social Psychology* XXXIII, 51–67

Fischer, J. L. (1958). 'Social influences on the choice of a linguistic variant', *Word* XIV, 47–56

Forby, R. (1830). *The vocabulary of East Anglia* (London)

Fowler, E. (1961). 'An English province and its capital', in Briers (ed.)

Francis, W. N. (1966). Review of Vachek: 'On the peripheral phonemes in modern English', *Language* XLII, 142–9

Fry, D. B. (1947). 'The frequency of occurrence of speech sounds in southern English', *Archives Néerlandaises de Phonétique Expérimentale* XX, 103–6

Fudge, E. C. (1967). 'The nature of phonological primes', *Journal of Linguistics* III, 1–36

(1969a). 'Syllables', *Journal of Linguistics* V, 253–86

(1969b). 'Mutation rules and ordering in phonology', *Journal of Linguistics* V, 23–38

(1972). Review of Postal: *Aspects of phonological theory*, *Journal of Linguistics* VIII, 136–56

Garman, M. A. (1973). *A Grammar of the Coorg Language* (University of Edinburgh: unpublished Ph.D. thesis)

General Register Office for England and Wales (1964). *Census 1961, England and Wales. County Report: Norfolk* (London: H.M.S.O.)

(1966). *Classification of occupations* (London: H.M.S.O.)

(1967). *Sample census 1966, England and Wales. County report: Norfolk* (London: H.M.S.O.)

Gimson, A. C. (1962). *An introduction to the pronunciation of English* (London: Arnold)

Glass, D. V. (ed.) (1954). *Social mobility in Britain* (London: Routledge & Kegan Paul)

Glass, D. V. & Hall, J. R. (1954). 'Social mobility in Great Britain: a study of inter-generation changes in status', in Glass (ed.)

Goldthorpe, J. & Lockwood, D. (1963). 'Affluence and the British class structure', *Sociological Review* XI, 133–63

Goode, W. J. & Hatt, P. K. (1952). *Methods in social research* (New York: McGraw-Hill)

Green, B. & Young, R. M. P. (1964). *Norwich – the growth of a city* (Norwich: Museums Committee)

Gregg, R. J. (1968). 'Notes on the phonology of a County Antrim Scotch–Irish dialect', *Orbis* VII, 392–406

(1964). 'Scotch–Irish urban speech in Ulster', in *Ulster dialects: an introductory symposium* (Holywood: Ulster Folk Museum)

Hägerstrand, T. (1951). 'Migration and the growth of culture regions', *Lund Studies in Geography Series B, Human Geography 3* (Lund: Royal University of Lund)

(1952). 'The propagation of innovation waves', *Lund Studies in Geography Series B, Human Geography 4* (Lund: Royal University of Lund)

(1965). 'A Monte Carlo approach to diffusion', *European Journal of Sociology* VI, 43–67

(1965). 'Quantitative techniques for analysis of the spread of information and technology', in Anderson & Bowman (eds.)

(1967). *Innovation diffusion as a spatial process* (Chicago: University of Chicago Press)

Haggett, P. (1965). *Locational analysis in human geography* (London: Arnold)

Hall, J. R. & Glass, D. V. (1954). 'Education and social mobility', in Glass (ed.)

Halle, M. (1962). 'Phonology in generative grammar', *Word* XVIII, 54–72

Halliday, M. A. K., McIntosh, A. & Strevens, P. (1964). *The linguistic sciences and language teaching* (London: Longmans)

Hamm, J. (ed.) (1967). *Phonologie der Gegenwart* (Vienna: Böhlaus)

Harris, Z. S. (1951). *Structural linguistics* (Chicago: University of Chicago Press)

Hatt, P. K. (1950). 'Occupation and social stratification', *American Journal of Sociology* LV, 533–43.

Hill, A. A. (ed.) (1969). *Linguistics today* (New York: Basic Books)

Hochbaum, G., Darley, J. G., Monachesi, E. D. & Bird, C. (1955). 'Socioeconomic variables in the large city', *American Journal of Sociology* LXI, 31–8

Hockett, C. F. (1958). *A course of modern linguistics* (New York: Macmillan)
Honikman, B. (1964). 'Articulatory settings', in Abercrombie *et al.* (eds.)
Houck, C. L. (1966). 'A computerized statistical methodology for linguistic geography: a pilot study', *Folia Linguistica* I, 80–95.
  (1967). *Methodology of an urban speech survey* (Leeds: University of Leeds, Institute of Dialect and Folk Life Studies, unpublished)
Hymes, D. H. (1971). 'Sociolinguistics and the ethnography of speaking', in Ardener, E. (ed.), *Social Anthropology and language* (London: Tavistock)
Johnson, J. H. (1967). *Urban geography* (London: Pergamon)
Joos, N. (1967). *The five clocks* (New York: Harcourt, Brace & World)
Kahl, J. A. & Davies, J. A. (1955). 'A comparison of indexes of socio-economic status', *American Sociological Review* XX, 317–25.
Kant, E. (1951). 'Umland studies and sector analysis', *Studies in Rural–Urban Interaction. Lund Studies in Geography Series B., Human Geography 3* (Lund: Royal University of Lund)
Keyser, S. J. (1963). Review of Kurath & McDavid: *The pronunciation of English in the Atlantic states, Language* XXXIX, 303–16
Kim, C.-W. (1970). 'Two phonological notes A$\sharp$ and B$\flat$' (Unpublished paper. University of Illinois)
King, R. D. (1969). *Historical linguistics and generative grammar* (Englewood Cliffs: Prentice-Hall)
Kiparsky, P. (1968). 'Linguistic universals and linguistic change', in Bach & Harms (eds.)
Kökeritz, H. (1932). *The phonology of the Suffolk dialect* (Uppsala: Appelberg)
Kornhauser, R. R. (1953). 'The Warner approach to social stratification', in Bendix & Lipset (eds.)
Kurath, H. (1939). *Handbook of the linguistic geography of New England* (Providence: Brown University)
Kurath, H. & McDavid, R. I. (1961). *The pronunciation of English in the Atlantic states* (Ann Arbor: University of Michigan Press)
Labov, W. (1964). 'The aims of sociolinguistic research' (unpublished mimeo)
  (1965). 'On the mechanism of linguistic change', *Georgetown University Monographs on Languages and Linguistics 18*, 91–114
  (1966a). *The social stratification of English in New York City* (Washington: Center for Applied Linguistics)
  (1966b). 'Some sources of reading problems for Negro speakers of non-standard English (unpublished paper) *N.C.T.E. Spring Institute on New Directions in Elementary English* (Chicago)
  (1966c). 'The effect of social mobility on linguistic behaviour', in Lieberson (ed.)
  (1966d). 'The linguistic variable as a structural unit', *Washington Linguistics Review* III, 4–22
  (1969). 'Contraction, deletion and inherent variability of the English copula', *Language* XLV, 715–62

Labov, W. (1970). 'The study of language in its social context', *Studium Generale* XXIII, 30–87

(1970 a). 'A quantitative study of sound changes in progress' (University of Pennsylvania Research Project Proposal)

(forthcoming). 'On the use of the present to explain the past', paper given at the 11th International Congress of Linguists, Bologna, 1972

Ladefoged, P. (1967 a). *Three areas of experimental phonetics* (London: Oxford University Press)

(1967 b). 'Linguistic phonetics', *Working Papers in Phonetics 6. UCLA*

(1971). *Preliminaries to linguistic phonetics* (Chicago: Chicago University Press)

Laver, J. D. M. (1968). 'Voice quality and indexical information', *British Journal of Disorders of Communication* III, 43–54

Lawton, D. (1968). *Social class, language and education* (London: Routledge & Kegan Paul)

Lehmann, W. P. & Malkiel, Y. (eds.) (1968). *Directions for historical linguistics* (Austin: University of Texas Press)

Lenski, G. E. (1954). 'Status crystallisation: a non-vertical dimension of social status', *American Sociological Review* XIX, 405–13

Levine, L. & Crockett, H. J. (1966). 'Speech variation in a Piedmont community: postvocalic *r*', in Lieberson (ed.)

Lieberson, S. (ed.) (1966). *Explorations in sociolinguistics* (The Hague: Mouton)

Lundberg, G. (1940). 'The measurement of socio-economic status', *American Sociological Review* V, 29–40

Lyons, J. (1968). *Introduction to theoretical linguistics* (London: Cambridge University Press)

Mabry, J. H. (undated). *Norwich 1961 – an analysis of census returns* (University of East Anglia: unpublished)

McDavid, R. I. (1966). 'Dialect differences and social differences in an urban society', in Bright (ed.)

(1967). 'Historical, regional and social variation', *Journal of English Linguistics* I, 1–40

(1969). 'Dialects: British and American standard and non-standard', in Hill (ed.)

Mack, R. W. (1951). 'Housing as an index of social class', *Social Forces* XXIX, 391–400

Martin, F. M. (1954). 'Some subjective aspects of social stratification', in Glass (ed.)

Martinet, A. (1952). 'Function, structure and sound change', *Word* VIII, 1–32

(1955). *Economie des changements phonétiques* (Berne: Francke)

Mayer, K. D. (1955). *Class and society* (New York: Random House)

Moser, C. A. (1958). *Survey methods in social investigation* (London: Heinemann)

Moser, C. A. & Hall, J. R. (1954). 'The social grading of occupations', in Glass (ed.)

Moser, C. A. & Scott, W. (1961). *British towns* (London: Oliver & Boyd)
Moulton, W. G. (1960). 'The short vowel systems of northern Switzerland: a study of structural dialectology', *Word* XVI, 155–83
(1962). 'Dialect geography and the concept of phonological space', *Word* XVIII, 23–33
Newmeyer, F. J. & Edmonds, J. (1971). 'The linguist in American society', *Papers from the 7th regional meeting of the Chicago linguistic society* (Chicago: Chicago Linguistic Society)
Nystuen, J. D. & Dacey, M. F. (1961). 'A graph theory interpretation of nodal regions', *Papers and proceedings of the Regional Science Association* 7, 29–42
Öhman, S. E. G. (1966). 'Coarticulation in VCV utterances: spectographic measurements', *Journal of the Acoustical Society of America* XXXIX, 151–68
O'Neil, W. A. (1963). 'The dialects of modern Faroese: a preliminary report', *Orbis* XII, 393–7
Orton, H. & Dieth, E. (1962–). *Survey of English dialects* (Leeds: Arnold)
Orton, H. & Tilling, P. M. (1969). *Survey of English dialects. Volume III East Midlands and East Anglia* (Leeds: Arnold)
Pickford, G. R. (1956). 'American linguistic geography – a sociological appraisal', *Word* XII, 211–33
Pike, K. L. (1947). *Phonemics* (Ann Arbor: University of Michigan Press)
Postal, P. M. (1968). *Aspects of phonological theory* (New York: Harper & Row)
Pulgram, E. (1964). 'Structural comparison, diasystems and dialectology', *Linguistics* IV, 66–82
Reading, H. K. (1963). *A glossary of sociological terms* (Athens: Contos)
Reiss, A. J. (1961). *Occupations and social status* (Glencoe: Free Press)
Robins, R. H. (1967). *A short history of linguistics* (London: Longmans)
Samuels, M. L. (1972). *Linguistic evolution* (London: Cambridge University Press)
Saporta, S. (1965). 'Ordered rules, dialect differences and historical processes', *Language* XLI, 218–24
Schwarz, E. (1950). *Die deutsche Mundarten* (Göttingen: Vandenhouck & Ruprecht)
Shuy, R. W., Wolfram, W. A. & Riley, W. K. (1967). *Linguistic correlates of social stratification in Detroit speech* (U.S. Office of Education: Final Report, Cooperative Research Project 6-1347)
(1968). *Field techniques in urban language study* (Washington: Center for Applied Linguistics)
Sivertsen, E. (1960). *Cockney phonology* (Oslo: Oslo University Press)
Smailes, A. E. (1944). 'The urban hierarchy in England and Wales', *Geography* XXIX, 41–51
(1957). *The geography of towns* (London: Hutchinson)
Spencer, J., Gregory, M. & Enkvist, N. (1964). *Linguistics and style* (London: Oxford University Press)

Tay, M. W. J. (1970). 'Hokkien phonological structure', *Journal of Linguistics* VI, 81–8.

Thomas, A. R. (1967). 'Generative phonology in dialectology', *Transactions of the Philological Society*, 179–203

Thomas, P. G. (1961). 'Commercial and professional services', in Briers (ed.)

Troike, R. C. (1969). 'Overall pattern and generative phonology', in Allen, H. B. & Underwood, G. N., *Readings in American dialectology* (New York: Appleton-Century-Croft)

(1970). 'Receptive competence, productive competence and performance', in Alatis, J. (ed.), *Georgetown Monographs on Languages and Linguistics 22* (Washington, D.C.: Georgetown University Press)

Trudgill, P. J. (1971). 'The social differentiation of English in Norwich' (University of Edinburgh: unpublished Ph.D. thesis)

(1972). 'Sex, covert prestige and linguistic change in the urban British English of Norwich', *Language in Society* I, 179–95

(1973). 'Phonological rules and sociolinguistic variation in Norwich English', to appear in Papers from the Colloquium on New Ways of Analysing Variation in English, Georgetown University, October 1972

Vasiliu, E. (1966). 'Towards a generative phonology of Daco-Rumanian dialects', *Journal of Linguistics* II, 79–98

(1967). 'Transformational versus biunique phonemic typology', in Hamm (ed.)

Wang, W. S-Y. (1969). 'Competing changes as a cause of residue', *Language* XLV, 9–25

Warner, W. L., Meeker, M. & Ellis, K. (1949). *Social class in America: a manual for procedure for the measurement of social status* (Chicago: Science Research Associates)

Weinreich, U. (1954). 'Is a structural dialectology possible?' *Word* x, 388–400

Weinreich, U., Labov, W. & Herzog, M. I. (1968). 'Empirical foundations for a theory of language change', in Lehmann & Malkiel (eds.)

Wetmore, T. H. (1959). *The low-central and low-back vowels in the eastern United States* (Alabama: University of Alabama Press)

Winford, D. (1972). 'A sociolinguistic description of two communities in Trinidad' (University of York: unpublished D.Phil. thesis)

Wolfram, W. A. (1969). *A sociolinguistic description of Detroit Negro speech* (Washington, D.C.: Center for Applied Linguistics)

Wood, A. A. (1968). 'City of unique quality', in 'Norwich – the Way Ahead', *Eastern Evening News*

Index